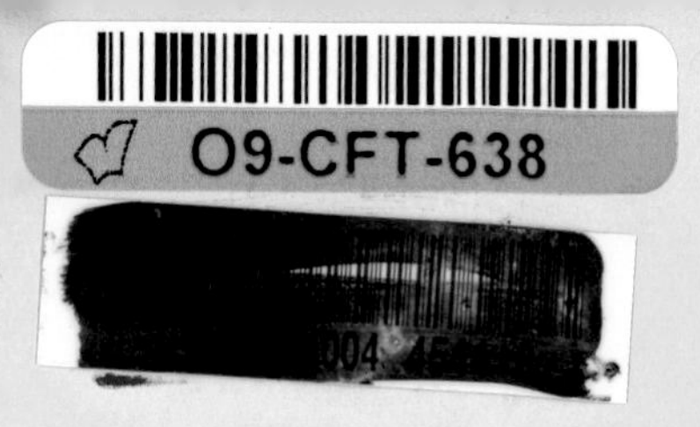
O9-CFT-638

818.52
R188
c.1
Randall Jarrell, 1914-1965
DISCARDED
COLLEGE OF THE SEQUOIAS
LIBRARY

Randall Jarrell

1914-1965

Randall Jarrell

1914-1965

EDITED BY

Robert Lowell, Peter Taylor,

& Robert Penn Warren

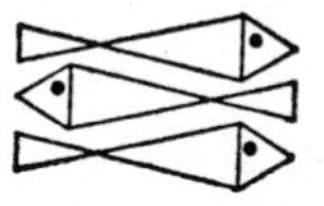

Farrar, Straus & Giroux

NEW YORK

Library of Congress catalog card number 67–13414
First printing, 1967
Published simultaneously in Canada by
Ambassador Books, Ltd., Rexdale, Ontario
Designed by Guy Fleming
Printed in the United States of America

ACKNOWLEDGMENTS

John Berryman's review of *Poetry and the Age* was first published in *The New Republic* (Copyright 1953 by *The New Republic*); his poem "Op. posth. no. 13," in the London *Times Literary Supplement* (Copyright © 1966 by John Berryman). Philip Booth's "Jarrell's Lost World" was first published in *The Christian Science Monitor* (Copyright © 1965 by Philip Booth). Cleanth Brooks's "Jarrell's 'Eighth Air Force' " was first published in *Literary Opinion in America,* edited by Morton Zabel, in a somewhat different form (Copyright 1951 by Harper & Row, Publishers, Incorporated). James Dickey's "Randall Jarrell" was first published in *The Sewanee Review* and then reprinted in Dickey's *The Suspect in Poetry* (Copyright © 1964 by The Sixties Press). R. W. Flint's "On Randall Jarrell" was first published in *Commentary* (Copyright © 1966 by R. W. Flint). Alfred Kazin's "Randall: His Kingdom" was first published in *The Reporter* (Copyright © 1966 by Alfred Kazin). Robert Lowell's review of *The Seven-League Crutches* was first published in *The New York Times Book Review* (Copyright © 1951 by The New York Times Company. Reprinted by permission); his essay "Randall Jarrell," in *The New York Review of Books* (Copyright © 1965 by Robert Lowell). "Metamorphoses in Randall Jarrell" by Sister M. Bernetta Quinn, O.S.F., was first published in a longer, somewhat different version in her *The Metamorphic Tradition in Modern Poetry* (Copyright © 1955 by Rutgers, The University Press. Reprinted by Gordian Press). John Crowe Ransom's "The Rugged Way of Genius" was first published in *The Southern Review* (Copyright © 1967 by John Crowe Ransom). Delmore Schwartz's review of *Poetry and the Age* was first published in *The New York Times Book Review* (Copyright © 1953 by The New York Times Company. Reprinted by permission); his review of *Little Friend, Little Friend,* in *The Nation* (Copyright © 1945 by Kenneth Schwartz). Karl Shapiro's lecture, "The Death of Randall Jarrell," was delivered under the auspices of the Whittall Poetry Fund and was first published by the Library of Congress in pamphlet form (Copyright © 1967 by Karl Shapiro); "Poem 68" ("Randall, I like your poetry terribly"), Copyright © 1963 by Karl Shapiro, is reprinted from his *The Bourgeois Poet* by permission of Random House, Inc. Peter Taylor's "Randall Jarrell" was delivered at the University of Michigan, the Hopwood Lecture Series, in a somewhat different version entitled "That Cloistered Jazz" and was first published in *Michigan Quar-*

NOTA BENE

All royalties on *Randall Jarrell, 1914–1965* will be donated, in the names of the editors, the contributors, and the photographers, to the Randall Jarrell Writing Scholarship at the University of North Carolina at Greensboro.

Contents

HANNAH ARENDT
Randall Jarrell / 3

JOHN BERRYMAN
On Poetry and the Age / 10
Randall Jarrell / 14
Op. posth. no. 13 / 18

ELIZABETH BISHOP
An Inadequate Tribute / 20

PHILIP BOOTH
Jarrell's Lost World / 22

CLEANTH BROOKS
Jarrell's "Eighth Air Force" / 26

JAMES DICKEY
Randall Jarrell / 33

DENIS DONOGHUE
The Lost World / 49

LESLIE A. FIEDLER
Jarrell's Criticism: A Footnote / 63

ROBERT FITZGERALD
A Place of Refreshment / 70

R. W. FLINT
On Randall Jarrell / 76

ALFRED KAZIN
Randall: His Kingdom / 86

STANLEY KUNITZ
Out of the Cage / 97

ROBERT LOWELL
Randall Jarrell / 101
On The Seven-League Crutches / 113

WILLIAM MEREDITH
The Lasting Voice / 118

Contents

MARIANNE MOORE
Randall Jarrell / 125

ROBERT PHELPS
For Randall Jarrell / 133

SISTER M. BERNETTA QUINN, O.S.F.
Metamorphoses in Randall Jarrell / 139

JOHN CROWE RANSOM
The Rugged Way of Genius / 155

ADRIENNE RICH
For Randall Jarrell / 182

DELMORE SCHWARTZ
On Little Friend, Little Friend / 184
On Poetry and the Age / 188

MAURICE SENDAK
For Randall Jarrell / picture facing 193

KARL SHAPIRO
The Death of Randall Jarrell / 195

ALLEN TATE
Young Randall / 230

ELEANOR ROSS TAYLOR
Greensboro Days / 233

PETER TAYLOR
Randall Jarrell / 241

P. L. TRAVERS
A Kind of Visitation / 253

ROBERT WATSON
Randall Jarrell: The Last Years / 257

MRS. RANDALL JARRELL
The Group of Two / 274

RANDALL JARRELL
A Man Meets a Woman in the Street / 299

Notes on the Contributors and the Editors / 305

BOOKS BY

Randall Jarrell

POETRY

The Rage for the Lost Penny (in *Five Young American Poets*)	1940
Blood for a Stranger	1942
Little Friend, Little Friend	1945
Losses	1948
The Seven-League Crutches	1951
Selected Poems	1955
The Woman at the Washington Zoo	1960
The Lost World	1965
The Complete Poems of Randall Jarrell	*edition in preparation*

ESSAYS

Poetry and the Age	1953
A Sad Heart at the Supermarket	1962
The Essays and Criticism of Randall Jarrell	*edition in preparation*

FICTION

Pictures from an Institution 1954

CHILDREN'S BOOKS

The Gingerbread Rabbit 1964
The Bat-Poet 1964
The Animal Family 1965
Fly by Night *edition in preparation*

TRANSLATIONS

The Golden Bird and Other Fairy Tales of the Brothers Grimm 1962
The Rabbit Catcher and Other Fairy Tales of Ludwig Bechstein 1962
The Three Sisters *edition in preparation*
Faust, Part I *edition in preparation*

ANTHOLOGIES

The Anchor Book of Stories 1958
The Best Short Stories of Rudyard Kipling 1961
The English in England (Kipling stories) 1963
In the Vernacular: The English in India (Kipling stories) 1963
Six Russian Short Novels 1963
Modern Poetry: An Anthology *edition in preparation*

Randall Jarrell

1914-1965

Hannah Arendt

Randall Jarrell

I MET HIM shortly after the end of the war, when he had come to New York to edit *The Nation*'s book section while Margaret Marshall was away, and when I was working for Schocken Books. What brought us together was "business"—I had been very impressed by some of his war poems and asked him to translate a few German poems for the publishing house, and he edited (translated into English, I should say) some book reviews of mine for *The Nation*. Thus, like people in business, we made it a habit of lunching together, and these lunches, I suspect but do not remember, were paid for in turn by our employers; for this was still the time when we were all poor. The first book he gave to me was *Losses*, and he inscribed it "To Hannah (Arendt) from her translator Randall (Jarrell)," reminding me jokingly of his first name, which I was slow to use, but not, as he suspected, because of any European aversion against first names; to my un-English ear, Randall sounded not a bit more intimate than Jarrell; in fact, the two sounded very much alike.

I don't know how long it took me to invite him to our home; his letters are of no help since they are all undated. But for some years he came at regular intervals, and when he announced his next visit he would for instance write, "You could enter in your engagement book Sat. Oct. 6, Sun. Oct. 7—American Poetry Weekend." And this is precisely what it always turned out to be. He read English poetry to me for hours, old and new, only rarely his own, which, however, for a time he used to mail as soon as the poems came out of the typewriter. He opened up for me a whole new world of sound and meter, and he taught me the specific gravity of English words, whose relative weight, as in all languages, is ultimately determined by poetic usage and standards. Whatever I know of English poetry, and perhaps of the genius of the language, I owe to him.

What originally attracted him not just to me or to us but to the house was the simple fact that this was a place where German was spoken. For

> I believe my favorite country's German.

The "country," obviously, was not Germany but German, a language he barely knew and stubbornly refused to learn. "Alas, my German isn't a *bit* better: if I translate, how can I find time to learn German? if I don't translate, I forget about German," he wrote after my last not very convinced attempt at making him use a grammar and a dictionary.

It is by Trust, and Love, and reading Rilke
Without *ein Wörterbuch,* that man learns German.

For him, all things considered, this was true enough, for he had read in this way Grimm's tales and *Des Knaben Wunderhorn,* and he was completely at home in the strange and intense poetry of German folk tales and folk songs, which are as untranslatably German as, well, *Alice in Wonderland* is untranslatably English. Anyhow, it was this folk element in German poetry that he loved and recognized in Goethe and even in Hölderlin and Rilke. I often thought that the country the German language represented to him was actually where he came from, for he was, down to the details of physical appearance, like a figure from fairyland; it was as though he had been blown down by some charmed wind into the cities of men or had emerged from the enchanted forests in which we spent our childhood, bringing with him the magic flute, and now not just hoping but *expecting* that everybody and everything would come to join in the midnight dance. What I mean to say is that Randall Jarrell would have been a poet if he had never written a single poem —just as that proverbial Raphael, born without hands, would still have been a great painter.

I knew him best during some winter months in the early fifties when he stayed at Princeton, which he found "*much* more Princetonian than—than Princeton, even." He came to New York on weekends, leaving behind, as he described it, a whole house of undone rooms and dishes and God knows how many street cats whom he had befriended. The moment he entered the apartment, I had the feeling that the household became bewitched. I never found out how he actually did it, but there was no solid object, no implement or piece of furniture, which did not undergo a subtle change, in the process of which it lost its everyday prosaic function. This poetic transformation could be annoyingly real when he decided, as he often did, to follow me into the kitchen to entertain me while I was preparing our dinner. Or, he might decide to visit my husband and engage him in some long fierce debate about the merits and the rank of writers and poets, and the voices of the two rang lustily as they tried to outdo and, especially, outshout each other: who knew better how to appreciate *Kim;* who was a greater poet, Yeats or Rilke—Randall, of course, voting for Rilke and my husband for Yeats; and so on, for hours. As Randall wrote after one such shouting match, "it's always awing (for an enthusiast) to see someone more enthusiastic than yourself—like the second fattest man in the world meeting the fattest."

In his poem about Grimm's tales, "The Märchen," he has described the land he came from:

> Listening, listening; it is never still.
> This is the forest

where

> The sunlight fell to them, according to our wish,
> And we believed, till nightfall, in that wish;
> And we believed, till nightfall, in our lives.

His was not at all the case of the man who flees the world and builds himself a dream castle; on the contrary, he met the world head on. And the world, to his everlasting surprise, was as it was—not peopled by poets and readers of poetry, who according to him belonged to the same race, but by television watchers and readers of *Reader's Digest* and, worst of all, by this new species, the "Modern Critic," who no longer exists "for the sake of the plays and stories and poems [he] criticizes" but for his own sake, who knows "how poems and novels are put together," whereas the poor writer "had just put them together. In the same way, if a pig wandered up to you during a bacon-judging contest, you would say impatiently, 'Go away, pig! What do you know about bacon?' " The world, in other words, did not welcome the poet, was not grateful to him for the splendor he brought, seemed unneedful of his "immemorial power to make the things of this world seen and felt and living in words," and therefore condemned him to obscurity, complaining then that he was "obscure" and could not be understood, until finally "the poet said, 'Since you won't read me, I'll make sure you can't.' " These complaints were ordinary enough, so ordinary indeed that I at first could not understand why he bothered with them at all. Only slowly did it dawn upon me that he did not want to belong among "the happy few, who grow fewer and unhappier day by day," for the simple reason that he was a democrat at heart, with "a scientific education and a radical youth," who was "old-fashioned enough to believe, like Goethe, in Progress." And it took me even longer, I must confess, to realize that his marvelous wit, by which I mean the precision of his laughter, was not only the simple outgrowth of his unbelief in cheapness and vulgarity of every kind or of his belief that everybody he came in contact with had his own absolute feeling (like absolute pitch) for quality, this infallible judgment in all artistic as well as human matters, but that there was also, as he himself pointed out in "The Obscurity of the Poet," the mocking and self-mocking "tone of someone accustomed to helplessness." I trusted the very exuberance of his cheerfulness, thought or hoped that it would be sufficient to ward off all dangers to which he was so obviously exposed, because I found his laughter so exactly right. How, after all, could any of the learned or sophisticated rubbish about "adjustment" hope to survive this one sentence of his: "President Robbins was so well adjusted to his environment that sometimes you could not tell which was the environment and which was President Robbins"? And if you can't laugh away the rubbish, what help is there? To disprove point by point all the nonsense our century has produced would demand ten life-spans, and in the end the disprovers would be as little distinguishable from their victims as was the college president from his environment. He, at any rate, had nothing to protect him against the world but his splendid laughter, and the immense naked courage behind it.

When I last saw him, not long before his death, the laughter was almost gone, and he was almost ready to admit defeat. It was the same defeat he had foreseen more than ten years earlier in the poem entitled "A Conversation with the Devil."

> Indulgent, or candid, or uncommon reader
> —I've some: a wife, a nun, a ghost or two—
> If I write for anyone, I wrote for you;
> So whisper, when I die, *We was too few;*
> Write over me (if you can write; I hardly knew)
> That I—that I—but anything will do,
> I'm satisfied. . . . And yet—
>   and yet, you *were* too few:
> Should I perhaps have written for your brothers,
> Those artful, common, unindulgent others?

John Berryman

On Poetry and the Age

This is, I believe, the most original and best book on its subject since *The Double Agent* by R. P. Blackmur and *Primitivism and Decadence* by Yvor Winters. Since the other ablest American critic of modern poetry in the generation now about forty, Delmore Schwartz, has not collected his essays, we may be specially glad that Jarrell has begun to, and the book is overdue. It does not, indeed, contain his most plunging criticism so far, which will be found in his articles and reviews and lectures on Auden, whose mind Jarrell understands better than anyone ought to be allowed to understand anyone else's, especially anyone so pleasant and destructive as Jarrell; these will make another volume. But it exhibits fully the qualities that made Jarrell the most powerful reviewer of

This review of *Poetry and the Age* was first published in The New Republic, November 2, 1953.

poetry active in this country for the last decade; and in its chief triumphs, the second essay on Frost and the first review of Lowell (I mean the first of the two here preserved) it exhibits more.

William Empson I suppose was Jarrell's master. An early piece on Housman, not reprinted, seems to prove this, and there are several handsome references here. His prose is not so manly as Empson's; it giggles on occasion, and nervous overemphasis abounds; but it sounds always like a human being talking to somebody—differing in this from nine-tenths of what other working American critics manufacture. It is cruel and amusing, undeniably well known for these qualities, which it developed so far beyond Empson's traces that that critic presents in comparison an icon of deadpan charity. But what really matter in Jarrell are a rare attention, devotion to and respect for poetry. These, with a natural taste in poetry hardly inferior to Tate's, restless incessant self-training, strong general intelligence, make up an equipment that would seem to be minimal but in fact is unique.

The second essay on Frost is nothing much but thirty pages of quoted poems and passages, with detailed comment. To see how astonishing it is, you ought first to read through a pallid assemblage called *Recogniton of Robert Frost*, to the authors of which (except Edward Garnett and Mark Van Doren) the Frost that Jarrell displays would be a horrifying stranger. Perhaps nothing of this vivid sort has ever surpassed the page on "Provide, Provide," unless it is the pages following on "Design."

Lord Weary's Castle was one of the stiffest books to review that has ever appeared. I have reason to know: Jarrell's was not only superior—far—to my own attempt: it is probably the most masterly initial review of an important poetic work, either here or in England, of this century so far. You have to compare it with wider-ranging reviews, like Eliot's of Grierson, or Dr. Johnson's of Soame Jenyns to feel its narrower but harder learning, its similar but submissive strength.

The studies of Ransom, Stevens, Marianne Moore (again especially the second piece on her), more conventional than those on Frost and Lowell, are nearly as good. A fine citation of Whitman, wittier even than usual, seems better now under a new, more modest title than it did originally, because it does not examine, as Jarrell usually does, substance or method or (save for a few remarks) style. This attention equally in him to matter and manner constitutes a development from what is called the New Criticism.

His general essays, on Obscurity and the Age of Criticism, which strike me as diffuse and making points rather familiar, will undoubtedly help many readers. At least the points made are right. A salient truth about Jarrell, for the present reader, is that he is seldom wrong. About William Carlos Williams's poetry, some of which I love too, he does, I think, exaggerate, and these papers are his weakest; even here he says much that is true, gay, and useful. One of his shrewdest, most characteristic remarks is apropos of a poet one might suppose he would not appreciate at all, the author of the beautiful "Song of the Mad Prince": "It is easy to complain that de la Mare writes about unreality; but how *can* anybody write about unreality?" One cannot but remark the healthy breadth of Jarrell's taste. Behind the writers here treated, perhaps his strongest obvious admirations are for Hardy, Rilke, and of course Eliot, and I hope he will treat them; and Proust, and I wish he dealt more with prose.

On the other hand, his neglect to theorize about poetry, and to theorize above all about criticism, is one of the most agreeable features of a prepossessing and engaging book. Criticism of criticism—at best a languid affair, as Irving Babbitt observed in the preface to one of his books about criticism—is probably best left to very young men and older men. The point is to deal with the stuff itself, and Jarrell does, nobody better. Everybody interested in modern poetry ought to be grateful to him.

Randall Jarrell

JARRELL'S DEATH hit me very hard. We were seldom together, but we were friends for a very long time. Our correspondence began in 1939. James Laughlin, editor of New Directions, was anxious to get five young poets together, and among them he wanted a woman—sales value, you see. So Jarrell and I, who were not the two stupidest people in the book, had a long correspondence about these women whom Laughlin was always turning up in all parts of the country. And Laughlin would write to us and say, "Tell me what you think of her 'Deathless, ah, deathless' verses, because I'm very eager to know her better." So that Jarrell and I began as a sort of team of two to produce standards in James Laughlin, and we may say that anything that New Directions has accomplished since then was influenced by Jarrell and me.

My favorite recollection of this amazing man was one time when he came to visit me in Princeton, New Jersey, and he came down from New York for dinner with Robert Lowell. And he had a hangover, and that was very amazing because Jarrell did not drink. He's the only poet that I've ever known in the universe who simply did not drink. So how did he get the hangover? Well, he'd been to a cocktail party the day before in New York and had eaten a poisoned canapé. So here's Jarrell walking up and down in my living room, miserable and witty. And very malicious, as he could certainly be, making up a brand-new Lowell poem full of characteristic Lowell properties, Lowell's grandfather and Charon, and the man who did not find this funny at all was Lowell. There was a complete want of humor at that point. At last we calmed Randall down, and he stopped making up this wonderful apocryphal poem by Lowell; we stationed him on the couch, and I gave him a book of photographs of the Russian ballet (he was very keen on ballet). While the rest of us had dinner, he lay there and made witty remarks about the photographs of the Russian ballet.

He was a terror as a reviewer. My own feeling would be that we're going to witness during the months to come an unusual spate of publication of really bad poetry. That is, let's say, people who have been holding their books up for years while they waited for Fate to come and deal with that terrible person, Randall Jarrell. He was immensely cruel, and the extraordinary thing about it is that he didn't know he was cruel.

One time his cruelty was made public. That rather sweet-souled man, Conrad Aiken, wrote a letter to, I think, *The New Republic* or some other respectable journal saying that Jarrell's reviews went beyond decency—that he was a sadist. I was very fond of both Conrad and Randall. Jarrell's reviews did go beyond the limit; they were unbelievably cruel, that's true. Conrad was quite right. But, on the other hand, Jarrell then wrote a letter in a rather aggrieved tone—and the word aggrieved handles a lot of Jarrell's tone, both in prose and in verse. He himself hated bad poetry with such vehemence and so vigorously that it didn't occur to him that in the course of taking apart—where he'd take a book of poems and squeeze, like that, twist—that in the course of doing that, there was a human being also being squeezed. Well, he wrote in to the journal, saying that he couldn't understand why Mr. Aiken thought that his reviews were cruel, whereas they really were remarkably cruel. However, it is to be said, as Mr. Lowell said in his piece, a beautiful piece [see pages 101–112], that the real point of Jarrell's criticism is not destructive, but—well, I'm not too keen on the word constructive—but that his criticism of praise was what mattered. Sometimes overpraise—Jarrell overrated William Carlos Williams, for example, I think considerably. I'm very fond of Bill Williams's poetry, but not as fond as Jarrell was. And Jarrell sort of lost heart over this, over the years, as I think he finally came to see that he had overpraised Williams. But the essays on Marianne Moore and on Frost and on Whitman, above all on Whitman, are sort of paeans of joy with nothing of the black wit that characterizes the rest of his criticism.

Then, I'll tell you one other story about Jarrell. This is secondhand, and it comes from Jean Stafford, a woman so witty that you can't trust her stories. You mustn't be that witty, but this is apparently a true story. I'll tell it to you, and then I'll comment on it. Randall was staying one time at the house of one of Jean Stafford's best friends, and he played croquet with the children in the afternoon and lost. He didn't like that at all. He was very grumpy at dinner and went to bed early. Next morning, Jean's friend woke very early and went downstairs to put on coffee or something, and she was going down her spiral staircase with the window that faced on the front lawn where the wickets were, and she found Randall out there. (This is about five o'clock in the morning.) Randall was studying the ground—changing the wickets. It's a good thing that he had a very successful career, as he did, because he was a hard loser. He wasn't a man who liked to lose at all.

Op. posth. no. 13

In the night-reaches dreamed he of better graces,
of liberations, and beloved faces,
such as now ere dawn he sings.
It would not be easy, accustomed to these things,
to give up the old world, but he could try;
let it all rest, have a good cry.

Let Randall rest, whom your self-torturing
cannot restore one instant's good to, rest:
he's left us now.
The panic died and in the panic's dying
so did my old friend. I am headed west
also, also, somehow.

In the chambers of the end we'll meet again
I will say Randall, he'll say Pussycat

and all will be as before
whenas we sought, among the beloved faces,
eminence and were dissatisfied with that
and needed more.

Elizabeth Bishop

An Inadequate Tribute

RANDALL JARRELL was difficult, touchy, and oversensitive to criticism. He was also a marvelous conversationalist, brilliantly funny, a fine poet, and the best and most generous critic of poetry I have known. I am proud to remember that, although we could rarely meet, we remained friends for twenty years. Sometimes we quarreled, silently, in infrequent letters, but each time we met we would tell each other that it had meant nothing at all; we really were in agreement about everything that mattered.

He always seemed more alive than other people, as if constantly tuned up to the concert pitch that most people, including poets, can maintain only for short and fortunate stretches.

I like to think of him as I saw him once after we had gone swimming together on Cape Cod; wearing only bathing trunks and a very queer straw cap with a big visor, seated on the crest of a high sand dune, writing in a notebook. It was a bright and dazzling day. Randall looked small and rather delicate, but bright and dazzling, too. I felt quite sure that whatever he was writing would be bound to share the characteristics of the day and of the small man writing away so busily in the middle of it all.

Philip Booth

Jarrell's Lost World

ADMITTING HIMSELF to a fine dramatic monologue in his great new book, Randall Jarrell says, almost as if in a casual aside: "But I identify myself, as always, / With something that there's something wrong with, / With something human."

Stressed by his own speech patterns, these charged lines come from a poem called "The One Who Was Different." In the book of which that poem is a part, *The Lost World*, Jarrell (that always "different" poet) has finally found the open language and flexible rhythms which make humanly one the world of his poems and the world these poems now speak to.

The titles of Jarrell's earlier collections of essays, *Poetry*

This review of *The Lost World* was first published in The Christian Science Monitor, March 11, 1965.

and the Age and *A Sad Heart at the Supermarket*, implicitly define his concern for, and his reaction to, the mid-century America he knows that poetry (now, if ever) must reach to redeem. As the most human critic of his age, and even as the cheaply tagged "war poet" of such famous poems as "The Death of the Ball Turret Gunner" and "Good-bye, Wendover; Good-bye, Mountain Home," Jarrell has constantly stretched himself to find a language commensurate with his affectionate sadness for the human condition, and his reserved belief in human joy. His imagination has, from the beginning, been flawless; but his full concern for speaking no less than the truth has sometimes (almost prosaically) flattened his lines, and (because the truth was ever complex) his poems have sometimes seemed confused in their always dramatic structure.

Now, not altogether newly, but in a clearly new depth, Jarrell dramatizes his sense of humanity with an absolute precision. Humanity may still be "what there's something wrong with," but these human poems are, in themselves, close to holy: they make painfully lovely sense of a world we've much confused but just might, because of poems like these, finally survive.

The fashion, momentarily, in "modern" poetry, is confessional: to make of one's appendectomy or psychoanalysis a narcissistic (and perhaps masochistic) first-person-singular poem. As his first six books of poetry generously attest, Jarrell can speak for his own losses as well as the next man. But even in this book, rightfully called *The Lost World*, Jarrell continues to refuse the selfish mode of programmatic despair.

Because his poetry understands that pain is a universal experience, Jarrell can identify with people beyond himself: in finding a language which dramatizes how people hurt, want, and try to define themselves, he peoples his poetry with those human beings who are, for him, what the great poem of the world is primarily about.

Frost did something of this in *North of Boston.* As Frost's most illuminating critic, Jarrell must surely have learned from Frost how speech stress, cutting across meters, can make a poetry of how people speak. But even Frost was less flexible than Jarrell in finding, shaping, and informing the various rhythms of individual experience.

Jarrell not only speaks for himself (recovering, perfectly, the "impotent omnipotence" of "The Lost World" of boyhood); he can write as Everyman in that singular poem called "Woman"; he can speak as a mother to "The Lost Children," and be wife to supermarkets in the poem called "Next Day." In all of these, there is an emotional precision comparable to that in Frost's "A Servant to Servants": there is compassion which lends its redemptive perspective to how (on the world's bare stage) people short of stardom walk on to speak for themselves.

The twenty-two poems of *The Lost World* would seem few were they not so full. Most of them are long by contemporary standards, yet none is padded; each explores its meanings with such a quiet flexibility that even the careful rhymes of the title poem seem natural. Within such technical brilliance (never greater than in "The Old and the New Masters," which reconstitutes, and then turns the theme of

Auden's "Musée des Beaux Arts"), the final value of Jarrell's new poetry lies in its seemingly casual wisdom. Jarrell has always been "bright" (witness the shining wit of his academic novel, *Pictures from an Institution*); yet where some of his previous effects seemed merely to ornament knowledge, what's lapidary in *The Lost World* feels almost self-surprising, so wisely (in context) is it earned.

Randall Jarrell's new book is so surely wise, so demonstrably honest, and so purely human, that it's tempting to play Jarrell the critic: to name the names of sustaining poems, to praise them with grateful adjectives. But these new poems deserve the better thanks of the words that Jarrell himself once wrote to honor Frost: ". . . to have this whole range of being treated with so much humor and sadness and composure, with such plain truth; to see that a man can still include, connect, and make humanly understandable . . . so *much*—this is one of the freshest and oldest of joys, a joy strong enough to make us forget the limitations and excesses and baseness that these days seem unforgettable, a joy strong enough to make us say, with the Greek poet, that many things in this world are wonderful, but of all these the most wonderful is man."

Cleanth Brooks

Jarrell's "Eighth Air Force"

ONE OF THE salient qualities of Randall Jarrell's poetry is a freshness of observation, a sense of direct and immediate and unhackneyed response. Doubtless this quality is related to a kind of innocence in Jarrell as a person, an innocence that one would be tempted to call childlike except that Jarrell was preternaturally articulate and thoroughly tough-minded. It was this or a related quality that made his critical essays so bright and refreshing. Yet his spontaneity and innocence (whether turned toward lyrical freshness or satirical acerbity) could, because they are so prominent in his poetry, blind the casual reader to the presence of other important qualities, qualities that one tends to associate with another kind of mind and with another order of talents. I am thinking of Jarrell's architectural quality, his ability to build the lofty rhyme, or—since we don't need to limit ourselves to Milton's precise phrasing—to build other sorts of rhyme, but in any case, to give us poems that are intricate and rich in their varying tonalities. One of the best instances of this quality to be found in Jarrell's poetry is his "Eighth Air Force." (His note on the poem tells us that it was the Eighth Air Force that bombed the cities of the Continent from British bases.) Here is the poem:

> If, in an odd angle of the hutment,
> A puppy laps the water from a can
> Of flowers, and the drunk sergeant shaving
> Whistles *O Paradiso!*—shall I say that man
> Is not as men have said: a wolf to man?
>
> The other murderers troop in yawning;
> Three of them play Pitch, one sleeps, and one
> Lies counting missions, lies there sweating
> Till even his heart beats: One; One; One.
> *O murderers!* . . . Still, this is how it's done:
>
> This is a war. . . . But since these play, before they die,
> Like puppies with their puppy; since, a man,
> I did as these have done, but did not die—
> I will content the people as I can
> And give up these to them: Behold the man!
>
> I have suffered, in a dream, because of him,
> Many things; for this last saviour, man,
> I have lied as I lie now. But what is lying?
> Men wash their hands, in blood, as best they can:
> I find no fault in this just man.

The poem when read "innocently," and even hurriedly, registers with tremendous impact. It declares its power almost in the first rush. But under a more meditative reading, the poem grows in depth and richness. One notices very quickly that the poem is truly wrought: there are simply no superfluous parts here, no dead or empty details.

The airmen in their hutment are casual enough and honest enough to seem convincing. They have domesticated the raw building in which they are quartered: there are flowers in water, from which a puppy laps. There is the drunken sergeant, whistling an operatic aria as he shaves. These "murderers," as the poet is to call the airmen in the next stanza, actually display a rather touching regard for the human values. How then, in view of the fact that these men "play, before they die, / Like puppies with their puppy," can one say that man is a wolf to man? The question put seems reasonable, and yet the presence of the puppy in the hutment is far from certifying Man's essential humanity, for the dog is a kind of tamed and domesticated wolf and the presence of the puppy in this scene may prove that the hutment is merely the wolf den. After all, the timber wolf plays with its puppies too.

The second stanza takes the theme to a perfectly explicit conclusion. If three of the men are playing pitch, and if one is asleep, one at least of the group is awake, and awake to the moral issues. He calls himself and his companions murderers. But his unvoiced cry "O murderers!" is met, countered, and dismissed in the next two lines: ". . . Still, this is how it's done: / This is a war. . . ."

The note of casuistry and cynical apology prepares for a brilliant resolving image, that of Pontius Pilate, which is announced specifically in the third stanza:

> I will content the people as I can
> And give up these to them: Behold the man!

Yet if Pilate, as he is first presented, suggests the jesting Pilate of the Scriptures, who asks "What is truth?" it is a bitter and grieving Pilate who concludes this poem. The integrity of Man himself is at stake. Is Man a cruel animal, a wolf, or is he the last savior, the Christ of our secular religion of humanity?

The Pontius Pilate metaphor, as the poet uses it, becomes a device for tremendous concentration. For the speaker (presumably the young airman who cried "O murderers!") is himself the confessed murderer under judgment, and also the Pilate who judges, and, at least as a representative of Man, the savior whom the mob would condemn. He is even Pilate's better nature, his wife, for the lines "I have suffered, in a dream, because of him, / Many things" is merely a rearrangement of Matthew 27:19, the speech of Pilate's wife to her husband. But this last item is more than a reminiscence of the scriptural scene. It reinforces the speaker's present dilemma. The modern has had high hopes for humanity. Are the hopes merely a dream? Is man, after all, incorrigible, merely a cruel beast? The speaker's torment springs from that hope and from his reluctance to dismiss it as empty. This Pilate is harder pressed than was the Roman magistrate. For he must convince himself of this last savior's innocence. But he has lied for him before. He will lie for him now.

> Men wash their hands, in blood, as best they can:
> I find no fault in this just man.

What is one to make of the statement that "Men wash their hands, in blood, as best they can"? It is thoroughly equivocal. It is rich in possible meanings. It could mean: Since my own hands are bloody, I have no right to condemn the rest. It could mean: I know that men can love justice, even though their hands are bloody, for I love justice and there is blood on mine. It could mean: Men are essentially decent; they try to keep their hands clean even if they have only blood in which to wash them. But it could also be a cry of desperation: How can one expect men to keep their hands clean when so often they are given only blood in which to wash them?

None of these meanings, it seems to me, quite cancels out the others. All are at some level relevant, and each meaning contributes to the total meaning of the poem. Indeed, there is hardly a facet of significance that does not receive illumination from this figure of a modern Pilate who would like to evade rendering judgment.

Some of Jarrell's weaker poems are weak, so it seems to me, because they lean too heavily upon this concept of the essential goodness of man. But in "Eighth Air Force" the affirmation of man's innate justness by a Pilate who washes his hands in blood as he pronounces that he finds no fault in the accused seems to me to supply every qualification that is required. The sense of one's own guilt, the yearning to believe in man's justness, the knowledge of the almost intolerable difficulty in so believing—all work to render accurately and dramatically the total situation that the poem presents.

In this poem the tone is complex with ironies. One might argue that the ironical inflections pare the theme of man's goodness down to acceptable dimensions. That is, the poet has here so qualified the theme that it is evident that he himself does not really believe in it. But to put matters in this way would distort what I want to say about the poem. We do not ask, and we ought not to ask, a poet to bring his poem into line with our own personal beliefs. What it is fair to ask is that the poet dramatize the situation with which he is concerned, and that he dramatize it so accurately, so honestly, with such fidelity to the total situation, that the issue is no longer a question of our beliefs but of our participation in the process through which the poet arrives at his declaration of belief or unbelief. In his best poems—and they are numerous—Jarrell manages, as he does here, to bring us, through an act of imagination, to the most penetrating insight. Participation in that insight doubtless involves us in a deeper examination of what we really believe and ultimately corrects and refines our beliefs. It may even make us better citizens. One of the "uses" of poetry, I should agree, is to make us better citizens—but it does so through its own mode and not by preaching to us. For poetry is not the eloquent rendition of the good citizen's creed. Poetry must carry us beyond the stated creed and into the very matrix out of which, and from which, our creeds are abstracted. That is what "Eighth Air

Force" does. That is what, it seems to me, all good poetry does.

For the theme in a genuine poem does not confront us as an abstraction—that is, as one man's generalization from the relevant particulars. Finding its proper symbol, defined and refined by the participating metaphors, the theme becomes a part of the reality in which we live—an insight, rooted in and growing out of concrete experience, many-sided, three-dimensional. Even the resistance to generalization has its part in this process—even the tension of opposing themes plays its part in the processes of revelation.

James Dickey

Randall Jarrell

A. Why are we Two?

B. I find that my opinions of Randall Jarrell's poetry are so violent that I have summoned you, or created you, out of niggling and Opposing Winds, to furnish me with arguments against which my own will stand forth even stronger, which I should like them to do.

A. I am glad you have created me. I think it good for writers to have the most violent possible arguments brought into play against them. Even unfair arguments. If the work is strong enough, all these will be overcome. Now, I was moved by Jarrell's poems even when I was Wind. Now that I am a Voice therefrom, I find I am moved even more, for I am nearer the human things he writes about.

This essay was first published in The Sewanee Review, Spring 1956.

B. I take it, then, that I have brought forth a satisfactory Opposing Self, for you seem to like Jarrell's poems.

A. I do. I think his book [*Selected Poems*] is, or should certainly be, the occasion of a Triumph. He has been writing for twenty years now, and this book contains a fair portion of all he will do as a writer: that is, the book is a monument, if not to Jarrell *in toto*, then at least to his "early phase," no matter what he may do later.

B. And why is the book a Triumph, may I ask?

A. Because it is the work of an honest, witty, intelligent, and deeply gifted man, a man who knows more about poetry, and knows it in better, more human ways, than any other of our time. If you add to these other things that he has a rare *poetic* intelligence which works, not for itself, but totally in the service of human beings, in compassion and love, then you will have an idea of the kind of Triumph I'm talking about. All you can do about a book like this, as Herbert Read said of Dylan Thomas's *Deaths and Entrances*, is to praise it.

B. I must tell you, then, that to me the book is dull beyond all dullness of stupefaction or petrifaction; that when I read it from end to end I know more of boredom than the dead do. "In plain American that dogs and cats can read" the poems are the most untalentedly sentimental, self-indulgent, and insensitive writings that I can remember; when I read them I cry and laugh helplessly all night, over the reputation that has come out of such stuff.

A. I would say, in answer, that you have missed the entire point of Jarrell's contribution, which is that of writing about real things, rather than playing games with words. He is set like a kind of laughing death against the technique-on-principle people that fill the quarterlies. His world is *the* World, and People, and not the cultivated island of books, theories, and schools. Can't you see that?

B. Would you give me an example of this attitude at work in one of Jarrell's poems?

A. I'll just pick up a random sample. This is from "The Night before the Night before Christmas." He speaks of "the big old houses, the small new houses." Don't you see. . . .

B. That's real enough, all right, if that's what you mean by real. That is, there *are* big old houses and small new houses, and perhaps this observation tells us something about the economic and social changes that have taken place in the time between the building of the two types of houses. But isn't the statement pretty much of a commonplace? After all, we don't need a poet to point *this* out to us. Am I to believe that you and Jarrell think that comment of this rather tame and obvious kind constitutes Triumphal Poetry? I should be sorry to think so.

A. You certainly *are* to believe it. It is, for instance, far more important than surrealist poems, or those of García Lorca's *Poet in New York*, or any other poetry that uses objects as counters to whirl into and out of bizarre images, simply for the sake of the images, and the bizarreness. Jarrell's poems are far too respectful of experience, of life as it is lived by people, for that to happen. Their world is *our* world.

B. Now this word "real." Hadn't we better examine it a

little more closely. Is it actually as important as you say to Jarrell's writing?

A. It *is* his writing. He writes about the things we know; that is, he writes about cats, common soldiers, about the dilemmas of children, and . . . and the small man, the man "things are done to," usually by the State, to the man's almost willing detriment and slow consternation.

B. "Reality," though, is what, exactly? The philosophers have gone into cold graves, for ages, still arguing about the nature of Reality, and probably will do so forever. Do you mean to tell me that if I read Jarrell's poems "in the right spirit" I will have the answer to all these vexing questions the Ages have turned back from with only provisional, unsatisfactory solutions?

A. Yes; in a sense, you will. Like any poet's, Jarrell's is an experiential reality. I believe that, without becoming entangled in metaphysics, we can assume that his reality is "the common ground of experience" of twentieth century man, especially the American, but not confined to him. Through poems about what has happened to this man (or to his child) in this time, we get, in an extremely detailed, moving, and "true" way, the experience of our time defined. And that is Reality enough.

B. "Reality," then, is what everybody knows and feels it is, since we all have roughly the same experiences as human beings living under (approximately) the same conditions. When there is a war, for instance, we all react to it.

A. That's right.

B. And you think that it's important that Jarrell appeals

to others' participation in this common ground of experience: that his poems draw their strength at least in part from this appeal?

A. I do. Can you deny that you have undergone many of the things he writes about?

B. No. I have undergone them. But so have newspapers, mediocre movies, soap operas, and bad poems. So has my old Aunt Virgie, on television. It is not enough that the poet's world be that of "all of us." Of course he must begin there, but that fact doesn't make him a poet, or his writings valuable.

A. Nobody is asserting anything of *that* kind. You oversimplify much too drastically.

B. Jarrell himself seems to assume something of this nature, though. In his criticism he speaks frequently, even obsessively, of a poet's evoking not "a" but "the" real world; he says of Whitman's world that it "so plainly *is* the world" (italics Jarrell's), and so on.

A. You are still missing the point. The poet must evoke a world that is realer than real: his work must result in an intensification of qualities, you might say, that we have all observed and lived, but the poet has observed and lived most deeply of all. This world is so real that the experienced world is transfigured and intensified, through the poem, into itself, a deeper *itself*, a more characteristic *itself*. If a man can make words do this, he is a poet. Only men who can do this *are* poets.

B. Isn't it, though, what all poets are trying to do? Or at least half of them, anyway. There are some poets who are on the side of the World against Art, like Jarrell, and there are others, like the surrealists, Mallarmé, and Valéry, who are for Art against the World. Nietzsche said that no true artist would tolerate for an instant the world as it is. Some artists want to characterize the world, and some to change it and make use of it in their own ways. Assuming for the moment that I, like you and Jarrell, think that the world ought to be characterized, let me ask you an important question: does Jarrell's work in fact *do* this intensifying and typifying you claim for it?

A. You bet it does. His realm is one of pity and terror, of a kind of non-understanding understanding (which I'll explain later), and above all of helplessness. All his people, the wounded soldiers, the children, the cancer patients, all these are people in predicaments that happen all the time. They are the things that our situation as human beings can't help bringing to bear on us. It is through the kind of compulsion that these things force up in us that Jarrell writes his poems. He is saying, in almost every poem, "There is no explanation for what is happening to you. *I* don't understand why it is; I can tell you nothing. But I know how it must be for you." The poems are moving in the way life is, when these things happen in it. And there is the compassion of a *man* in them, a man who knows that his helpless pity won't do any good, won't change anything, but who keeps pouring it out anyway because he can't help it. There is your real helplessness, and there is your poet Jarrell. And if you read him in a little less cynical manner than you have done, you would know this; you would become fully Human.

B. But these are *poems* he is trying to write. If you ignore that, you substitute sentimentality and special pleading (admirable though it be) for the poet's true work, which is to put down words in a certain order. You get, in fact, *my* Jarrell. Tell me, my Compassionate friend, with all these fine things that happen to you when you read a Jarrell poem, can you honestly tell me that you think Jarrell has a good ear, or is very perceptive or even accurate in his use of *language*?

A. Yes, I think he has, and is, in an unexceptional, unobtrusive way.

B. (reads)

> The yaks groaning with tea, the burlaps
> Lapping and lapping each stunned universe

Now, how about those "burlaps / Lapping and lapping"? What put *that* one past him if not laxity and not-hearing? Come, now; has he really the poet's deep, instinctive feel of language, the sense of language as a *mode* of experience?

A. He has, but he has a more important commitment, which is to humanity. And that is better.

B. Not in poetry, it isn't. Language and experience have got to be interactive at a deeper (or higher) level to make poetry happen. Deeper or higher than Jarrell commands, I mean. I maintain that Jarrell doesn't have in more than the slightest and rather synthetic and predictable degree this kind of grasp on language. He has a good sense of the poetically profitable situation, which by itself is by no means enough. It won't do, when you write a bad poem, a poem that doesn't "raise to consciousness" (to paraphrase Collingwood) a given segment of experience, to say, "Well, the World told me to say it that way. I looked at the Thing, the War, the Child, the Wounded Man, and it looked back, and the World told me, 'Son, what you see, *is*,' And so I put it down without Artifice, or with only a little, and I felt Compassion for the subject, and I had a poem. And that's what poetry is, by gum." No; that won't wash. Let Jarrell write a single phrase that has the harnessed *verbal* energy of Valéry's *"La mer, la mer, toujours recommencée"* and I'll begin to see him as a poet. And let me add that that line, as far as I'm concerned, has more of "the World" in it than all of Jarrell's; it has because the poet has *put* it there.

A. Do you think that Jarrell's criticism operates from the same assumptions as the poetry?

B. Yes, and these assumptions are infinitely more valuable to him there. He says, in effect, that the poet has to get into *rapport* with his world, which, if he is a real poet, will turn out to be part of Jarrell's definitional (but nowhere defined) World.

A. I believe him.

B. Well, the first part, yes. When he says of Marianne Moore that she has "the poet's immemorial power to make the things of this world seen and felt and living in words," I rejoice. When he says of Richard Wilbur (himself a far better poet than Jarrell) that a certain passage was "only an excuse for some poetry," I can see the justice of the remark, applied not so much to Wilbur, but to other poets Wilbur's age or a little younger: Anthony Hecht, James Merrill, W. S. Merwin. But when we turn to Jarrell's own poems to see what exemplifies, necessarily most centrally in attempt, if not in performance, these principles of writing about "real things," we sense immediately that something is gravely wrong. In reading them you have a feeling of great and self-satisfied relief in thinking, "Is *that* all there is to it? Me for Reality." For the "Real World" is far too often merely called on, and not created at all, by descriptions that would not be remarkable in an ordinary naturalistic short story or novel. This is in part the case, I suppose, because Jarrell evidently considers it a particular virtue, in his espousal of the "real," to cling like death to the commonplace, as though the Real were only the Ordinary, after all, and the solution that artists have sought for centuries were resolved in that recognition. But when García Lorca says, "Your belly is a battle of roots," is that Ordinary?

A. Jarrell might not admit it as poetry.

B. I can't judge as to that. But I admit it. Furthermore, it seems to me to be almost fearfully "real," Jarrell be damned. It comes down to this: I don't think you can impose your own notion of "reality" as everyone's, no matter how much you assume and take for granted that everyone is like you, or should be like you. You can't legitimately offer your *personal* interpretation of "reality" *as though it were* universally acceptable, and write criticism and poetry out of an agreement with yourself that this is the case.

A. But that is what you *have* to do, *especially* in your own work.

B. There is a difference between offering a view and attempting to impose *the* view.

A. I don't think that is arguable, really.

B. Perhaps not, but think of what I have said, anyway, the next time Jarrell says to you, "Surely everyone will want to read. . . ." or "Anyone knows that. . . ." or "Nowadays we all learn from. . . ."

A. I suppose I am at liberty to believe in Jarrell's as a real world, as a world that is probably as near as a poet can bring me to *the* World, whatever that is (but I *feel* it!).

B. You are. Realer, though, than Dylan Thomas's?

A. Well, yes. Not so good, though, as poetry. But Jarrell's world is nearer what I know.

B. How about what Thomas knows? You appear to be willing to accept this business of Ordinariness as Reality. Tell me, then, why you believe Thomas's to be the better poetry?

A. He does something, well, something *else* to the world. Changes it, maybe.

B. Yes, birds fly through water, stars burst out of bearing mothers' ears (this from the prose), hunchbacks turn into tall young women, and so on. He plays pretty fast and loose with your Ordinary Reality, doesn't he?

A. Yes, I guess so. But what you're saying is that *anyone* who plays fast and loose with things is *thereby* a poet, which is just as untrue as any of the assumptions you say Jarrell makes.

B. I don't intend that inference at all. Would you admit

that Thomas's successes depend at least in part on these qualities of changing and shaping?

A. Yes, and so would Jarrell, probably. He says of Whitman that he is "the rashest, the most inexplicable and unlikely—the most impossible, one wants to say—of poets." Doesn't that knock out almost everything you've said?

B. Not at all. Consider the kinds of individualities he thinks *relevant* to poetry. All, or almost all the poets he likes, Frost, Williams, Elizabeth Bishop, Robert Lowell, Corbière, even poets mentioned, as it were, in passing, like Adam Drinan and Niccolò degli Albizzi, have what qualities in common?

A. I should say (except possibly of Lowell) that they use simple diction, different kinds of unpoetical offhandedness, and are preoccupied largely with. . . .

B. Everyday objects, scenes, and so on: brooms, cats, garbage cans, broccoli patches, chickens, squirrels, rabbit-hutches, socks, boxes. If someone has a simile comparing defeated soldiers to ". . . barrels rolling, jolting," Jarrell will be more likely to approve it than if the soldiers were likened to dispossessed kings, unless the kings were homey ones. But mightn't kings be more effective, in some conceivable instances?

A. Aren't you just assuming all this?

B. I don't think I am, entirely. Most of the metaphors Jarrell cites as good are of this type. Almost all of his own are. "His raft's hot-water-bottle weight," for instance. There are hundreds. If you make a metaphor, Jarrell seems to be telling you, the second term of it, the thing the first term is being compared *to,* must be something homey, something ordinary, or else you are not dealing with "reality" and therefore not writing poetry.

A. Are you asserting that poetry shouldn't or can't be made with these things?

B. Of course not. Only that it can be made with other things as well.

A. Tell me, do you think these objections hold true of the war poems?

B. Yes, more even than of the others, if that is possible. They have all the attitudes that most people think ought to be shown by poets during wars. Can you imagine a poet loving war, or not pitying the individual soldiers?

A. Does that prevent Jarrell from *really* pitying them?

B. No, and he does pity them. I am disturbed, though, that despite all the pity he shows, none of it is actually brought to bear on any*one.* Did Jarrell never love any *person* in the service with him? Did he just pity himself and all the Others, in a kind of monstrous, abstract, complacent, and inhuman Compassion? I don't think there are really any *people* in the war poems. There are only The Ball Turret Gunner, A Pilot from the Carrier, The Wingman, and assorted faceless types in uniform. They are just collective Objects, or Attitudes, or Killable Puppets. You care very little what happens to them, and that is terrible.

A. It seems to me that Jarrell is writing mostly *about* the impersonal side of war: about the fact that wars are fought, now, almost entirely by machines, and that men suffer more or less as an irrelevant afterthought of the machines.

B. Yes, but men, not Man, suffer. You do get, however, in Jarrell's war poems, some sense of this vast and impersonal aspect of modern warfare, but little of it is realized dramatically. Most of the stuff about aircraft carriers, for instance, is like watching a good film on the subject, like *The Fighting Lady*. If I had to choose between the film and the poems, I would choose the film. I can think of no film I would prefer to Thomas's "Ceremony After a Fire Raid." Jarrell's secondhand Reality simply does not do enough.

A. So far you've been doing most of the talking. Just let me have the floor for a few minutes and I'll explain all this to you, so that you'll see Jarrell for what he is: a serious, important poet, with a great deal to say, a style of his own, and all the rest.

B. Go ahead.

A. In the first place, I think you've been seduced (although maybe that's not the word) by Jarrell's criticism.

B. I think it informs the poetry. Or perhaps the criticism and the poetry are two manifestations of the same attitude. Therefore I assume there is some point in connecting them.

A. No, let me go on. My belief is that there is an honest fellow under the smart-aleck, the fashionable, giggled-over-in-seminars trickster who can quote anything to his purpose much as the devil must be able to quote Scripture. From the evidence of the poems he is an honest, responsible human being, and, as in every poet's essential way, innocent. Let me read you something.

(Reads "The Truth")

B. Well?

A. You mean you're not *moved* by that? Now, goddamn it, B., if that doesn't move you, you ought to be boiled down for soap. Look here; there's this little boy whose father and sister have been killed in a bombing raid on London. . . .

B. I understand all that. Perhaps that "slow, grave, choking voice" you read it in is supposed to do part or all of the poem's work. But the thing seems to me to be as sentimental as Eugene Field; after all, he wrote about death and children, too, if you remember. Jarrell certainly doesn't need me to be embarrassed for him, but I am anyway when I hear what you've just read.

A. It takes *courage* to be sentimental nowadays. Besides, the real things are *like* that.

B. Not like *that.* That is just sophisticated journalism; it is craft, in Collingwood's definition: working up a predictable emotion, and damned poor metrically, too. In these later poems, do you suppose Jarrell cares, any more, that poetry is supposed to display at least some degree of rhythmic concentration?

A. He is *beyond* those considerations. He is not Yvor Winters, you know. He is not your mechanical stressmonger. He is a Man, as he says in the last line of the book. He has broken away from all that petty finger-and-toe-counting, those neat, rectangular stanzas. He is past being concerned with those mechanics. He has attained a realm "where only necessary things are done, / With that supreme and grave dexterity that ignores technique" (though I may be misquoting from Kirkup here, in a word or two).

B. You say he's "broken through" these things, that he knows enough, now, not to have to worry about technical matters. Yet it seems to me that he hasn't really reached them at all, in any significant way, or has fallen progressively away from the very slight acquaintance with them evidenced in his first book. The unstated and insistent principle underlying the later poems is "The situation is enough." But, as I keep saying, he has not the power, or the genius, or the talent, or the inclination, or whatever, to make experience rise to its own most intense, concentrated, and meaningful level, a level impossible without *that* poet's having caught it in *those* words. And there the matter rests, as far as I'm concerned.

A. I can see that there's no arguing with you. But I believe that Randall Jarrell will have something to say to people for a very long time to come, especially as the world tries increasingly to survive by inhumanity (assuming you agree with me on this). The poems give you the feel of a time, our time, as no other poetry of our century does, or could, even. They put on your face, nearer than any of your own looks, more irrevocably than your skin, the uncomprehending stare of the individual caught in the State's machinery: in an impersonal, invisible, man-made, and uncontrollable Force. They show in front of you a child's slow, horrified, magnificently un-understanding and growing loss of innocence in which we all share and can't help: which we can neither understand nor help in ourselves in the hands of the State any more than can the children in *our* hands. The poems are one long look, through this expression, into a child's face, as the Things of modern life happen around it, happen to it, so that you see the expressions change, and even feel the breath change over you, and you come to be aware that you are staring back in perfect and centered blindness, in which everything to pity is clear as death, and none of the reasons for any of it. Now *that* is our time. It is humanity in the twentieth century. Or whatever is good, worth saving, there. And that is your poet Randall Jarrell, to stand against any objections, even legitimate ones. He gives you, as all great or good writers do, a foothold in a realm where literature itself is inessential, where your own world is more yours than you could ever have thought, or even felt, but is one you have always known.

Denis Donoghue

The Lost World

One of Randall Jarrell's favorite poems was "During Wind and Rain." Hardy's poem invokes the lost worlds, the songs of *Under the Greenwood Tree*, the English villages, the gallantry of bright things on the lawn. In each stanza there are seven lines, five to bring back the old images, two to concede their loss; but these two have the last word, the "sick leaves," the "white storm-birds," the "rotten rose," and the rain cutting the names on the gravestone. "Ah, no; the years, the years." It is a noble poem, keeping up appearances when there is nothing else to be done. The stanzas begin with a lift of feeling: to every dog his day of remembered ease. The loss is held at memory's length, but in the last two lines the years break in upon reverie. It is easy to guess that the poem pleased Jarrell because of its gallantry, the bravery of its tone in defeat. Gallantry: as in *King Lear* when Edgar says:

Men must endure
Their going hence, even as their coming hither:
Ripeness is all. Come on.

and Gloucester answers

And that's true too.

This is the burden of Jarrell's poems: "And that's true too."

The poems begin with loss. The lost world is, to use Eliot's phrase, "the ground of our beseeching," Act I. An entire book is called *Losses.* In "When I Was Home Last Christmas . . ." the poet says:

There is no one left to care
For all we said, and did, and thought—
The world we were.

"Never again," the voice in "Moving" says, recalling dear dead schooldays, "Never again / Will Augusta be the capital of Maine." "Children's Arms" calls to "this first Rome / Of childhood," and several poems are elegies for the penny world of Pop, Mama, and Dandeen "in her black / Silk." In "The Lost Children" a mother, observing that her daughter has grown up and that the air of home is thin, reflects:

She makes few demands; you are grateful for the few.

In "Woman":

A girl hesitates a moment in mid-air
And settles to the ground a wife, a mother.

There is more to be said, and the poet says it in the same poem, but this is Act I, the cause of all. The figure the feeling makes is given in "Thinking of the Lost World":

> Back in Los Angeles, we missed
> Los Angeles.

The terms of loss are the inveterate relationships: father, mother, child, wife, husband. Jarrell's poetry is a sequence of Mutability Cantos, tracing the crucial situations back to the point at which, changing, they withered into a new and darker truth. The tracing is done, mostly, in fear. In "The Märchen," "the darkness quakes with blood." Sometimes the tone tries to hold itself well back from the edge. There is a time for speaking of the woe that is in marriage, but Jarrell tries to postpone that speech; meanwhile, keep the cry muted. In "Next Day" a woman at the supermarket, her pilgrim's progress confined to a choice of Cheer, Joy, and All, is troubled by what she has become, "commonplace and solitary." Life makes few demands upon her and perhaps, like the other mother, she is grateful for those few. The demands she makes upon life are not exorbitant:

> Now that I'm old, my wish
> Is womanish:
> That the boy putting groceries in my car
>
> See me. It bewilders me he doesn't see me.

Not "enrages" or even "annoys"; just "bewilders." In this first act there is bound to be a moment in which the bewilderment is complete and fixed. In Jarrell's poetry it occurs when the voice says something and then, since the something said is disconsolate, says the opposite, hoping that this is the trick, the key; and finds that it makes no difference.

> The husband answers, "Life is life,"
> And when his wife calls to him from the kitchen
> He tells her who it was, and what he wanted.
> Beating the whites of seven eggs, the beater
> Asks her her own opinion; she says, "Life
> Is life." "See how it sounds to say it isn't,"
> The beater tempts her. "Life is not life,"
> She says. It sounds the same. Putting her cake
> Into the oven, she is satisfied
> Or else dissatisfied: it sounds the same.

I have spoken of this as Act I, where the dramatist gives the first hints. With the wisdom of hindsight we can say, looking at Jarrell's poetry: there, there is where it began. The poems in *Blood for a Stranger* and *Little Friend, Little Friend* are not his choice work. In these the feeling is raw, and Jarrell was not good with raw wounds. He needed, for the good of the poetry, a wound not quite healed and yet as close to healing as it would ever come. He needed to be able to go a little way off, far enough to talk about the experience. He was not a dramatic poet. Reading his poems is not like seeing *King Lear:* it is like the relief of breaking a wounded silence, letting the pain drain away in words, in companionable talk. When we say that his idiom is conversational, we mean that it is like the conversation that helps, in trouble; balm to hurt minds.

Meanwhile there is Act II, since we cannot live forever in loss even if the loss lives forever in us. As Gloucester says, "O cruel! O you Gods!" Act II is the place for blame, recrimination, fighting back. As Jarrell says, "Oh, it's not *right*," the italics the fury in the words of "The Night before the Night before Christmas," heard again in "The Face." Some of Jarrell's most celebrated poems come from this second act: cadences of protest, as in "The Prince." "A man dies like a rabbit, for a use"; followed by: "What will they pay me, when I die, to die?" The war poems are here, and poems like "Jews at Haifa" about the war after the War. Some years later we hear the protest, rueful now, *diminuendo,* in the prose of *A Sad Heart at the Supermarket* and many of the poems in *The Woman at the Washington Zoo.* Perhaps it is the residue of the war feeling which, turning sour, sets the cruel moments astir in *Pictures from an Institution.* In "The Snow-Leopard" Jarrell speaks of "the brute and geometrical necessity." In "Siegfried" this necessity is reported as dull fact:

> *It happens as it does because it does.*
> It is unnecessary to understand; if you are still
> In this year of our warfare, indispensable
> In general, and in particular dispensable
> As a cartridge, a life

This is the "murderous / Dull will" invoked in "1945: The Death of the Gods," arranging, as in "The Sick Nought," that the soldier is "something there are millions of." "The book is finished. I tell you you're not in it," the poet says to the men in the Overseas Replacement Depot. Reading the protest poems again when another protest is in the air, I find that those which have not survived intact are dead in their public manner. They sound as if, for a proper reading, they need a megaphone and Hyde Park, a public-address system and Madison Square Garden:

> Man is born in chains, and everywhere we see him dead.
> On your earth they sell nothing but our lives.
> You knew that what you died for was our deaths?

There is nothing wrong with these lines, in principle, except that they come from a poetic world that Jarrell never owned. He did not lose it, because he never had it. The lines witness a failure of the feeling to secure its proper voice, its proper form. In an early poem Jarrell invokes "that strange speech / In which each sound sets out to seek each other." In poems like "The Emancipators" the sounds set out to seek each other but, not finding, settle for other sounds, more accessible, merely because they are there. The sounds have a better chance when they are less portentously directed, left to find their own companions. This is to say that Jarrell's poems are best when scored for a voice, like Cordelia's, "soft, gentle, and low"; even when the words are large in content:

> nothing comes from nothing,
> The darkness from the darkness. Pain comes from the
> darkness
> And we call it wisdom. It is pain.

There is nothing remarkable in these lines except the tone of their delivery. The crucial moment is in the gap between the last two sentences: what is said, in the words, is only important because it frames the silence between one apprehension and the next. Among the modern poets Eliot is the greatest master of these silences. But Jarrell is more than Eliot's pupil in this resource. He is particularly vivid in the relation between silence and speech, the flow of feeling between them. So he does wonderful things with a full stop, a colon, a question mark. In "A Street off Sunset" the voice speaks of Mama, her face "half a girl's," wringing a chicken's neck; and the child thinking:

> . . . Could such a thing
> Happen to anything? It could to a rabbit, I'm afraid;
> It could to—
> "Mama, you won't kill Reddy ever,
> You won't ever, will you?"

This experience, which recurs in several poems, is beautifully registered. Its horror is domestic: this is not to say that the horror is small. Jarrell's special area of feeling is the private loss, held but not resolved in the structure of daily things; where the domestic order conceals—but not really, and not for long—the private anarchy; where speech is bewildered in silence. His sad hearts are most warmly felt at the supermarket, his wounded souls at the Washington Zoo. This is why the conversational idiom is so close to the shape of the poems, the shape of their feeling; why, too, this poet got so much, in this way, from Hardy, Yeats, and Frost. Saying "Oh, it's not *right*" is momentous when things seem to be right: right, meaning normal, ordinary, daily. There is no point in saying "Oh, it's not *right*" if you are in Hiroshima. In "Three Bills" we are to imagine a man, the poet perhaps, in the restaurant at the Plaza, breakfast time, overhearing a conversation between a man, his wife, and another woman, all rich. The man goes off to the lavatory and his wife complains to her friend:

> "We can't stay anywhere. We haven't stayed a month
> In one place for the last three years.
> He flirts with the yardboys and we have to leave."

The friend is sorry; and the poet in turn, is sorry; sorry that the wife, the blonde, "the suffused face about to cry / Or not to cry—"

> was a face that under different
> Circumstances would have been beautiful, a woman's.

I.e.: "Oh, it's not *right*."

Act III: "An English Garden in Austria"; a voice asking, "And how shall we bear it?" The first answer is: by recalling everything else. Jarrell is a little Proust to whom, as someone has said, the only real paradises are lost paradises, spectrally recovered in memory and vision. Memory is compulsive in this poet, as if he feared that by losing anything he would lose everything. This is why so much of Jarrell's experience is seen under glass, and the death of the ball turret gunner, in a famous poem, is a sinister version of the boyhood image, the magic gone wrong. In "Children's Arms":

> The glass encloses
> As glass does, a womanish and childish
> And doggish universe. We press our noses
> To the glass and wish

In "The One Who Was Different" the poet thinks of a dead woman and, rearranging the conditions, thinks of her, instead, lying

> Encased in crystal, continually mortal,
> While the years rolled over you . . .

Hence the mirror's magic, sometimes black, sometimes the whitest white; as in "Woman," where the morning sun, "grayer for its mirroring," is "perfected" in the wife's shining eyes. Hence also the dream poems, sometimes nightmare, sometimes what we see when we press our noses to the glass and wish. In "A Sick Child" the child longs so hard for things to be different that they must be different, mustn't they?

Jarrell has a wonderful feeling for dreams and for the children who attend them, for those countries to which a child creeps "out of his own life." He wrote many poems to chart those countries, planting them with their proper vines. In the nightmare poems the proof of desolation is the thought that the dream things are just the same as daily things. In "The Truth," when the bombs on London drive a child away from father and mother and the father is lost in one way and the mother in another, the child knows that the mother is no longer the same:

> Sometimes she was the same, but that was when I
> dreamed it.
> I could tell I was dreaming, she was just the same.

The wounded soldier in "A Field Hospital" comes out of his dream: "the old mistake." Dream is a way of bearing it. So is fiction, anything to make it new. Jarrell wrote several poems about children seen in a lending library. He speaks of "one cure for Everychild's diseases / Beginning: *Once upon a time there was.*" We live, the same poem has it, by "trading another's sorrow for our own"; trading "another's / Impossibilities, still unbelieved in, for our own. . . ." Stevens said of the Supreme Fiction: "It Must Change." To Jarrell, that kind of change is the fiction itself, "dear to all things not to themselves endeared." So in "Children's Arms" the island sings to the child: *"Believe! Believe!"* We bear it, if we can, by make-believe, dreams, figments, fictions. The verbal equivalent, in the detail, is wit; where the poet, almost a child, creeps out of his own life, fighting the good poetic fight, slaying the prosaic dragon. Mostly the dragon comes as authority, the way of the world, Army Regulations, public cliché. The poet bears these things by gulling them, tripping them on their own banana skins. In "A War":

> There set out, slowly, for a Different World,
> At four, on winter mornings, different legs . . .
> *You can't break eggs without making an omelette*
> —That's what they tell the eggs.

When the poet asks, "And how shall we bear it?" his answer is: "Lightly, lightly." This is his way into Act IV, the place where, traditionally, the dramatist releases "the pity of it all." Jarrell is lavish in pity. Indeed, he is never afraid of his feelings, or ashamed of them, or even proud of them. He is always pleased to appreciate the natural thing, liking the way a baby bat holds on tight to its mother's tail and the different ways an owl tests the corners of the night. The poet's special feeling in Act IV is care; its particular cadence, "And yet, and yet." He does not parade his care. Simply, he cares. It is typical of his sensibility that in an art gallery he notices the guard before he looks at the pictures; that when a girl talks of "the dailiness of life," he saves the day with an image of water:

> Water, cold, so cold! you cup your hands
> And gulp from them the dailiness of life.

After the cruelty of the gods we have to care for what remains, such as it is. If the rules of the game are unjust, so much the worthier those men of chance who play it well. Character is a game splendidly played: therefore good like the other good things, "to go on being," life itself with all its cruelty, ordinary things like sunshine, rain, childhood, the life of Nollekens. Or literature, one of the best ordinary things. In criticism, in teaching, praise was the highest form of Jarrell's care. Robert Lowell has written that eulogy was Jarrell's glory as a critic, praise that moved mountains of inertia and condescension. Who has ever spoken so well for Whitman's lists merely by saying of them: yes, but what lists! Jarrell's own lists make an impeccable anthology, the classic unexpected poems from Hardy, Ransom, Rilke, Frost,

Williams, Shakespeare, Marianne Moore. When he was wrong, as I think he was wrong in that early essay on Stevens, he found an occasion to try again and this time got it right. Indeed, his reading of favorite poets was so devoted that he seemed to think his response a paltry effort until he had almost made himself over in their image. So I think of "A Soul" as a Ransom poem, "To the New World" an Auden poem, "The Märchen" a Tate poem. And if someone loved Hardy so much that he wanted to write a Hardy poem, could he do better than Jarrell in "The Blind Sheep"? I am often surprised that Jarrell did not write a Yeats poem, but there are Frost poems, like "Money" and "Field and Forest." These poems are thank-you notes mailed to the poets who showed Jarrell what might still be done.

I am not sure about Act V. We are accustomed to muted endings, as in *King Lear* when Edgar says simply, "The weight of this sad time we must obey." In Jarrell's Act V the crucial poem is "Thinking of the Lost World." A man goes back, in reverie, to California, finding smog in Los Angeles where a child knew sunshine. "The orange groves are all cut down. . . ." So he tries to bear it, lightly:

> I say to my old self: "I believe. Help thou
> Mine unbelief."

The images of boyhood, the strangled chicken and the woman with the lion, are now parts of science fiction: this is not to say that they have been replaced, in belief, by anything else. There is a moment in *Timon of Athens* when Timon, who has been composing his epitaph, says to Flavius:

My long sickness
Of health and living now begins to mend,
And nothing brings me all things.

It is a moment entirely in keeping with that all-or-nothing play. "Thinking of the Lost World" is also written, imaginatively, at the end of the line. So it goes back to the old images and gestures: one thing copying its opposite, a shadow miming a shadow, trading one emptiness for another. The poem ends, the last poem in Jarrell's last book:

Where's my own hand? My smooth
White bitten-fingernailed one? I seem to see
A shape in tennis shoes and khaki riding-pants
Standing there empty-handed; I reach out to it
Empty-handed, my hand comes back empty,
And yet my emptiness is traded for its emptiness,
I have found that Lost World in the Lost and Found
Columns whose gray illegible advertisements
My soul has memorized world after world:
LOST—NOTHING. STRAYED FROM NOWHERE.
NO REWARD.
I hold in my own hands, in happiness,
Nothing: the nothing for which there's no reward.

Gloucester speaks to Edmund of "the quality of nothing." Stevens speaks, in "The Snow Man," a poem dear to Jarrell, of the "mind of winter," the superbly qualified mind of one who willingly sees wintry things:

> the listener, who listens in the snow,
> And, nothing himself, beholds
> Nothing that is not there and the nothing that is.

This second nothing is the one that brings all things, Timon's nothing in Act V. In "Prologues to What Is Possible" Stevens writes of

> The way the earliest single light in the evening sky, in
> spring,
> Creates a fresh universe out of nothingness by adding
> itself.

This is what the mind of winter comes to, after the long sickness. Where there is nothing, Stevens implies, there is man, there is his imagination. Stevens thinks of it as a wonderful resilience of perception. It is what Jarrell comes to, at the end: winter, and then, "in happiness," the mind of winter. In his case I think of it as a resilience, equally wonderful, of love. Call it gallantry. As Yeats sang:

> Man is in love and loves what vanishes,
> What more is there to say?

Leslie A. Fiedler

Jarrell's Criticism: A Footnote

THERE IS a certain irony in insisting that, after all, Randall Jarrell was a good critic, even if one hastens to qualify by adding a good critic, *too;* for one of his most admired essays was an attack upon criticism and his own age, which had come to admire that art almost more (Jarrell said simply "more," being accustomed to eschew "almosts") than poetry or fiction. But precisely the irony of the observation would have redeemed it for Jarrell, who was a lover of the double tone, the tongue in the cheek, the wry joke on oneself. Yet he was quite serious when he said in the essay in question, in the very midst of criticism of criticism, deadliest of all literary forms: "Readers, real readers, are almost as wild a species as writers; most critics are so domesticated as to seem institutions—as they stand there between reader and writer, so different from either, they remind one of the Wall standing between Pyramus and Thisbe."

So, perhaps, we should settle for saying that Jarrell was not *quite* a critic finally, but rather a "real reader" joined in a single body to a compulsive talker, who could never resist any editor's invitation to turn his conversation into an article, a "piece," even an "omnibus review," though without ever losing the sense of breathlessness or the intimacy of the human voice. It is, at any rate, that conversational voice which lives again in our ear, when we turn after Jarrell's death to the two collections of such articles which he was also persuaded to make: *Poetry and the Age,* which appeared in 1953, and *A Sad Heart at the Supermarket,* published nearly a decade later in 1962.

The second volume contains nothing quite so fresh or acute as many things in the first (the wit has grown too nervously aggressive, the tone bullies a little); but in neither does he anywhere betray his own speaking voice and responding heart. He is everywhere the man who has *just* read something he loves or hates, sometimes the man baffled by what surprised him into admiration or exacerbated him beyond patience by its ineptitude; but always the man speaking his passion, rather than an embodied institution pronouncing judgment. He is resolutely unsystematic, committed to no methodology or aesthetic theory—responsible only to his own responses, hushed only before the mystery of his own taste. And what unfailing taste he possessed; though its roots were in something nearer to madness than to method, given or endured rather than earned or sought, and therefore often offensive, as any talent is offensive, to those who resist believing in predestination.

Because—trusting to insight and depending on his feeling and talking self as a sufficient source of unity—he preferred stringing apothegms together to constructing logical sequences, it is finally phrases rather than whole essays out of Jarrell which stay in the mind. They seem, however, neither at first nor in retrospect mere gags or wisecracks, but rather gnomic utterances made to be puzzled over and remembered —to be got "by heart," as the apposite phrase has it. "If we were in the habit of reading poets their obscurity would not matter; and, once we are out of the habit, their clarity does not help." "But here I am not only left helpless to say whether this is slight or not, I don't even want to know: I am too sure of what I have even to want to say what it is, so that I will say if you ask me, as St. Augustine did about Time: 'I know if you don't ask me.' " "Having wonderful dreams, telling wonderful lies, was a temptation Whitman could never resist; but telling the truth was a temptation he could never resist, either. When you buy him you know what you are buying." "From his children and ghosts one learns little about children and nothing about ghosts. [Jarrell is talking about Walter de la Mare, in case anyone cares], but one learns a great deal of the reality of which his ghosts and his children are projections, of the wishes and lacks and love that have produced their 'unreality.' " "Contemporary criticism has not done very well by Williams; most of the good critics of poetry have not written about him, and one or two of the best, when they did write, just twitched as if flies were crawling over them." ". . . Frost has little of Hardy's self-effacement, his matter-of-fact humility; Frost's tenderness, sadness, and humor are adulterated with vanity and a hard complacency."

But there is no point (though much pleasure) in going on; since one can never quite quote enough; and anyhow there is more in Jarrell than a handful of aphorisms—buttressed by a habit of quotation, which is, obviously enough, catching. He was a critic, a reader bent on freeing himself and *his* readers from the literary canons of his own time, the rigid set of all-right books compiled and certified by his mentors, those New Critics, whom he loved (expecially John Crowe Ransom) short of idolatry. The books certified by any age, he knew to be a prison for the spirit—and it is his praise of currently unfashionable writers which especially delights and refreshes us, providing hope, if not absolute reassurance, that even from the current mode there may be avenues of escape.

I suppose it is in light of this, of Jarrell's perception that an essential function of the critic is to free the loving reader from all orthodoxies as well as all methodologies, that I admire most those essays of his which deal not with poets sufficiently admired by others in his own time (Ransom, let's say, or Marianne Moore, or even Auden—about whom he wrote so much which he left quite uncollected—or Richard Wilbur, or even Robert Lowell), but with those condescended to or excluded by reigning criticism: William Carlos Williams, for example, and especially Walt Whitman and Robert Frost.

With Whitman we have come to feel at home once again, forgetting that only a couple of decades ago he had been declared officially dead by literary commentators sufficiently acute and perceptive (i.e., obtuse only beyond their own self-imposed limits): Tate and Blackmur and Yvor Winters and all the small fry they spawned, whose Criticism was thought of deep into the fifties as being somehow still New.

In a sense, the rediscovery—reinvention is probably more precise—of Whitman belongs to the years just after the one hundredth anniversary of *Leaves of Grass* in 1955, and is largely the work of a single poet of eminent talent, Allen Ginsberg, in whom Whitman was improbably reborn. But as early as 1951, Jarrell had, as it were, anticipated him, begun to prepare for him by combing through the pages of Whitman's overlong poem—which no responsive reader has ever really wished a line shorter all the same—finding, with his typical uncanny precision, precisely the lines capable of rekindling our interest and providing a paradigm for new work. Especially he minded us of the wit everywhere at play in lines we had long persuaded ourselves in our dullness were themselves as dull as our perceptions. It is Whitman the comic poet whom he gave back to us, perhaps gave to us for the first time.

How odd to discover, rereading Jarrell, that he had to *sell* us Whitman just over fifteen years ago by recalling to us that Gerard Manley Hopkins (himself then safely okay) had been fond of his odd American counterpart; and how humiliating to be reminded that even so recently—a scant five years before the return of Whitmanian verse to the center of our tradition—Jarrell had felt obliged to write: "I have said so little about Whitman's faults because they are so plain: baby critics who have barely learned to complain of the lack of ambiguity in *Peter Rabbit* [it was another of Jarrell's favorite forgotten books] can tell you all that is wrong with *Leaves of Grass*. But a good many of my readers must have felt that it is ridiculous to write an essay about the obvious fact that Whitman is a great poet. . . . Critics have to spend half their time reiterating whatever ridiculously obvious things their age or the critics of their age have found it necessary to forget."

But though Whitman has been repossessed, Frost, it seems to me, has tended to become more and more invisible, except as resurrected for political reasons—to adorn the ceremonies at a Presidential Inauguration, for instance, or to raise the tone of a campaign speech intended to be received by those to whom a quotation from any other poet would seem a cultural affront. It is, I fear, still true that "Ordinary readers think Frost the greatest poet alive, and love some of his best poems almost as much as they love some of his worst ones"; and it is, I suspect, equally true that the more advanced readers of currently fashionable verse tend to condescend to him just as loftily as their opposite numbers in the earliest fifties. ". . . the reader of Eliot or Auden usually dismisses Frost," Jarrell wrote then in an essay called "The Other Frost," "as something inconsequentially good that *he* knew all about long ago"; and I am sure that if we substitute, say Charles Olson for Eliot, and Allen Ginsberg for Auden (our Old Men for theirs), the observation would still hold.

For most readers and writers of "projective verse," Jarrell's "other" Frost, that vanity-ridden and gifted monster—able to evoke the "strange ordinariness" as well as the "ordinary strangeness" of things, without betraying either those things or the spoken language he inherited—remains still quite as unavailable as he formerly was to the worshippers at the shrine of "metaphysical conceits" and "serious wit." Yet Jarrell specified the poems in which that "other" Frost was to be found: "The Witch of Coös," "Neither Out Far nor In Deep," "Directive," "Design," "A Servant to Servants," "Provide, Provide," etc., etc.; and in a second essay, "To the Laodiceans," actually quoted for the lazy or reluctant the relevant passages, including that terrifying final quatrain of "Neither Out Far nor In Deep," which is Frost's comment on those readers (which is to say, on us) whom he cannot help insulting even as he woos them:

> They cannot look out far.
> They cannot look in deep.
> But when was that ever a bar
> To any watch they keep?

So, what then if this Frost remains still undiscovered, undiscoverable? It is merely another irony to please the spirit of Jarrell, who learned a taste for irony surely from Frost among others. And it is a kind of triumph, too; since to the critic, better even than having anticipated (as Jarrell did in the case of Whitman) a shift of taste just over the horizon, is having perceived a hidden goodness with which critical fashion has not yet caught up, and perhaps never will.

Robert Fitzgerald

A Place of Refreshment

IF I COULD have my way in the matter, I would prefer to see Randall again in the quarry pool near Bloomington, Indiana, where we used to swim almost every afternoon in the summer of 1952. He and I and Leslie Fiedler were holding classes at the School of Letters there, and it was nice to have a swimming hole to resort to when the heat waves made our eyebrows crawl. The abandoned limestone quarry at the edge of town was filled with clear green spring water, always cool, and crossed by a smooth rock ledge a foot or so above the water, very handy for diving and sunning. You drove down a country road, walked a quarter of a mile or so, and found yourself approaching this place, which was off limits, we were told, for town and university people—and in fact rarely visited except by ourselves and our friends. Our friends were a few students, the most constant of whom were two bright and not at all uncomely girls. That sounds interesting, and it was, but it would have had very slight interest for the well-known Kinsey Institute at the university. If there had been no other considerations, I suppose the awful presence of the Institute would have been enough to make all three of us refrain from so much as brushing those girls with a daisy, in the fine Ransom phrase. Prelapsarian if not prenatal were our pleasures, cavorting in that pool with our naiads, whom I can still see pale and blurry underwater or emerging, hair streaming, to shake and bat the blearing drops from their eyes. And I see Randall just as vividly, coming up for air, his hair plastered over his forehead, his line of mustache dripping, eyes shut tight in the delicate sallow bony face that at those times and at others had what I thought of as a *Confederate* look—old-fashioned and rural and honorable and a little toothy or hungry. Once up and paddling and often laughing, he would talk about what had crossed his mind underwater, so to speak. Long ago he had done at least one passionate essay to wake people up to Robert Frost, but that summer he was still waking up, himself; hanging on a floating log in the quarry pool, he began one day to quote aloud the poem, "Provide, Provide," and to his growing astonishment and delight succeeded in going straight through it from memory. "Why, *I* didn't know I had memorized *that*!" Randall is one of the few men I have known who chortled. He really did. "Baby *doll*!" he would cry, and his voice simply rose and broke in joy. As I say, I would like to see him again in that happiness, in the cool Midwestern water.

It is the chronological centerpiece in my memories of him. At Sarah Lawrence in the first year after the war we met as part-time teachers and became friends. Randall had agreed to edit the literary section of *The Nation* that winter while Margaret Marshall was on leave, so he was living in Manhattan as I was, and I could often give him a ride back from Bronxville in my olive-drab old Ford. We talked about poems and people on those trips, as the parkway unrolled before us back to the great Hudson scene, or we talked at lunch together in the college cafeteria or over coffee in the college tuck-shop. I can see him plainly in that place, too: young and tallish and a bit gangling but with dignity, his long throat distinctly angled, his dark eyes in repose proud and solemn, the lids drooping slightly toward the outer corners. More often they were animated, exceedingly gay and bright, but in conversation they could shadow swiftly with recognition, looking less at you than at some depth in himself that had been stirred, becoming hooded eyes where memory and mockery lurked. He loved his job at *The Nation,* or at least he certainly loved the game of matching reviewers and books, and he did it so well that in Mr. Ransom's later judgment his editorship deserved a Pulitzer Prize. He made me aware of the work of his old Kenyon friends, Peter Taylor and Robert Lowell. He got me to do some reviews. It turned out that besides the vocation we had in common, Randall and I also shared a devotion to tennis. We would have liked, almost more than anything, to play well enough for national ranking, but we had been born to be only fair tennis players. In those days Randall used to remind people that he had been trained as a psychologist—at Vanderbilt, before he switched to English—and competitive tennis fascinated that side of him; then, too, he relished the craft and lore of the game, as of everything he took up. When he dropped the ball for his first forehand shot in practice, you saw a small ritual performed with attention and gravity.

I had the impression that for Randall this interest in tennis represented an attachment to common life, as later on sports cars did and later still professional football, and that he placed a peculiar value on these hobbies. He was, after all, precocious and a prodigy; he simply had genius; he must have known that at times he was not only lonely but faintly monstrous, as those who were fondest of him regularly agreed. Well, he wished not to be, and the wish was appealing. How many times he must have curbed his tongue! I never had to endure Randall's famous disdain, at least not the full brunt of it, but I have seen it rudely bestowed. The saving grace by which one forgave him in advance, and always, lay in his loyalty to his admirations and beyond them to the wisdoms and wonders of art.

Those were the first days of our acquaintance, in 1946–47. The summer in Indiana was six years later; six years later still, in 1958, after his term as Consultant to the Library of Congress, he brought his family to spend the summer in Liguria near the Peter Taylors and ourselves. He had acquired a full bushy beard and denied that it made his face hot. In some ways it proved to be an inharmonious summer. Randall and I were even outclassed in a local tennis tournament that we entered, both in singles and in doubles. But no incidental failures could outweigh the great pleasure of seeing one another again and exchanging our tidings and somewhat riper thoughts. One literary affection we were able to renew in company was that for Kipling. While reading the Jungle Books to my children in Italian, I had found, in the marvelous oceanic story about the white seal, a great and timely reminder of what may be done with sheer invention; the oaths that Kipling had thought up for that seal were somehow liberating to me at a moment when my own work demanded this. No one alive could have understood the case better than Randall. He may have been rereading the stories with a view to editing them for Anchor Books, because he remarked one evening that there wasn't a page of Kipling that he hadn't read, and most of them many times. He had been working on his translation of *Faust,* and as I was then working on Homer he made me a present of his Roget and, even more helpfully, of one admirable perception on the way diction can be modulated, but must not be abruptly changed, from high to low. After taking the Jarrells to the train one summer day, I was never to see him in this world again—except as I have been seeing him in the course of this reminiscence.

Lately in London I came across the new edition of Christina Stead's novel, *The Man Who Loved Children,* bearing Randall's long introduction, and it was like seeing a capstone fall into place, for it seemed to me that having done that essay, he had, in a way, completed the arch of his appreciative writing and had imparted to the rest of us the sum of his brilliant insights and delights. What he could do in poetry he did early and with prodigious security; he was one of our true poets for thirty years and practically the only American poet able to cope with the Second Great War; many of us both younger and older would acknowledge him as a master in one degree or another. It was this gift of true pitch as a writer that made his teaching voice, his critical voice, as penetrating as it was. I do not deny that he could be too chattery and too exclamatory; everyone can be too something. But his work again and again enhanced the life of poetry and gave the age, in its degradation, a great example of sensibility and wit. I hope that he has found his place of refreshment, as we found it in that quarry years ago.

R. W. Flint

On Randall Jarrell

PORT OF EMBARKATION

Freedom, farewell! Or so the soldiers say;
And all the freedoms they spent yesterday
Lure from beyond the graves, a war away.
The cropped skulls resonate the wistful lies
Of dead civilians: truth, reason, justice;
The foolish ages haunt their unaccepting eyes.

From the green gloom of the untroubled seas
Their little bones (the coral of the histories)
Foam into marches, exultation, victories:
Who will believe the blood curled like a moan
From the soaked lips, a century from home—
The slow lives sank from being like a dream?

Randall Jarrell was in many ways the wonder and terror of American poetry during the late 40's and early 50's. Like Shelley, as Robert Lowell fondly describes him after a friendship of thirty years, in his "harsh luminosity," he could glide for days against the sun, swooping down every so often with murderous effect on the warblers and thrushes. Not many readers knew where to find him, or indeed sometimes, to their dismay, where not to find him. After the publication of his novel, *Pictures from an Institution*, in 1954, and his critical collection, *Poetry and the Age*, in 1953, books so amusing, high-spirited, accurate, original, and humane that they often confirmed an easy prejudice (of which I have been guilty) that he was a better critic than poet, he apparently retired to his private Weimar at Greensboro, North Carolina, to teach, write poetry, prefaces, children's books—seemingly a domesticated lion. To say that he had been a disturbing figure during his years as poetry editor of *The Nation* would be a rash understatement. Not since Poe had an American poet of his distinction laid down the law in quite such a carnival spirit. He reached maturity at the climax of the New Critical era, whose excesses he both relished and deplored with brilliant finality, and could not have been the kind of poet he was had he not been an equally good critic. To look back on his ascendancy when the connective tissue between the beauty and magnanimity of much of his writing and the bacchic exhilaration of his rejections and dislikes may have been hard to discern—impossible for a few of his unlucky victims—is, for me, to rediscover how quickly he had won my trust without my knowing exactly why, and how much in his debt many of us were.

There were two peaks, at the beginning and end of his public life, when his full quality was active in his poetry. I agree entirely with Lowell that "His gifts, both by nature and by a lifetime of hard dedication and growth, were wit, pathos, and brilliance of intelligence. These qualities, dazzling in themselves, were often so well employed that he became, I think, the most heartbreaking English poet of his generation." He made his debut as a war poet of astonishing poise and fullness for so young a man; for several older critics who had recognized his quality immediately and done it justice, but who lost him in the radical-pastoral, romantically nostalgic, bittersweet idylls of his middle career, Randall Jarrell remained *the* poet of the war.

Returning to the war poems twenty years after their appearance in *Blood for a Stranger*, *Little Friend, Little Friend*, and *Losses*, is something of a revelation. I had taken them in, a few whole poems and many wonderfully effective images, but had somehow missed the magnificence they have for me now, perhaps vaguely expecting an equal magnificence from another poet in a style more congenial to my experience of the war. There was no other poet, none who came within shouting distance of Jarrell. That he had been, like Whitman, very lucky in his circumstances, neither too far in the fighting nor too far out, a true airman in every figurative sense, and even better prepared by genius and training to render the particulars of war by diffraction from a radically civilized and simple philosophy (or "strategy," if you prefer John Crowe Ransom's hallowed term)—all this was obscured from some of us who had been closer to the action and wore a veteran's foolish pride not quite lightly enough, forgetting that the civilian Whitman and Melville had been the Civil War poets, resisting a repetition of the mud-soaked griefs of Wilfred Owen and Isaac Rosenberg in World War I, looking perhaps for poetry more in the jaunty style of Howard Nemerov in America or Keith Douglas in England; something abrupt and hard-bitten, steeped in romantic disillusion and military slang; brief, sweeping, dismissive ironies, like the crushing out of a last cigarette before take-off.

By 1945 everyone knew what the motto of the war had been . . . *hurry up and wait.* Jarrell knew it. But the long patience of outfacing a worn-out myth of heroism took, on the surface where most war poetry gets written, a very different form in the average serviceman's mind than it did in Jarrell's. For the soldier, the flyer, especially the carrier-based flyer (I had been a ship's-company gunner on a carrier for the last year in the Pacific), it was a matter of killing boredom by devotion to the technical niceties of the job, for which we were truly but ambiguously grateful. Nothing in my ship's distant engagements with the Japanese (we were protected by an immense screen of other ships) matched, for ship's-company gunners, the excitement of shooting down drone planes with our ultra-new, line-of-fire-radar fire-control system hot off Norbert Wiener's drawing board at M.I.T. I realize now that only Jarrell's poetry was equal to expressing the weird congeries of horrors and distractions the war became in its final months; yet, on the "front," we lacked either the whole heart or the whole mind to make his splendidly simple sense of it. As possible poets, he judges us retrospectively among the losses.

The idea grew, therefore, among younger readers that he had taken the soft option for a poet of the 40's, had been culpably sentimental, even patronizing. He had moved backward to the pitying spirit of Owen and behind that to the radically pessimistic, panoramic, world-historical spirit of Hardy, or the great, scathing war episodes in Byron's *Don Juan.* What one least expected, I think, was this intensely private, learned, sure, *ready* voice of Jarrell, sounding now like Hardy's Ancient Spirit of the Years, Spirit of the Pities, Spirits Sinister and Ironic (of *The Dynasts*), now in the high Parnassian of some Leconte de Lisle of the prairies, now pathetic to the verge of baby talk, now ferociously graphic. Above all, it took time to absorb the poems' general monotony of effect, the mind they make, their static grandeur of sentience. A ground tone of swaying iambics varied by spondees and syncopation, paired and tripled adjectives in wistful or angry clumps, a recurring litany of abstractions: the State, the States, Death, Dream, fire, the years, the cities—the soldier-prisoner-patient, his wife, mail, and cat. A fastidiously inhibited poet, finding in a world gone nearly insane with distraction the "blind" certainties of unlettered feeling he had recently absorbed from Whitman, Hardy, and Rilke; a very American epic of acceptance. No poet was better prepared, these peculiarities notwithstanding, to swallow the war whole, to make it his, to provide so many vivid, oblique glimpses of an existence whose official aspect he knew all too well.

What was it, then, that saved him from drowning in his

influences and gave him strength to extend a powerful arc of vision over World War II to Korea, Vietnam, and the new age of technocratic wars? Firsthand knowledge, of course, as a land-based flight instructor who had flown himself, but more essentially, a passion to make the reader *see,* to concentrate his whole moral effort in an act of sight, leaving to "philosophy" those tenuous exchanges of condition and role —Life into Death into Dream into Death again—that encompass his plain, original, very poetic idea of knowledge.

I quote two of the best short poems that show his movement from a masterly but still fairly traditional pathos to a full-scale pathos of concrete vision:

A FIELD HOSPITAL

He stirs, beginning to awake.
A kind of ache
Of knowing troubles his blind warmth; he moans,
And the high hammering drone
Of the first crossing fighters shakes
His sleep to pieces, rakes
The darkness with its skidding bursts, is done.
All that he has known

Floods in upon him; but he dreads
The crooked thread
Of fire upon the darkness: "The great drake
Flutters to the icy lake—
The shotguns stammer in my head.

I lie in my own bed,"
He whispers, "dreaming"; and he thinks to wake.
The old mistake.

A cot creaks; and he hears the groan
He thinks his own—
And groans, and turns his stitched, blind, bandaged head
Up to the tent-flap, red
With dawn. A voice says, "Yes, this one";
His arm stings; then, alone,
He neither knows, remembers—but instead
Sleeps, comforted.

A FRONT

Fog over the base: the beams ranging
From the five towers pull home from the night
The crews cold in fur, the bombers banging
Like lost trucks down the levels of the ice.
A glow drifts in like mist (how many tons of it?),
Bounces to a roll, turns suddenly to steel
And tires and turrets, huge in the trembling light.
The next is high, and pulls up with a wail,
Comes round again—no use. And no use for the rest
In drifting circles out along the range;
Holding no longer, changed to a kinder course,
The flights drone southward through the steady rain.
The base is closed. . . . But one voice keeps on calling,
The lowering pattern of the engines grows;

The roar gropes downward in its shaky orbit
For the lives the season quenches. Here below
They beg, order, are not heard; and hear the darker
Voice rising: *Can't you hear me? Over. Over—*
All the air quivers, and the east sky glows.

I have avoided those somewhat coercive adjectives, "tender" and "compassionate," not, God knows, that the poetry is not all of both in an ultimate sense, but because in the best poems these qualities are so much the whole story that it seems indecent to mention them, extended beyond the usual limits to literally everything; men, machines, landscape, women, children—everything. He moves beyond the avuncular-idyllic manner of Whitman's *Drum Taps,* beyond the lovable Kipling fantasy of marching, campfires, and taverns, beyond even the comradeliness of Owen, to a place that mixes pity and philosophy, exact knowledge of war and sympathy for its victims, on a grand scale; a fresh visionary tension. The air force is the new military elite. In addition to its usual disciplines, it seems to foster an anarchy of spirit that begets its own antidote—distaste for war—more readily than earlier kinds of militarism. After the first Futurist inanities of Italian flyers over Ethiopia, no airman has, to my knowledge, written anything good that might be construed as glamorizing war. What Jarrell imagined with great clarity and force was this final detachment of the flyer, the dumb animism of his life among the planes and the planes' lives among themselves, the rarefaction and dissolution of most of the earth-bound certitudes of earlier wars. He thereby gives us a new measure of war altogether, in spite of the persistence of its older forms.

I remember being shown on the carrier a movie in color about carriers called *The Fighting Lady*, some of it shot earlier from my gun mount. It had a sickly sweetness around the edges that must have revolted Jarrell if he saw the film at home, as I imagine he did. His splendid long poem, "Pilots, Man Your Planes," is a demonstration of how the same thing should be done. Here are the last eleven lines:

> The planes fly off looking for a carrier,
> Destroyers curve in their long hunting arcs
> Through the dead of the carrier: the dazed, vomiting,
> Oil-blackened and fire-blistered, saved or dying men
> Cling with cramped shaking fingers to the lines
> Lowered from their old life: the pilot,
> Drugged in a blanket, straining up to gulp
> From the mug that scrapes like chalk against his mouth,
> Knows, knows at last; he yawns the chattering yawn
> Of effort and anguish, of hurt hating helplessness—
> Yawns, sobbingly, his head falls back, he sleeps.

This reaching back for an older mode of writing about war was also a reaching forward to the solitary terrors of the "small-scale" professional wars to come, fought by the new soldier-technician with his elaborately absorbing gear, somewhere beneath the headlines about burning Caribbean cruise ships and the almost normal politics and holidays of home. It is a world where islands on a map are dragons, where planes are "green, made beasts run home to air," where the soldier is set before a blackboard to learn, "the rifle steady at his back, / The functions of a variable: to die." In other words, a pure and *evil* irrationality. The poet's deepest pity is for what these clumsy mechanical animals and their child-guardians might become in rational circumstances, free of the ugly necessity, at just this time and place, of a fire birth into mere legend.

Alfred Kazin

Randall: His Kingdom

I DID NOT know Randall Jarrell very well—and the first time we met, at the house of a friend to both of us—we had a bitter argument. In later years, reading Randall with appreciation and observing him with a sympathy I would not have expected to feel at our first meeting, I realized better what it had been about him that first night that had so provoked me—the smart, bristling, military air with which he had put his passionate literary allegiances on the agenda, before company, with the impressive passion of a commander arguing an *absolutely necessary position.*

For Randall, conversation with new people, people he had only *read,* seemed to be a matter of his affirming his literary allegiances and his expecting you to join him in passionate avowal of his cause. And for me the odd thing about our first meeting, our intense, yet really symbolic disagreement over Eliot, was not that we disagreed but that we were so haughty in reaction to each other's literary pieties and sacred cows. We had expected to disagree with each other; almost we met in order to disagree; we disagreed. And at least on my side I could see, thinking it over, that what had fascinated me, provoked me, even made me envious, was the overwhelming, inexpressible importance that Randall attached to taste, to his own taste, to right reading and to right thinking about what one had read.

I am a professional critic—but Randall was a poet-critic. Despite Proust's devastating exposure of Sainte-Beuve's failure to spot the really great men of his time—despite his proof that Sainte-Beuve lacked character, courage, and intelligence—I find it hard to believe that professional critics (who on the whole usually do miss the really great men of their time) are, in consequence, simply contemptible. Sainte-Beuve survives, as Edmund Wilson will survive, as a writer, not as a lawgiver to the age, not as a taste-maker. Despite what critics in general are supposed to do for the age, it is a fact that professional critics do not shape the taste of an age; they are themselves not prophetic enough. (Professional critics in art and music may be different; they certainly think they are; but they miss as many first-raters as they discover, for they tend to back a possibly dominating style, not the individual genius for his own sake.)

Professional critics are read as moralists, observers from the side lines, chroniclers, biographers—even autobiographers; they line the figures up, they retrace the passion of a period, they write "marvelous essays." But just as Sainte-Beuve was wrong about Flaubert and Baudelaire, just as Van

Wyck Brooks was wrong about Joyce and Eliot, just as Wilson has been wrong about Kafka and much modern poetry, just as Trilling has been stuffy about Dreiser and other strong if uncouth talents, so the poet-critic, who works not from the side lines but has to be right in the middle of the parade (and if he is good enough, he will be leading it), obviously has to be "right"—that is, he has to make the vital choices, in advance of everybody else, that get people to *see* differently, to hear differently, to read the new people and in a sense to be new people themselves. Everybody knows—Randall knew nothing else so well—that T. S. Eliot's early essays turned literary opinion in English away from certain poets and toward other poets who hadn't been read with so much interest and affection until Eliot came along. It *mattered* what Eliot thought about Shelley and Donne and Milton; he made his opinions matter because in some vital sense his opinions about literature supported, made possible, the kind of odd poetry he alone could write. Superb as Edmund Wilson is, it does not really matter to the taste of our age, so congenial to Kafka, that Wilson does not like Kafka. Edmund Wilson is a great man of letters, a unique temperament in letters, a great scholar, a marvelously deft chronicler. We read him for himself; we love him even for his "faults" of taste, which we dote on because they are so obstinate and individualistic. Randall did not feel that *he* could afford to be wrong.

I did not realize it then, but that was the background of our argument. For professional critics, even if they are firm, clear, coherent, and constantly in touch with their inmost promptings of taste, are never as firm, clear, coherent, and involved in their literary judgments as poet-critics are. They do not identify enough. To Randall, "Wordsworth" was not a name, a career—all he is to most cultivated people; he was not a writer whose style and central vision of life one might "like" or "disagree" with or "enjoy," as auditors now say about the most intellectual lectures. Wordsworth was a fundamental stage through which the human imagination had to pass; he incarnated fundamental virtù; he was a metaphor of human progress; he was the sacred wood through which Randall's childhood had passed. As it happens, I attach all these virtues to Blake; everyone has his sacred objects. But my work does not depend on my affirmation of Blake; I do not write poetry. In a very real sense, Randall's poetry did depend on his right understanding of Wordsworth—and of many, many poets besides, not forgetting the short-story writers and novelists whom Randall could love almost as much as he did Wordsworth and Frost and Hardy, and whom (the prose writers) he learned from and put into his poems.

Randall lived in a world whose sacredness consisted in his images of certain beloved writers, in certain poems, novels, stories; in the happiest lines and passages from these. In the collections of his critical pieces and lectures, *Poetry and the Age* (1953) and *A Sad Heart at the Supermarket* (1962), he adored the writers he adored—Whitman, Frost, Stevens, Kipling—with such a rapt readiness to *show* them off to everyone, to show their greatness off, to show them off against inferior poets and even the inferior sides of themselves, to show them off against ordinary experience, ordinary, mean, nonreading people!—that the performance, so rooted in love, in the need to praise, in boundless affirmation, was witty, as love so often is witty, when in its joy it mocks the not-lovable. No doubt the unwisely confessional lady who set for one poem the impossible task (for her) of describing sexual transport did not appreciate Randall's wit as much as other readers did when Randall, in his review, quoted the lines back to her in mockery of her innocent self-congratulation. Randall could be cruel as a child is cruel—but he was wittily so. Yet even the poet whose misses were more than his achievements must have grinned a little to be told by Randall that to extract his good things was *work*: like getting at "the gold in sea water." (I must have read *that* Jarrell review as long ago as 1940, and have never forgotten the literary talent behind it.)

So, if you felt about Frost as Randall came to feel about Frost (taking on all the doubters about Frost left in the United States):

> Frost's virtues are extraordinary. No other living poet has written so well about the actions of ordinary men . . . It is easy to underestimate the effect of this exact, spaced-out, prosaic rhythm, whose objects have the tremendous strength—you find it in Hardy's best poems—of things merely put down and left to speak for themselves. . . . [Frost] makes the reader feel that he is not in a book but in a world, and a world that has in

common with his own some of the things that are most important in both.

then you could *not* but feel, and say—out, out, damned spot! —that "an Irving Babbitt was a man who, tenanted by all nine of the muses, still couldn't create a couplet." From Randall's kingdom it looked as if others lived in a country of the blind, not only without genius but also without geniuses. They were simply without it, *it,* the goldenness of art, the hallowing touch, the thing that Goethe had, that Mies van der Rohe has, that Keats had, that Schubert had, that Chekhov had, that Robert Lowell has. . . . Randall was as full of quotations as a Unitarian minister—they were his theology, too. He quoted Goethe as constantly as any German refugee, and he quoted *his* touchstones (who were the great writers themselves, talking about anything), in their letters and personal pronouncements, with all the adorable old-fashioned admiration for the general wisdom of the man of letters that Van Wyck Brooks, I used to think, was the last man to practice in his footnotes. "The work of art, Rilke said, says to us always: 'You must change your life.' " "Goethe says, when he is talking about slum children, 'No person ever looks miserable who feels that he has the right to make a demand on you.' " "Bismarck says that you can do anything with children if you play with them." (I have this from memory, and it is probably not word perfect; but who but Randall would have quoted Bismarck on how to manage children?) "Hofmannsthal says, with awful finality, 'The world has lost its innocence, and without innocence no one creates or enjoys a work of art'; but elsewhere he says more hopefully, with entire and not with partial truth, that 'each of us lives in an innocence of his own which he never entirely loses.' "

Rapturously, boundlessly, scornfully, polemically, Randall believed not merely in literature—he believed in the *writer*, in many writers, in all possible good writers, with a breadth of allegiance actually more characteristic of professional critics than of poet-critics, but making the great writers his own with a love and praise and generosity that only a *poet* can muster. When you talk to *writers*, they are always ready to cry "Wonderful!" over the pleasure in creation that unites you in conversation. Not for Randall the peculiar poisonousness—unwitty, uncharming, bilious, spiteful, proud—that gets so many untalented professors of modern literature to write about contemporary literature with *hauteur*. Randall believed that the writer had and was a special persona, was a magician, was a liberator—his particular liberator, guardian of his kingdom. Randall, I think, was basically modest about his own poetry; he did not have the absorbed arrogance characteristic of absolute masters. His many quotations, his many enthusiasms, his many adjurations to his students and his attacks on the noncomprehending, his constant unhappy awareness of the Others in their country of the blind—all testified to a special faith in *literature* rather than to the vision in his own writing. In this, Randall, though different in kind from professional critics, though superb in his temperament, matchless and unforgettable in his verve, reminded me more of the "faith" so characteristic of critics than of the "works" identified with the poet. Randall, I think, was too conscious, too easily irritated, by the nonreaders, the non-comprehending readers, the critics who have no ecstasy to share. When I read such brilliant but *simpliste* essays in the poet's pathos as "A Sad Heart at the Supermarket," I can see why it provoked the philistine derision it is said to have done at the National Book Awards, for Randall was complaining to his audience about itself—almost as if to be justified by its unfriendliness. Of course we all do this—we writers who are paid to tell college audiences how uncultured they are—we writers who are so proud of the loneliness we suffer at conventions even as we suffer it, and them. But it is better to study the strangeness of the external world than to be outraged by it. There was a group that Randall and I belonged to for a time; they had many dinners; at these dinners I used to *feel* his extraordinarily self-defensive, barbed and bearded presence, as if it were blinking in loneliness at the festive table. God knows I am no one to talk, but a poet should be too busy being himself, writing, thinking, creating, always to worry in public lectures, even when he is witty in his outrage, about The Obscurity of the Poet, The Plight of the Poet.

Randall, it seems to me, became rather more of a professional poet and teacher and lecturer, and thus rather more of a generalizer, than a poet should have been. I was not greatly impressed by his sharp but unmistakable lamentations over the poet's fate, for by taking on so many large social issues in explanation, he assumed a responsibility for their "minute particulars" which he did not fulfill. When he bewailed the fate of poetry, the isolation of the poet, and how everybody who once upon a time could read at all read *poetry*, Randall was simply rhetorical: ". . . that long-continued, world-overturning cultural and social revolution (seen at its most advanced stage here in the United States) which has made the poet difficult and the public unused to any poetry, exactly as it has made poet and public divorce their wives, stay away from church, dislike bull-baiting, free the slaves, get insulin shots for diabetes . . ." This is smart delivery, recited to an audience . . . Randall was an extraordinary performer—in verse, in prose, and obviously (I never actually heard him in public) on the platform. He was never publicly defeated. Even his poorer things, deficient in actual vision, are professionally deft. Clearly, Randall was very dependent on an audience and identified with it. Many poets are glittering performers in public—they make a virtue of their difference from other men, as saints do, and the sick, and the conquerors. Yet even Dylan Thomas and Robert Frost, expert actors and lovable demagogues that they were, never identified themselves with this public so much as Randall did—even as he lamented the fate of poetry, of the poet, of *modern* poetry.

Well, Randall was not tough, not indifferent, nor blessed by negative capability. He was not so wrapped up in his thinking and his poetry as Auden has been—the poet on whom Randall wrote more pages than he did on any other poet, but who obviously bothered his unconscious. For though Randall felt certain affinities—of style, wit, aristocratic disdain—with Auden, it is clear that he was nowhere so independent-minded, so autarchical of imagination, so *lawless* . . . The writers Randall loved were usually moralists as decent as himself; he was a democratic Christian, in the country where democracy is our Christianity: so Whitman thought, so Wordsworth would have agreed, so William Carlos Williams believed . . . And beyond this, Randall loved *poets* more than other poets have loved *poets* in general. His comprehensive love of poets, his eloquent and witty love, the personal despair that by contrast is the story and tone of so many of his poems, shows that for him not his own poems but "poetry" was his kingdom.

It was this that made him the prince of reviewers. Such a combative reviewer he was, such a loving reviewer, such an incredibly feeling, teaching, exciting reviewer! When I read Randall's review of Robert Lowell's *Lord Weary's Castle*, I knew that I was reading something that Coleridge might have written about Wordsworth—it seemed to come out of an anthology, it was so blessedly decisive, straight, clever, true.

> When I reviewed Lowell's first book I finished by saying, "Some of the best poems of the next years ought to be written by him." The appearance of *Lord Weary's Castle* makes me feel . . . like a rainmaker who predicts rain, and gets a flood which drowns everyone in the country. A few of these poems, I believe, will be read as long as men remember English.

That is the way poets write about each other. That is authority.

That authority, I think, was Randall's greatest ideal. It was what made Goethe and Schubert wise. It filled his own heart and mind with so much eloquence—and at times so much bitterness against a world that seemed to deny it to him—that to read him was to vibrate with the excitement of his love, his ambition, his reading, his hope, and his despair. His best essays—the particular studies of Frost, Whitman, Stevens, Williams, Kipling, the art of the short story—communicate the perfection and authority that Randall seemed to be dreaming, dreaming alone, in his kingdom. Does anyone still have to say how different these studies were from the kind of criticism that reads, as Randall said, as if it had been written by "a syndicate of encyclopedias for an audience of International Business Machines"? Criticism that is not informed by an ideal of the highest professional competence is usually ungenerous as well as uninformed. In his kingdom, Randall was happier to belong with the poets than to triumph over them. It was pure intellectual love, an allegiance, a gift of the heart that filled him. That allegiance can sometimes make a man feel lonelier on a modern highway than if he were lost in the Antarctic.

Stanley Kunitz

Out of the Cage

I WISH I HAD known Randall Jarrell earlier. We met in the mid-fifties, when he called to discuss an abortive publishing project. There were others in my Village apartment, but his was the presence that filled and disturbed the room. He was bearded, formidable, bristling, with a high-pitched nervous voice and the wariness of a porcupine. That was my dominant image of him for a decade, until the turn of '65, when he came north for a visit from Greensboro, with his beard deleted, and I saw at dinner for the first and last time the naked vulnerability of his countenance. A few months later he was dead.

One of the most revealing poems that he ever wrote, and one of his best, was "The Woman at the Washington Zoo." The speaker is, of course, the woman of the title—one of the many female voices to whom he gave, in his poetry, a language:

The saris go by me from the embassies.

Cloth from the moon. Cloth from another planet.
They look back at the leopard like the leopard.

And I. . . .
this print of mine, that has kept its color
Alive through so many cleanings; this dull null
Navy I wear to work, and wear from work, and so
To my bed, so to my grave, with no
Complaints, no comment: neither from my chief,
The Deputy Chief Assistant, nor his chief—
Only I complain. . . . this serviceable
Body that no sunlight dyes, no hand suffuses
But, dome-shadowed, withering among columns,
Wavy beneath fountains—small, far-off, shining
In the eyes of animals, these beings trapped
As I am trapped but not, themselves, the trap,
Aging, but without knowledge of their age,
Kept safe here, knowing not of death, for death—
Oh, bars of my own body, open, open!

With a dramatic single stroke in the opening line—"The saris go by me from the embassies"—a colorful and cosmopolitan world is evoked. The next movement is toward the dark, for the speaker who stands before the cages, this government clerk in her "dull null navy," knows that the colors and the possibility of colors have been washed out of her life. She senses her kinship with and yet her difference from the animals.

The world goes by my cage and never sees me.
And there come not to me, as come to these,
The wild beasts, sparrows pecking the llamas' grain,
Pigeons settling on the bears' bread, buzzards
Tearing the meat the flies have clouded. . . .

Trapped in her lonely and defeated flesh, she is worse off than the captive beasts, for "the world goes by my cage and never sees me." Nor is she visited, as are the beasts, by those who feed on their leavings: sparrows, pigeons, buzzards. Her life is too starved for leavings. What a gray world! What a bleakness! And just when we are ready to turn away, Jarrell does something magical and triumphant with his woman at the zoo. He has her cry out, addressing the predatory bird who is the figure of lover-death, such words of shameless agony that the despair is transmuted into a fierce exaltation, as the true colors of the world, terrible though they may be, pour back into the poem:

Vulture,
When you come for the white rat that the foxes left,
Take off the red helmet of your head, the black
Wings that have shadowed me, and step to me as man:
The wild brother at whose feet the white wolves fawn,
To whose hand of power the great lioness
Stalks, purring. . . .
You know what I was,
You see what I am: change me, change me!

All the voices in all of Jarrell's poems are crying, "Change me!" The young yearn to be old in order to escape from their nocturnal fears; the old long for the time of their youth, no matter how poor and miserable it was, for "in those days everything was better"; life is moving toward the death; the dead are moving back into life, and wherever they come, they come in disguises. It is a world of shifts and changes, as in a fairy tale, and the only reason you suspect it is more is that Cinderella and the Dwarfs and the Frog Prince have had a curse put on them: they have real memories and real fears. Karl Shapiro once acutely observed that Jarrell's "almost obsessive return to the great childhood myths is sometimes as painful as psychoanalysis," and that the subtitle of his work might well be "Hansel and Gretel in America." What Hansel and Gretel tell us is that the woods are dark and that the creatures who inhabit them change their skins. In the mythic imagination metamorphosis is the great theme underlying all others. To the individual psyche it is the way out of the cage. "Self-transformation," said Rilke, whom Jarrell revered and translated, "is precisely what life is."

Robert Lowell

Randall Jarrell

WHEN I FIRST met Randall, he was twenty-three or four, and upsettingly brilliant, precocious, knowing, naïve, and vexing. He seemed to make no distinction between what he would say in our hearing and what he would say behind our backs. If anything, absence made him more discreet. Woe to the acquaintance who liked the wrong writer, the wrong poem by the right writer, or the wrong lines in the right poem! And how those who loved him enjoyed admiring, complaining, and gossiping about the last outrageous thing he had done or, more often, said. It brought us together—whispering about Randall. In 1937, we both roomed at the house of John Crowe Ransom in Gambier, Ohio. Ransom and Jarrell had each separately spent the preceding summer studying Shakespeare's *Sonnets*, and had emerged with unorthodox and widely differing theories. Roughly, Ransom thought that Shakespeare was continually going off the rails into illogical incoherence. Jarrell believed that no one, not even William Empson, had done justice to the rich, significant ambiguity of Shakespeare's intelligence and images. I can see and hear Ransom and Jarrell now, seated on one sofa, as though on one love seat, the sacred texts open on their laps, one fifty, the other just out of college, and each expounding to the other's deaf ears his own inspired and irreconcilable interpretation.

Gordon Chalmers, the president of Kenyon College and a disciple of the somber anti-Romantic humanists, once went skiing with Randall, and was shocked to hear him exclaiming, "I feel just like an angel." Randall *did* somehow give off an angelic impression, despite his love for tennis, singular mufflers knitted by a girlfriend, and disturbing improvements of his own on the latest dance steps. His mind, unearthly in its quickness, was a little boyish, disembodied, and brittle. His body was a little ghostly in its immunity to soil, entanglements, and rebellion. As one sat with him in oblivious absorption at the campus bar, sucking a fifteen-cent chocolate milk shake and talking eternal things, one felt, beside him, too corrupt and companionable. He had the harsh luminosity of Shelley—like Shelley, every inch a poet, and like Shelley, imperiled perhaps by an arid, abstracting precosity. Not really! Somewhere inside him, a breezy, untouchable spirit had even then made its youthful and sightless promise to accept—to accept and never to accept the bulk, confusion, and defeat of mortal flesh . . . all that blithe and blood-torn dolor!

Randall Jarrell had his own peculiar and important excellence as a poet, and outdistanced all others in the things he could do well. His gifts, both by nature and by a lifetime of hard dedication and growth, were wit, pathos, and brilliance of intelligence. These qualities, dazzling in themselves, were often so well employed that he became, I think, the most heartbreaking English poet of his generation.

Most good poets are also good critics on occasion, but Jarrell was much more than this. He was a critic of genius, a poet-critic of genius at a time when, as he wrote, most criticism was "astonishingly graceless, joyless, humorless, long-winded, niggling, blinkered, methodical, self-important, cliché-ridden, prestige-obsessed, and almost autonomous."

He had a deadly hand for killing what he despised. He described a murky verbal poet as "writing poems that might have been written *by* a typewriter *on* a typewriter." The flashing reviews he wrote in his twenties are full of such witticisms and barbs, and hundreds more were tossed off in casual conversation, and never preserved, or even repeated. Speaking of a famous scholar, he said, "What can be more tedious than a man whose every sentence is a balanced epigram without wit, profundity, or taste?" He himself, though often fierce, was incapable of vulgarity, self-seeking, or meanness. He could be very tender and gracious, but often he seemed tone-deaf to the amenities and dishonesties that make human relations tolerable. Both his likes and dislikes were a terror to everyone, that is to everyone who either saw himself as important or wished to see himself as important. Although he was almost without vices, heads of colleges and English departments found his frankness more unsettling and unpredictable than the drunken explosions of some divine *enfant terrible,* such as Dylan Thomas. Usually his wit was austerely pure, but sometimes he could jolt the more cynical. Once we were looking at a furnished apartment that one of our friends had just rented. It was overbearingly eccentric. Life-size clay lamps like flowerpots remodeled into Matisse nudes by a spastic child. Paintings made from a palette of mud by a blind painter. About the paintings Randall said, "Ectoplasm sprinkled with zinc." About the apartment, "All that's missing are Mrs. X's illegitimate children in bottles of formaldehyde." His first reviews were described as "symbolic murders," but even then his most destructive judgments had a patient, intuitive, unworldly certainty.

Yet eulogy was the glory of Randall's criticism. Eulogies that not only impressed readers with his own enthusiasms, but which also, time and again, changed and improved opinions and values. He left many reputations permanently altered and exalted. I think particularly of his famous Frost and Whitman essays, and one on the last poems of Wallace Stevens, which was a dramatic reversal of his own earlier evaluation. His mind kept moving and groping more deeply. His prejudices were never the established and fashionable prejudices of the world around him. One could never say of one of his new admirations, "Oh, I knew *you* would like that." His progress was not the usual youthful critic's progress from callow severity to lax benevolence. With wrinkled brow and cool fresh eye, he was forever musing, discovering, and chipping away at his own misconceptions. Getting out on a limb was a daily occurrence for him, and when he found words for what he had intuited, his judgments were bold and unlikely. Randall was so often right that sometimes we said he was always right. He could enjoy discarded writers whom it was a scandal to like, praise young, unknown writers as if he were praising and describing Shakespeare's tragedies, and read Shakespeare's tragedies with the uncertainty and wonder of their first discoverers.

He once said, "If I were a rich man, I would pay money for the privilege of being able to teach." Probably there was no better teacher of literature in the country, and yet he was curiously unworldly about it, and welcomed teaching for almost twenty years in the shade or heat of his little-known Southern college for girls in Greensboro, North Carolina. There his own community gave him a compact, tangible, personal reverence that was incomparably more substantial and poignant than the empty, numerical long-distance blaze of national publicity. He grieved over the coarseness, unkindness, and corruption of our society, and said that "the poet has a peculiar relation to this public. It is unaware of his existence." He said bitterly and lightheartedly that "the gods who had taken away the poet's audience had given him students." Yet he gloried in being a teacher, never apologized for it, and related it to his most serious criticism. Writing of three long poems by Robert Frost, poems too long to include in his essay, he breaks off and says, "I have used rather an odd tone about [these poems] because I feel so much frustration at not being able to quote and go over them, as I so often have done with friends and classes." Few critics could so gracefully descend from the grand manner or be so offhand about their dignity. His essays are never encrusted with the hardness of a professor. They have the raciness and artistic gaiety of his own hypnotic voice.

Randall was the only man I have ever met who could make other writers feel that their work was more important to him than his own. I don't mean that he was in the habit of saying to people he admired, "This is much better than anything I could do." Such confessions, though charming, cost little effort. What he did was to make others feel that their realizing themselves was as close to him as his own self-realization, and that he cared as much about making the nature and goodness of someone else's work understood as he cared about making his own understood. I have never known anyone who so connected what his friends wrote with their lives, or their lives with what they wrote. This could be trying: whenever we turned out something Randall felt was unworthy or a falling off, there was a coolness in all one's relations with him. You felt that even your choice in neckties wounded him. Yet he always veered and returned, for he knew as well as anyone that the spark from heaven is beyond man's call and control. Good will he demanded, but in the end was lenient to honest sterility and failure.

Jarrell was the most readable and generous of critics of contemporary poetry. His novel, *Pictures from an Institution,* whatever its fictional oddities, is a unique and serious joke-book. How often I've met people who keep it by their beds or somewhere handy, and read random pages aloud to lighten their hearts. His book, *A Sad Heart at the Supermarket*, had a condescending press. When one listened to these social essays, they were like *dies irae* sermons, strange ones that cauterized the soul, and yet made us weep with laughter. A banal world found them banal. But what Jarrell's inner life really was in all its wonder, variety, and subtlety is best told in his poetry. To the end, he was writing with deepening force, clarity, and frankness. For some twenty-five years he wrote excellent poems. Here I only want to emphasize two of his peaks: what he wrote about the war, and what he completed in the last years of his life.

In the first months of the war, Jarrell became a pilot. He was rather old for a beginner, and soon "washed out," and spent the remaining war years as an aviation instructor. Even earlier, he had an expert's knowledge. I remember sitting with him in 1938 on the hill of Kenyon College and listening to him analyze in cool technical detail the various rather minute ways in which the latest British planes were superior to their German equivalents. He then jokingly sketched out how a bombing raid might be made against the college. Nine-tenths of his war poems are air-force poems, and are about planes and their personnel, the flyers, crews, and mechanics who attended them. No other imaginative writer had his precise knowledge of aviation, or knew so well how to draw inspiration from this knowledge.

> In the turret's great glass dome, the apparition, death,
> Framed in the glass of the gunsight, a fighter's blinking
> wing,
> Flares softly, a vacant fire. If the flak's inked blurs—
> Distributed, statistical—the bombs' lost patterning
> Are death, they are death under glass, a chance
> For someone yesterday, someone tomorrow; and the fire
> That streams from the fighter which is there, not there,
> Does not warm you, has not burned them, though they
> die.

More important still, the soldiers he wrote about were men much like his own pilot-students. He knew them well, and not only that, peculiarly sympathized with them. For Jarrell, the war careers of these young men had the freshness, wonder, and magical brevity of childhood. In his poetry, they are murderers, and yet innocents. They destroyed cities and men that had only the nominal reality of names studied in elementary geography classes.

> In bombers named for girls, we burned
> The cities we had learned about in school—
> Till our lives wore out

Or

> In this year of our warfare, indispensable
> In general, and in particular dispensable

Finally, the pilot goes home for good, forever mutilated and wounded, "the slow flesh failing, the terrible flesh / Sloughed off at last . . . / Stumbling to the toilet on one clever leg / Of leather, wire, and willow." There, knowledge has at last come to him:

> And it is different, different—you have understood
> Your world at last: you have tasted your own blood.

Jarrell's portraits of his pilots have been downgraded sometimes as unheroic, naïve, and even sentimental. Well, he was writing beyond the war, and turning the full visionary powers of his mind on the war to probe into and expose the horror, pathos, and charm he found in life. Always behind the sharpened edge of his lines, there is the merciful vision, *his* vision, partial like all others, but an illumination of life, too sad and radiant for us to stay with long—or forget.

In his last and best book, *The Lost World*, he used subjects and methods he had been developing and improving for almost twenty years. Most of the poems are dramatic monologues. Their speakers, though mostly women, are intentionally, and unlike Browning's, very close to the author. Their themes, repeated with endless variations, are solitude, the solitude of the unmarried, the solitude of the married, the love, strife, dependency, and indifference of man and woman—how mortals age, and brood over their lost and raw childhood, only recapturable in memory and imagination. Above all, childhood! This subject for many a careless and tarnished cliché was for him what it was for his two favorite poets, Rilke and Wordsworth, a governing and transcendent vision. For shallower creatures, recollections of childhood and youth are drenched in a mist of plaintive pathos, or even bathos, but for Jarrell this was the divine glimpse, lifelong to be lived with, painfully and tenderly relived, transformed, matured—man with and against woman, child with and against adult.

One of his aging women says:

> When I was young and miserable and pretty
> And poor, I'd wish
> What all girls wish: to have a husband

But later, thinking of the withering present, she says:

> How young I seem; I *am* exceptional;
> I think of all I have.
> But really no one is exceptional,
> No one has anything, I'm anybody,
> I stand beside my grave
> Confused with my life, that is commonplace and solitary.

In so reflecting, she is a particular woman—one sad, particular woman reaching into Jarrell's universal Everyman, poor or triumphant. Speaking in his own person and of his own childhood, he says:

> . . . As I run by the chicken coops
> With lettuce for my rabbit, real remorse
> Hurts me, here, now: the little girl is crying
> Because I didn't write. Because—
> of course,

I *was* a child, I missed them so. But justifying
Hurts too

Then in a poem called "Woman," the speaker, a man, addresses the woman next to him in bed:

Let me sleep beside you, each night, like a spoon;
When, starting from my dreams, I groan to you,
May your *I love you* send me back to sleep.
At morning bring me, grayer for its mirroring,
The heavens' sun perfected in your eyes.

It all comes back to me now—the just under thirty years of our friendship, mostly meetings in transit, mostly in Greensboro, North Carolina, the South he loved and stayed with, though no agrarian, but a radical liberal. Poor modern-minded exile from the forests of Grimm, I see him unbearded, slightly South American-looking, then later bearded, with a beard we at first wished to reach out our hands to and pluck off, but which later became him, like Walter Bagehot's, or some Symbolist's in France's *fin de siècle* Third Republic. Then unbearded again. I see the bright, petty, pretty sacred objects he accumulated for his joy and solace: Vermeer's red-hatted girl, the Piero and Donatello reproductions, the photographs of his bruised, merciful heroes: Chekhov, Rilke, Marcel Proust. I see the white sporting Mercedes-Benz, the ever better cut and more deliberately jaunty clothes, the television with its long afternoons of professional football, those matches he thought miraculously more graceful than college football . . . Randall had an uncanny clairvoyance for helping friends in subtle precarious moments—almost always as only he could help, with something written: critical sentences in a letter, or an unanticipated published book review. Twice or thrice, I think, he must have thrown me a lifeline. In his own life, he had much public acclaim and more private. The public, at least, fell cruelly short of what he deserved. Now that he is gone, I see clearly that the spark from heaven really struck and irradiated the lines and being of my dear old friend—his noble, difficult, and beautiful soul.

On The Seven-League Crutches

RANDALL JARRELL is our most talented poet under forty, and one whose wit, pathos, and grace remind us more of Pope or Matthew Arnold than of any of his contemporaries. I don't know whether Jarrell is unappreciated or not—it's hard to imagine anyone taking him lightly. He is almost brutally serious about literature and so bewilderingly gifted that it is impossible to comment on him without the humiliating thought that he himself could do it better.

He is a man of letters in the European sense, with real verve, imagination, and uniqueness. Even his dogmatism is more wild and personal than we are accustomed to, completely unspoiled by the hedging "equanimity" that weakens the style and temperament of so many of our serious writers.

This review of *The Seven-League Crutches* was first published in The New York Times Book Review, October 7, 1951.

His murderous intuitive phrases are famous; but at the same time his mind is essentially conservative and takes as much joy in rescuing the reputation of a sleeping good writer as in chloroforming a mediocre one.

Jarrell's prose intelligence—he seems to know *everything* —gives his poetry an extraordinary advantage over, for instance, a thunderbolt like Dylan Thomas, in dealing with the present; Jarrell is able to see our whole scientific, political, and spiritual situation directly and on its own terms. He is a tireless discoverer of new themes and resources, and a master technician, who moves easily from the little to the grand. Monstrously knowing and monstrously innocent—one does not know just where to find him . . . a Wordsworth with the obsessions of Lewis Carroll.

The Seven-League Crutches should best be read with Jarrell's three earlier volumes. *Blood for a Stranger* (1942) is a Parnassian tour-de-force in the manner of Auden; nevertheless, it has several fine poems, the beginnings of better, and enough of the author's personality for John Crowe Ransom to write in ironic astonishment that Jarrell had "the velocity of an angel." *Little Friend, Little Friend* (1945), however, contains some of the best poems on modern war, better, I think, and far more professional than those of Wilfred Owen, which, though they seem pathetically eternal to us now, are sometimes amateurish and unfinished. The determined, passive, sacrificial lives of the pilots, inwardly so harmless and outwardly so destructive, are ideal subjects for

Jarrell. In *Losses* (1948) and more rangingly in *The Seven-League Crutches*, new subjects appear. Using himself, children, characters from fairy stories, history, and painting, he is still able to find beings that are determined, passive and sacrificial, but the experience is quiet, more complex, and probably more universal. It's an odd universe, where a bruised joy or a bruised sorrow is forever commenting on itself with the gruff animal common sense and sophistication of Fontaine. Jarrell has gone far enough to be compared with his peers, the best lyric poets of the past: he has the same finesse and originality that they have, and his faults, a certain idiosyncratic willfulness and eclectic timidity, are only faults in this context.

Among the new poems, "The Orient Express," a sequel, I think, to "Dover Beach," is a brilliantly expert combination of regular and irregular lines, buried rhymes, and sestinalike repeated rhymes, in which shifts in tone and rhythm are played off against the deadening roll of the train. "A Game at Salzburg" has the broken, charmed motion of someone thinking out loud. Both, in their different ways, are as skillful and lovely as any short poem I know of. "The Knight, Death, and the Devil" is a careful translation of Dürer's engraving. The description is dense; the generalizations are profound. It is one of the most remarkable word pictures in English verse or prose, and comparable to Auden's "Musée des Beaux Arts."

"The Contrary Poet" is an absolutely literal translation from Corbière. The original is as clearly there as in the

French, and it is also a great English poem. "The Night before the Night before Christmas" is long; it is also, perhaps, the best, most mannered, the most unforgettable, and the most irritating poem in the book. Some of Jarrell's monologues are Robert Frost for "the man who reads Hamlet," or rather for a Hamlet who had been tutored by Jarrell. In "Seele im Raum," he masters Frost's methods and manages to make a simple half-mad woman speak in character, and yet with his own humor and terror.

My favorite is "A Girl in a Library," an apotheosis of the American girl, an immortal character piece, and the poem in which Jarrell perhaps best uses both his own qualities and his sense of popular culture. The girl is a college student, blond and athletic.

> (But not so sadly; not so thoughtfully)
> And answer with a pure heart, guilelessly:
> *I'm studying. . . .*

I quote the ending:

> Sit and dream.
> One comes, a finger's width beneath your skin,
> To the braided maidens singing as they spin;
> There sound the shepherd's pipe, the watchman's rattle
> Across the short dark distance of the years.
> I am a thought of yours: and yet, you do not think . . .
> The firelight of a long, blind, dreaming story
> Lingers upon your lips; and I have seen

Firm, fixed forever in your closing eyes,
The Corn King beckoning to his Spring Queen.

"Belinda" was once drawn with something of the same hesitating satire and sympathy.

William Meredith

The Lasting Voice

As I PUT together these, my profoundly felt if not profoundly original remarks about Randall Jarrell, I listened several times to a recording of his. Perhaps we still underestimate the importance of this innovation in the preservation of poetry. The poets' voices which began to be recorded in our century will retain for future readers rhythms and tones which have died with all previous poets. These sounds are surely subordinate in importance to that permanent voice which is written into the words and is proof against declamation by actors, recitation by school children, and impersonation by school teachers and other poets. Nevertheless the living voice may have contributed to the contemporary understanding of a poet and perhaps to the real voice, as that voice was first established among contemporaries and intimates of the poet.

At the memorial service held at Yale University for Randall Jarrell the February after his death, for example, the voices of two of his friends and contemporaries must have struck most hearers as much as they did me. Robert Lowell's readings carry always a slight tone of complaint, as though he would make some disappointment heard beyond that of man's tragic predicament. This disappointment, half modest, half the reverse, seems to express: although I am the man of remarkable vision who has seen and said this, am I not sadly unremarkable? John Berryman's voice, more sharply than his poems, conveys continuously astonishment and intermittently outrage: is this predicament to be believed or to be borne? To have heard either of these men read is to learn some final secrets about the enduring voice on the page and the enduring vision of the man.

The vision of a serious artist is a very individual matter. Perhaps the most important thing he has to learn is, what am I clairvoyant about, what do I see *into* that other people simply see? The minor artist is, by comparison, a beachcomber. He lives off the discovery of novel beauties and horrors; he sees them *first,* but he sees them with the flat eyes of just anybody. Novelty in this sense is nothing to the serious artist, or worse than nothing, a temptation to desert his individual vision. We can't imagine Wallace Stevens trying to penetrate the complacencies of an oven bird, or Frost the complacencies of a peignoir. Artists like that know who they are and what they can see into.

Randall Jarrell's progress, volume by volume, seems to have been toward greater awareness of what he could call his own. For many years he was clearly one of our best poets, in the company of Wilbur, Berryman, Roethke, and Lowell, but he wasn't perfectly sure what to do with his restless gift. He wrote a number of brittle, chilly poems that detach themselves from life with an irresponsible irony—poems like "The State," "Sears Roebuck," and "Variations"—which may be all right as poems but never seem to be quite Jarrell. At the same time he was consistently producing marvelous, deep-running dramatic poems that from the first were stamped with his voice and his eye for subjective imagery: "Second Air Force," "Seele im Raum," "The End of the Rainbow."

The recognition of his especial vision, which was complete with his fine last book, *The Lost World,* involved two things, though perhaps they were a single act: abandoning a timid, mechanical skepticism and embracing a wide human involvement. The accomplishment of these seems to have confirmed another fact: his gift was essentially dramatic, like Browning's.

Comparing poems that span a number of years, we can see his dramatic talent grow brighter as though controlled by a rheostat. He returns to characters, images, even to lines. "A Hunt in the Black Forest" in *The Lost World* opens with the same lines that had opened, seventeen years before in *Losses,* "The Child of Courts." And the returns to apparently autobiographical events of childhood are even more striking. There are things a man goes over and over until he gets them right.

Take a character that Jarrell finds in many guises, the woman whose growing old is an inexplicable and brutal mystery to her. Three poems on this theme, spaced over a number of years, conclude as follows:

But it's not *right*.
If just living can do this,
Living is more dangerous than anything:

It is terrible to be alive.

[THE FACE]

Vulture,
When you come for the white rat that the foxes left,
Take off the red helmet of your head, the black
Wings that have shadowed me, and step to me as man:
The wild brother at whose feet the white wolves fawn,
To whose hand of power the great lioness
Stalks, purring. . . .
You know what I was,
You see what I am: change me, change me!

[THE WOMAN AT THE WASHINGTON ZOO]

I am afraid, this morning, of my face.
It looks at me
From the rear-view mirror, with the eyes I hate,
The smile I hate. Its plain, lined look
Of gray discovery
Repeats to me: "You're old." That's all, I'm old.

And yet I'm afraid, as I was at the funeral
I went to yesterday.

My friend's cold made-up face, granite among its flowers,
Her undressed, operated-on, dressed body
Were my face and body.
As I think of her I hear her telling me
How young I seem; I *am* exceptional;
I think of all I have.
But really no one is exceptional,
No one has anything, I'm anybody,
I stand beside my grave
Confused with my life, that is commonplace and solitary.

[NEXT DAY]

Granted that some of the differences come from the subjects' differences: the woman in "The Face" seems to have an aristocratic beauty, and her epigraph identifies her with the Marschallin in *Der Rosenkavalier*; the woman at the zoo seems to be an unmarried office worker; the woman in the final passage, the conclusion of the opening poem in *The Lost World*, is a suburban wife. (Of the woman in the Washington zoo, Jarrell wrote that she is "a distant relation of women I have written about before, in "The End of the Rainbow" and "Cinderella" and "Seele im Raum.") But the final passage above is, in the first place, free of the glamour of violence. It makes its point, it involves us, without a Marschallin on the one hand or a vulture on the other. Dailiness has been seen as its drama, rather than rank or sexuality. ("Vulture is a euphemism," Jarrell wrote about this.) And the attitude of the poet in "Next Day" seems therefore a great deal more compassionate. Instead of crying, *beauty*!

horror! he seems to be saying, *life*, *life*, with a vision that elevates that remark to wisdom—that is to say, with a kind of wondering acceptance. He says this explicitly in the poem called "Well Water":

> What a girl called "the dailiness of life"
> (Adding an errand to your errand. Saying,
> "Since you're up . . ." Making you a means to
> A means to a means to) is well water
> Pumped from an old well at the bottom of the world.
> The pump you pump the water from is rusty
> And hard to move and absurd, a squirrel-wheel
> A sick squirrel turns slowly, through the sunny
> Inexorable hours. And yet sometimes
> The wheel turns of its own weight, the rusty
> Pump pumps over your sweating face the clear
> Water, cold, so cold! you cup your hands
> And gulp from them the dailiness of life.

The irony in this poem, and in most of the poems in the last book, turns as much toward himself as it turns outward, and adds to the compassion which inflects his true voice. Some of his reputation, a part I still cannot applaud, came from an acid humor which he turned on people and things from whom he withheld sympathy. He could be very funny under these circumstances, if you shared his unsympathy, but he never wrote as skillfully then as he did in appreciation.

Listening now to his early reading of "Lady Bates," an early poem, is a painful experience. So much feeling and understanding beyond what is on the page emerges from his delivery. "These are the bones of stories, and we shiver at them," he wrote about two poems by Blake and Stephen Crane. The voice of all his best poems is that of a storyteller almost too deeply involved to speak. The stories themselves, though, lie exactly right for his voice, as they say of certain songs for certain singers.

A man of his intellectual brilliance must have known better than most of us the consequences of such wide and unguarded sympathy. Many of the stresses of his life must have come from checking, and from failing to check, a great generosity of heart. The poems he left behind seem to me to speak in the most compassionate voice of any of his generation. What you would hear if you stood outside a door and could not make out the words the voice was saying (*the sound of sense*, Frost called this) might be what St. Irene's hands convey in "The Old and the New Masters":

> Revealing, accepting, what she does not understand.
> Her hands say: "Lo! Behold!"

With this voice he was able to say beautiful, tentative things no one else could say.

Marianne Moore

Randall Jarrell

Like Randall Jarrell's bats, we live by hearing, by vibrations; by having heard what makes us happy—his way of saying what he says. I cannot think of anyone who gives me more incentive than Randall Jarrell, as I read him or think about him.

Even a touch of affectation would have spoiled it—what he says in "The Lost World" of himself as a child, reading at bedtime, "Forced out of life into / Bed." Safe in his naturalness, he says, "I'm not afraid," and goes on in his glow of gratitude to existence.

> There off Sunset, in the lamplit starlight,
> A scientist is getting ready to destroy
> The world. "It's time for you to say good night,"
> Mama tells me; I go on in breathless joy.

"Remember, tomorrow is a school day,"
Mama tells me; I go on in breathless joy.

. . .

Then I go back
To my bedroom; I read as I undress.
The scientist is ready to attack.
Mama calls, "Is your light out?" I call back, "Yes,"
And turn the light out.

Randall Jarrell's evaluation of others is descriptive of himself. He says, ". . . the poems of Miss Bishop or Mr. Williams or Mr. Graves are a lonely triumph of integrity, knowledge, and affection."

War engulfs him. "The engines rise to their blind laboring roar."

"The great drake
Flutters to the icy lake—
The shotguns stammer in my head.
I lie in my own bed,"
He whispers, "dreaming"; and he thinks to wake.
The old mistake.

. . .

The tags' chain stirs with the wind; and I sleep
Paid, dead, and a soldier. Who fights for his own life
Loses, loses: I have killed for my world, and am free.

No; the dead are not afraid, cannot refute

The grave's cross, the grave's grass, the grave's polished granite
THESE DIED THAT WE MIGHT LIVE
—that I may live!—

Like Jonah, the soldier is vomited into life from the grave—not bitter or with uncertainty but with emphasized comprehension.

"Integrity, knowledge, and affection." Of these attributes it seems as though affection, affection unaided, might have demonstrated the abounding unsnobbishness of his heart. He says, "In my / Talk with the world,"

how strange that I
Know nothing, and yet it tells me what I know!—
I appreciate the animals, who stand by
Purring. Or else they sit and pant. It's so—
So *agreeable.*

One might say here something about an art of appreciation that does not estrange the beneficiary from the giver. Randall Jarrell could invest a creature with romance which makes it seem the counterpart of a luna moth with seagreen wings that have violet crescents on them—a creature that was a worm, and that only respects compliments which respect modesty.

Randall Jarrell's integrity is inescapably graphic in the testfire of anomalous associates described by him in his *Pic-*

tures from an Institution. The Institution was Benton College; and Dwight Robbins was its President. He had inherited Camille Batterson, teacher of creative writing, "and there was nothing he could do about her. Nothing, that is, that wouldn't have been cruel and inexpedient . . . the University of Iowa, or Illinois, or Indiana . . . had offered Miss Batterson a better job, a Chair in fact . . . [The President] hid the joy he felt, and expressed . . . the sorrow he did not feel."

The Head of the Department that had made the offer "was the informing intelligence of the committee that revised the English curriculum of the secondary schools of his state." "His field was Cowper." "When you pronounce Cowper properly, you say Cooper. . . . But when people who didn't know how to pronounce Cowper heard the head referred to by people who did . . . *they* thought him an authority on Cooper and spoke of him as such." ". . . before long he and his wife were spending evenings with deans." ". . . it did no good to remind himself that Cowper had been, for a good deal of his life, insane."

"Nobody except the English Department had thought it sensible of him to be interested in Cowper; now everybody thought it sensible of him to be interested in the English Department. Each member of the Department did something that seemed to the world impractical at best, idiotic at worst; to be in charge of the whole idiocy and impracticality seemed impractical or idiotic to no one."

His wife was a daughter and granddaughter of Justices of the Supreme Court of Virginia. "She was Miss Batterson's oldest and dearest friend. She . . . had heard Ellen Glasgow refer to Miss Batterson as 'a woman of the finest sensibility.' " After she left Benton, Miss Batterson sent postcards "home to Benton." "It was as if she were attending the University, not teaching at it."

"In March, the first spring after she left Benton, she died." "The next day, when the first girls came to Dr. Rosenbaum's office for their conferences, there was only a note on the door postponing these . . . Dr. Rosenbaum was looking out the window of a plane . . . on his way to a funeral."

Dr. Gottfried Rosenbaum and Mrs. Rosenbaum seem the most lovable residents of Benton. "And [yet] they did not like America so well as one would have wished them to like it . . . Irene, for instance, had a name that is pronounced *i RA ne,* more or less, over most of Europe; here in America she was called I REEN." Dr. Rosenbaum "had published three volumes of an immense work showing how content gets expressed in, and modified by, the forms of its time." He was composer in residence, known for his *Joyous Celebration of the Memory of the Master Johann Sebastian Bach.*

One cannot degrade the Rosenbaums' house by calling it exotic. ". . . there were, badly arranged on its rarely dusted bookshelves, books in English, German, Russian, French, Latin, Greek—all the languages of the earth . . . printed scores, photostats of scores, scores in manuscript, scores in Esperanto, almost. . . . a pale engraving of Vivaldi, Beethoven and Liszt letters in stand-up frames, glass on both sides so that one could see both sides of the page. There was no end to the confusion and richness of the house." A student friend "would close her eyes, and then open them again and look at the Rosenbaums 'like puzzled urchin on an aged crone / Who keepeth closed a wond'rous riddle-book.' "

Gertrude Johnson (English Department) was a spoiled one, spoiled beyond repair, marred forever in the making—a novelist who "listened only as A Novelist." Her books "did not murder to dissect, but dissected to murder. The blush on the cheek of Innocence is really—one learned this from Gertrude—a monomolecular film of giant levorotatory protein molecules, and the bonds that join them are the bonds of self-interest."

In Randall Jarrell, we have an author who somehow unshackled himself from *self* and could have a good time; have as companions a bat, a chipmunk, a bird. This was in the South and a mockingbird frequented the yard. He was somewhat mercurial. ". . . on his bad days he'd dive on everything that came into the yard—on cats and dogs, even. . . . The day the bat went to him the mockingbird was perched on the highest branch of the big willow by the porch, singing with all his might. . . . every part of him had a clear, quick, decided look about it. He was standing on tiptoe . . . sometimes he'd spring up into the air. This time he was singing a song about mockingbirds.

"The bat fluttered to the nearest branch, hung upside down from it, and listened; finally when the mockingbird stopped for a moment he said in his little high voice: 'It's beautiful, just beautiful! . . . I listen to you every night. Every day too. I—I . . . could listen to you forever.' " [The bird was pleased.] "'I'll sing it for you again.' . . . When the mockingbird had finished, the bat thought: 'No, I just can't say him mine. Still, though—'"

Later "the bat said: 'Sometimes when I wake up in the daytime I make up poems. Could I—I wonder whether I could say you one of *my* poems?'"

"Till a bat is two weeks old he's never alone: the little naked thing . . . clings to his mother wherever she goes. After that she leaves him at night; . . . almost dreaming, the bat began to make up a poem about a mother and her baby."

A bat is born
Naked and blind and pale.
His mother makes a pocket of her tail
And catches him.

. . .

She lives by hearing.
The mother eats the moths and gnats she catches
In full flight; in full flight
The mother drinks the water of the pond
She skims across. Her baby hangs on tight.

. . .

at daybreak
The tired mother flaps home to her rafter.
The others are all there.

. . .

Bunched upside down, they sleep in air.

The bat-poet's art is like Randall Jarrell's—never forced, but a thing of integrity, knowledge, affection. The weak rhymed foot not always matching the strong foot ("the moonlight" and "beak is bright"); "through the night / Doubling and looping, soaring, somersaulting"—as inconspicuous as prose; or "In full flight; in full flight / . . . Her baby hangs on tight," emphasized as if giving directions to an inexperienced child.

(After seeing Maurice Sendak's pictures of Randall's animals—of the bat fleeing from the owl, while "the night holds its breath" as the owl "calls and calls"; or a mother possum with all her baby possums holding tight to her, in the moonlight where apples have fallen under the apple tree—I am sure that if he were not an artist, he would not work for an exterminator.)

"The X-Ray Waiting Room in the Hospital," "In Galleries," *The Bat-Poet,* "They All Go"—no "steps echoing along the corridor." These story-dramas are not labored; they ignite imagination and just stop; they have no end. But the magic *never* ends.

Robert Phelps

For Randall Jarrell

I NEVER KNEW HIM; never heard him lecture; never even glimpsed him. Once, during the year in which he replaced Margaret Marshall as literary editor of *The Nation*, I went down to Vesey Street and stood in front of the building where his office must have been. But I didn't have the nerve to go up and have a look at him, or ask him to let me try reviewing a book.

(On the other hand, it was this very bout of cowardice, recalled years later, which operatively convinced me that courage is the only virtue that counts.)

He began publishing in the late thirties. His first collection of poems was called *The Rage for the Lost Penny*, and appeared, along with a sweetly dimpled photograph and a brisk, bright, bookish but entirely unacademic *apologia pro poetica sua*, as one fifth of a New Directions omnibus in 1940.

In 1942, he had a book all to himself, *Blood for a Stranger.* But it was with *Little Friend, Little Friend* (1945) that I discovered him. Its opening poem, "2nd Air Force," contained lines I shall always be haunted by.

And the green, made beasts run home to air.

*

How emptily the watchers see them gone.

*

The head withdraws into its hatch (a boy's)

*

It also taught me, exampled me, more about the art of poetry, and the difference between writing in sentences and writing in lines, than any other preceptor I had known until then.

I didn't buy my copy of *Little Friend, Little Friend* until it was being remaindered in Miss Frances Steloff's Gotham Bookmart. That same day, and on Jarrell's recommendation, I also bought a copy of Robert Lowell's *Land of Unlikeness.* This was not remaindered; in fact, it was a limited edition, hand-set, and very expensive (for me, at least), and it speaks for the power of Jarrell's persuasiveness that I had hitchhiked one hundred miles and carried a lunch of hard-boiled eggs in my pocket to save the money to buy it.

At that time, I was living in Woodstock, New York, a populous art colony in the summer, a quiet Catskill village in the winter, and year-around possessor of the dearest library I have ever known. Its contents were shelved in two or three rooms of a tiny, early-ninetenth-century farmhouse on the west periphery of the town, across a meadow from the undertaker and set well back from the Bearsville road, under elderly maples. Most of its several thousand books had been gifts, either from the generation of patrician and rather precious idealists who had settled in Woodstock about the turn of the century, or from a later generation who had spent the twenties abroad. There was very little trash. The books were highbrow, high-minded, polylingual, and often bore nameplates on their flyleaves. The result was more like an exceptional private library than the sort set up for public use, and the librarian was a wry and wiry little lady named Mrs. Thompson, who loved books and book-loving more than the Dewey decimal system.

Upstairs there was a low-ceiling, unheated attic where the overflow—duplicates, music, books Mrs. T. simply hadn't gotten around to cataloguing—were stored. It was here that I saw for the first time the score of Charles Ives's Fourth Symphony (or at least the single movement printed in green covers by the New Music Press). There were shelves of Bostonians, Henry and Brooks Adams, James Russell and Amy Lowell, William James and Henry; I remember the silky beige bindings of the original Scribner's editions of *The Golden Bowl* and *The Sacred Fount* and *The Better Sort.* There were cardboard boxes of the old *Dial*, *Transatlantic Review, Hound & Horn, transition*, and there was the "Plain Edition," which Gertrude Stein published herself, of *Lucy Church Amiably*. There were odd volumes in assorted languages: Rémy de Gourmont's *Promenades Littéraires*; Unamuno in Spanish; d'Annunzio in Italian. There was the only copy I have ever seen anywhere of William Carlos Williams's *The Great American Novel*; and ranked in knee-high stacks along the walls, there were back issues of *The New Republic*, *Partisan Review*, *Life*, and *The Nation*.

Especially during the winter of 1948–49, I spent many afternoons up in that attic, and it was here that, so to speak, I came to know Randall Jarrell. I would sit on the floor, or on a carton containing the complete works of Wilkie Collins. The library was open from two to six, though at that time of the year the only visitors usually came about four, on their way to the post office and the day's shopping. I would hear their snow tires crunching on the drive outside, and now and then a murmur of voices below. Some days I could see my own breath. Below the dormer window on my right lay an acre of frozen white, tinted rose on sunny days, with a blue shadow moving in as the sun settled behind a row of hemlocks to the west. It was when that advancing shadow reached an old pump that I knew I'd better start for home, or else I'd have to walk the last of my two miles in the dark. It was a quiet attic, far from the center of anything, hardly the place for a young man to make connections, or launch a career, or practice courage. But it was a perfect place to know Randall Jarrell.

I still have a flaky and yellowing sheaf of his poetry chronicles from *The Nation*, which Mrs. Thompson eventually gave me. (There used to be three times as many, but about 1952 I lent them to a young man named Burks, who thought

Jarrell every bit as wonderful as I did; and understandably he never returned them.)

I don't think I could measure how much I must owe them. But whenever I have to fill out one of those forms which asks me to specify my "education," I am tempted—instead of putting Oberlin College and the University of Chicago—to say:

> Randall Jarrell on Poetry; James Agee on Film; Virgil Thomson on Music. The latter two circa 1944, when I began to read their weekly columns in the storeroom of an army supply depot in Hialeah, Florida. The former circa 1948, in the attic of the Woodstock library.

At the least, though, Randall Jarrell's personality on the printed page gave me two important experiences.

(1) He was my first encounter with real taste: not good taste, correct taste, or charitable taste, but taste *tout court*: zest abounding, appetite that follows its own nose, one man's unfearful relish and delight, dismay or indignation, before something he loves. Jarrell loved language and all the uses of it which we call poetry. I shall never forget how intoxicating it was to share his joy—that's the only adequate word—over Corbière and Elizabeth Bishop and Robert Frost, over Robert Graves's poem "To Juan at the Winter Solstice" and the first book of *Paterson* and Robert Lowell's line about the Pilgrim Makers who take a lathe "And point their wooden steeples lest the Word be dumb." In fact, I am not sure I shall ever have a reaction to these poets and these poems which I can quite call my own. It may be that a little bit of Randall Jarrell's original reverence and delight simply continues to echo

in me, and that whenever I think of Williams's line "Butterflies settle on his stone ear" it will be with Jarrell's shiver of wonder. I am grateful, though, whatever the case.

(2) Something more elusive. Jarrell could praise but he could also devastate. He was not vindictive or cruel or willful. He simply saw what he saw, with the serene, fierce, unflinching disinterest of a recording angel. He was intelligent. He knew the score and the ropes and the rules. But he was also pure, formidably pure. Sooner or later, most of us compromise, water down, lean over backwards, pull punches; and we tend to call it kindness, or worldliness, or accepting things as they are. Jarrell remained innocent of this tactic. Someone once told me he had been shocked, even hurt, on hearing that one of his most overwhelming (to pull a punch) reviews had angered the author in question.

But it is possible that a poet's most precious, his least dispensable gift may not be his talent, or his vision, not even his luck; but his maddening and awesome assumptiveness, his incapacity to imagine that, just as he sees and breathes and is, he may not be wanted, eagerly. It amounts to a state of grace. A poet cannot ordain it, calculate it, earn it. It must be "given." It was what Baudelaire was yearning for when he spoke of wanting to lose himself "in an impeccable naïveté." Jarrell had it, wondrously, all his poetic life, and in Baudelaire's sense of the word, he remained blessedly "naïve," blessedly "impeccable," in everything he wrote.

Sr. M. Bernetta Quinn,
O. S. F.

Metamorphoses in Randall Jarrell

Un enfant accroupi plein de tristesses, lâche
Un bateau frêle comme un papillon de mai.

RIMBAUD

A CHILD FULL OF sadness and weariness gives one the feeling of a boat frail as a butterfly. Butterflies *are* metamorphosis. They act its drama. Jarrell has been, is, will be many things to many, among them a child who lives in the kingdom of metamorphosis. To find the heart of each of his protean songs we must struggle as did Menelaus with the Old Man of the Sea. If we are successful we shall have attained to prophecy. Like clues the poems Jarrell left drift back from the boat's journey, especially certain ones, such as "The Märchen" with its urgent "to change, to change!"

Such a magical world is in many ways a far more satisfactory one than that of real life. Though it does not exclude evil, it permits supernatural help to man in his eternal struggle against it, help which inevitably leads to happiness if the rules of the game are observed. It is hardly strange, indeed, that psychoanalysts early seized upon the *Märchen* as objectifications of the wish-fulfillment principle. In these, merit in the strict sense does not determine reward.

A striking feature of this world of fairy tale is absence of death. To a dead friend, Jarrell writes (in "The One Who Was Different"):

> "We shall not all sleep, but in a moment,
> In the twinkling of an eye,
> We shall be changed.

Spenser, in his Mutability Cantos, gets around the fact of dissolution through metamorphosis. Fairy tales contrive even for their villains euphemisms for death: petrifaction and other types of transformation.

Imagery from the fairy tales helps too in an explanation of the poetic process as Jarrell sees it. In discussing "What Are Years" by one of his favorite writers, Marianne Moore, he makes the following comparison, reminiscent of Grimm's "Rumpelstiltskin":

> She not only can, but must, make poetry out of everything and anything: she is like Midas, or like Mozart choosing unpromising themes for the fun of it, or like one of those princesses whom wizards force to manufacture sheets out of nettles.

Jarrell has clearly been influenced by these Germanic popular stories, the *Märchen*, as he himself acknowledges in *Mid-Century American Poets*, an anthology edited by John Ciardi, where he lists them as furnishing subjects for some of his poems. In his collection entitled *Losses*, "The Märchen" appears with "Grimm's Tales" as a subtitle; again in "Deutsch Durch Freud" he pictures himself as sitting on a sofa reading Grimm. In the first poem, allusions occur to many of the best-known tales, such as "Hänsel and Gretel" in which Hänsel is startingly identified with Christ. (The story of Hänsel and Gretel figures conspicuously in two other Jarrell poems, "The Night before the Night before Christmas" and "A Quilt-Pattern.") Metaphor rather than metamorphosis dominates the introduction of the poem, the forest pictured as a sea which stands for life as a whole, considered as the kingdom of Necessity. But in the final lines Jarrell sums up the metamorphic lesson we ought to have learned from the *Märchen*:

> Had you not learned—have we not learned, from tales
> Neither of beasts nor kingdoms nor their Lord,
> But of our own hearts, the realm of death—
> Neither to rule nor die? to change, to change!

"It is just here," Robert Humphrey says in introducing Charles M. Adams's 1958 Jarrell bibliography, "in the universal will to change focus and shape that much of the appeal of Jarrell's poetry lies."

The most ambitious and complete handling by Jarrell of

the metamorphosis theme is "Hohensalzburg: Fantastic Variations on a Theme of Romantic Character." All during the summer of 1948 Jarrell lived under the shadow of this famous castle, supposed to be haunted by ghosts who, like the wizards of folklore, have power to change whomever they meet into something else.

In sketching the background of the ghost whose visit forms the heart of the poem, Jarrell touches delicately on one form of metamorphosis of anthropological interest, petrifaction. He represents a stone maid who was once a young girl of exceptional loveliness, now sunk in the waters of the earth and whispering to the child who has run all evening on the beach. Transformation into stone is as catholic a belief as that into animal shape. Here the stone maid symbolizes the skeletal future of man. The child's wish for invisibility which immediately follows the allusion to petrifaction is of course a reference to another variety of metamorphosis and is a foreshadowing of the final passage in the poem.

Waking at night in a house near the castle, the protagonist is first aware of a strange visitor by a touch, swallow-light, on his hand. Next, he hears her speak. At first he sees only the moonlight. From moonlight, the "ghost" changes, at least in the way he talks about her, into the enchanted princess of the Grimm story, lying asleep "in the last, least room." The Briar Rose story, a favorite with Jarrell, appears in at least six of his other poems; the protagonist here is merely one drop of Sleeping Beauty's blood, one drop of the immense quantities that death has sucked. Then follows a most effective creation of suspense, fright; in a breathless dialogue, the princess describes to her victim how, some day, she will come to him and kiss his throat.

Then, as he kisses her, she takes on the taste of the lime tree, flower and fruit, and finally—horrible fulfillment of her prophecy—turns to a vampire who fixes her teeth into his throat and sucks all his blood into herself. The victim's dreadful predicament is dramatized through a crucifixion image; the moonlight pierces his extended arms as if with nails. Just as Christ's Body and Blood are separated on Calvary, so are the speaker's here. The terror recedes, and his guest is a girl again. The speaker, too, grows backwards until he reaches his own childhood. In a passage included in the *Poetry* first publication of the poem but omitted in *The Seven-League Crutches*, the whole meaning of the experience is now clarified: "The past is a child that sucks our blood / Back into the earth." Here the man grows tender toward his "Little Sister," for he sees that she is really his life; somberly, she adds to his voicing of this truth that she is also his death.

It would seem as if this stratified intepretation of death were rich enough, without further deepening. Yet, to understand Jarrell's lyric, one must take under examination a final metamorphosis. The moonlight > princess > vampire > girl ("Little Sister") > life > death becomes next a star. Foreshadowing of this last change has occurred in the line "Your cold flesh, faint with starlight"; the process is again suggested in the earlier version of the poem by "as all my blood / Flows from your starry limbs into your heart—"; it is at the end defined thus:

We shall change; we shall change; but at last, their stars,
We shall rest in the branches of the antlers
Of the iron deer.

The poem closes with a declaration that there is something more, something unexplained in the above account of reality, something best represented by the Christian concept of the world. All these things which appear to be so different—"at the last, all these are one, / We also are forever one: / A dweller of the Earth, invisible." In these lines the two chief characters in the poem become one and achieve invisibility, the metamorphosis which is the consummation of the girl's childhood wish.

In "Hohensalzburg," dream and folklore are combined. No image, not even that of blood or of ghosts, is more integral to Jarrell's work than that of the dream, which appears in more than half of the lyrics published by him in book form.

Randall Jarrell in his poetry almost always identifies death with dreaming. The most extensive expression of this identification, "The Night before the Night before Christmas," is a poignant case history of adolescent heartbreak. It begins with the simplicity and generality of a fairy tale, one set in an apartment house significantly called the Arden Apartments. Throughout its twelve pages, the principal character is referred to only as "the girl"; her mother has been dead for two years and she lives with her father, her invalid brother, and an aunt. Jarrell supplies obliquely the dreary intercourse of her daily life in a series of poignant details.

The girl's first dream, upon falling asleep the night before the night before Christmas, is a grotesque scene in which a big squirrel teaches lines from *Romeo and Juliet* to six others with radiator-steam-valve voices, an application of the Communist panacea of education which will at last destroy all evil. Then: "She whispers: 'I'm awake. / No, I'm not dreaming, I'm awake.'" The girl thinks of the vertiginous expanse of the universe; from her window she stares at the evergreens, stars, the bushes covered with snow that stand like Hänsel and Gretel, sparkling as brightly as Lot's wife after her metamorphosis to salt. She sees herself and her brother look at the squirrel dead in the snow.

The passage just following conveys in a brief dialogue, partly through manipulation of tenses, the children's bewilderment at this mixture of fantasy and truth. The leaves and the birds—a skillful use of motor imagery—have become the snow; the boy and girl, buried in their graves of snow, are radiantly transformed to the wings of the bird of the snow.

The snowbirds increase in magnificence in the poem till their great starry wings spread like the Milky Way itself. As in "Hohensalzburg," they have been changed after death into stars. Looking back to earth, both of the children whisper of the time when they were alive. The motto hanging in their father's office—*To Travel Hopefully Is A Better Thing Than To Arrive*—becomes *To End Hopefully Is A Better Thing—A Far, Far Better Thing*, the girl's memory of Sidney Carton from her English book. The motherless girl's crying, with which the poem ends, belongs not to the world of death and dream which she has created but to the problems that Christmas Eve will bring. But actually no one evades heartaches. Perhaps the reason why children appear so often is that, as in "Thinking of the Lost World," Jarrell tries through his poet's craft to turn age—the oncoming of old age—into childhood, "that calm country / Through which the stream of my life first meandered."

"The Black Swan" is still another child's attempt to understand death by way of the hallucinatory imagination, its title is the name usually given to a *pas de deux* from the metamorphic ballet *Swan Lake.* Instead of facing the fact that her sister is dead, the little girl in the poem makes up a fairy tale about her: the swans have turned her into a swan. At sunset, when chores are done, the girl goes in search of her transformed sister, down to the lake across which even the sun has become a swan with a red beak huge enough to contain the night.

The reeds by the edge of the lake are not reeds, but clusters of little voices whispering an incantation intended to metamorphose the living girl into the same form as her dead sister. The pathetic child leaves her own body waiting with the bowl of porridge on the shore and finds herself to be a swan, at the center of the lake, where the laugh had come from: through the intensity of her longing and loneliness she becomes her sister. Across the lapping water—the very waves hissing like swans—comes her own voice, faintly calling and now, from the other side of death, she learns the impossibility of any reconciliation. It is as if the white tombstones of the cemetery where they had laid her sister come swimming up from the lake's bottom—the low green mounds, the named white stones.

But all this hasn't happened, no, not really happened; in her dreams, the little girl has created even the trip to the lake; actually she is home in bed, though the moon, stars, frogs, waves, swans are all about her in the darkness as her dead sister soothes her to rest (or calls her to death). There is a great tenderness here, with a willingness to present emotion without apology, unique among poets of today. Sentimentality is avoided by the union of dream and fantasy, both of which refuse to be bound by the precepts of waking, practical life. Memory as experienced by the poet himself is a blend of these (title lyric of *The Lost World*); more and more as his writing reflects his inner landscape Jarrell goes back to his childhood as to a still-existing state, building a crescendo of pain when we see him unable to accept "losses" for change.

In "The Venetian Blind" Jarrell again works the difficulty of separating dream from reality (this problem, posed by Calderón's title, seems to him to call for assent or denial) and discovers that the true nightmare is the wide-awake one. Here also he utilizes the technique of metamorphosis. The person waking has the illusion that he is in Eden on the first day of the world. Falling in the shape of bars of a musical staff, the sunlight becomes his face. Then: "His dreams / Have changed into this day, this dream." He cannot remember where he is—a common enough experience—and imagines that his limbs are curled about space. The implications of this attitude, as they affect the question of personal identity, are echoed in many of Jarrell's lyrics.

Another type of dream analysis is illustrated in the final lines of "A Hunt in the Black Forest," wherein a child dreams a complete fairy story, one in which a tyrannical king is poisoned by a deaf-mute whose tongue has been cut out by a royal order; after the crime, the mute and a dwarf who has led the king to the trap prepared for him gaze through the window at the corpse until their two faces merge into the face of the child (the one dreaming the story) who knows that something is dreadfully wrong without understanding precisely what and is all the more fascinated on that account: "Their blurred faces, caught up in one wish, / Are blurred into one face: a child's set face." The murder by the mute and the dwarf in the dream is equivalent to the child's passionate wish to destroy some part of the grown-up world that oppresses him.

"A Quilt-Pattern" is another dream of an unhappy child, an invalid whose subconscious tries to compensate for the agonies of his conscious life. The title is drawn from the actual quilt on his sickbed; on it is blocked out the Tree of Life, gray as the light fades. On seven-league crutches the boy travels into "the oldest tale of all," sleep. In his dream he sees his mother dead and transformed into a house; her "scaling face" is "square in the steam of a yard." He hates her demanding, possessive love that pursues him every moment of his waking life; only by such a stratagem can he evade it.

Death itself, the mystery at the heart of "A Hunt in the Black Forest" and "A Quilt-Pattern," has lost its reality in these days of abstraction, where the targets of the bombardiers are only names learned in geography classes. In "A Conversation with the Devil," even Lucifer is appalled by modern man's attitude toward death. Indeed, Mephistopheles is a changed devil, an anachronism whose occupation is gone. Contemporary warfare has removed from man his freedom of choice, leaving no room for a devil's operations. And death, which used to have dignity, ritual, cannot be believed in; we only dream that we die. Thus the flier in "Losses," horrified at the contrast between actuality and the stereotyped war reports, blends dreaming and dying: "It was not dying—no, not ever dying; / But the night I died I dreamed that I was dead."

The life-is-a-dream motif so usual in Jarrell's poetry finds one of its best articulations in "The Dream of Waking," the first two stanzas of which represent what goes through the mind of a wounded soldier in a hospital as he dreams he is a child waking; he is back home again—the water around the drifting boat from which he was picked up changes into light, then into laughter, then into a blend of himself, his room, and the tree outside the window. In that earlier day, his sun is gold mixed with air, is his own life. Then he really wakes, remembering back to the boat, to the origin of his present plaster cast brown with dried blood, the boat where his friend died in spite of his own frenzied begging. The reality he wakes to now is gruesomely different from the childish reality he woke to in the dream and once used to wake to in life. The interpenetration of self with environment continues throughout the last stanza:

> the boat is bodies
> And the body broken in his broken arms
> And the voice, the old voice: *Please don't die—*
> His life and their death: oh, morning, morning.

The situation described so movingly here is very much like that in "A Field Hospital," where the patient thinks that he is dreaming after he has awakened—the "old mistake."

In "Absent with Official Leave," the soldier escapes to life through sleep, escapes to civilian lands where death is not organized; where roads hop aimlessly instead of leading to objectives; where hunters sprawl for birds, not men; where fires are lit not to burn down cities but to dry "His charmed limbs, all endearing from the tub." Near the end of the poem Jarrell's devotion to Grimm finds voice in "He moans like a bear in his enchanted sleep," with its overtones of the Snow White and Rose Red story. The soldier wakes from the spell not to a princess but only to the night, its silence broken by the sighs and breathing of his co-sufferers.

The prose poem "1914," reminiscent of Auden, as is much of Jarrell's earlier work, represents World War I thus:

> Now the forts of Antwerp, broken into blocks, slide into a moat as bergs break off into the sea; the blocks, metamorphosed into the dead, sprawl naked as grave-mounds in the stalky fields

It reiterates the life-is-a-dream motif discussed above by picturing minutely a photograph of a dead soldier and then pointing up the significance in these words: "Underneath his picture there is written, about his life, his death, or his war: *Es war ein Traum.*" Jarrell goes on to say, fusing the opposites life and death with their meeting place, war: "It is the dream from which no one wakes."

A clear example of mutation caused by war is Jarrell's lyric called "The Metamorphoses." Between the first and the second stanzas, peace has been converted into war. The peace was a degenerate, not a healthy one: surplus commodities were being destroyed as an artificial way of keeping up prices (the oranges thrown into the harbor, the burning coffee); idle ships were riding the waters; the protagonist, too, was idle. Once war breaks out, with its acceleration of the country's economic life, the scene springs to action: oil-tankers dot the bay, crated bombers cover the wharves, the unemployed "I" works all day in the rush caused by war needs. The significance of the title is underlined in the final quatrain. In a ghastly perversion of the prince-flounder idea in Grimm's "The Fisherman and His Wife," the speaker has been changed into a fish—Jarrell's way of describing a swollen corpse, floating upon the "oil-black bay," with wounds in his sides which gape like gills. The "rust of the freighters" has been replaced by the "blood of the transports"; however, whereas the rust blended into the tide, the blood remains separate with a frightful distinctness.

The whole poem emphasizes an idea which permeates

several of Jarrell's pieces: war metamorphoses men into things. "The Lines" develops this thought, pursuing it up through the time of discharge from service, when the "things" are changed back into men again: "After the naked things, told they are men, / Have lined once more for papers, pensions." The horror of regimentation over, the "things" are free, human beings once again.

World War II brought into the focus of popular attention the truth that a man is at least two persons: the soldier but also the civilian of the past who still exists in the minds of those back home and in his own dreams. In the days of Ovid's Rome, personal identity was not so fleeting a thing as it is today, after Berkeley's idealism, Locke's sensism, James's flux, Bergson's intuitionism, Sartre's existentialism, and all the other attempts to break down the notion of an abiding self. The rise of atomic science, with its emphasis on the underlying similarity of all things, may be partially responsible for our modern difficulties in forming a definite idea of personality.

With the self-consciousness of the artist, Jarrell approaches this problem of identity, subjects it to poetic examination. One of his favorite symbols in so doing is the mirror, as in "Next Day," for example. Earlier he did something similar on a higher social level: *Die alte Frau, die alte Marschallin* in "The Face" (a character borrowed from *Der Rosenkavalier*) repudiates what she sees in the looking glass, reflecting: "It is terrible to be alive," when what you are and what you appear to be are so different; this creature in the mirror cannot be she. So does the speaker in "Hope" (from *The Lost World*): "*But, married, I turn into my mother* / Is the motto of all such sundials." The protagonist in "A Ghost, A Real Ghost" thought that he could never survive looking in the mirror and finding the room empty; yet this happens and he keeps on existing. Someone in "An Old Song" speaks of "the mirror's lamentable change." The speaker goes on to wonder, looking into a grave, if the soul might be deceived into thinking it could escape punishment or praise in such depths, where it "might endure / The altering ages in that altered shape." "The Venetian Blind," already mentioned in connection with dreams, reveals a man groping frantically for his identity, for his niche in the cosmos; for that inexplicable *something* which is his true self, left out in every account of the world:

> And yet something calls, as it has called:
> "But where am *I*? But where am *I*?"

The italicizing of the personal pronoun shows upon which facet of the mental agony Jarrell wishes accent to fall.

In "The Mockingbird" he feels equally unsure about that world itself. At night, when the mockingbird imitates the creatures it has all day been chasing away, it succeeds so well that the poet asks, for a moonlit moment, "Which one's the mockingbird? which one's the world?"

That Randall Jarrell is concerned with philosophical explanations of inner and external reality is further evident in "The Place of Death," which portrays a student walking, his

Spinoza in hand, among the tombstones of a cemetery which is reminiscent of Robert Lowell's Quaker graveyard in Nantucket:

> He has felt the boundaries of being fade,
> These long-outmoded, mounded, dewy modes
> Lapse to the seeding and inhuman Substance
> Whose infinite, unchanging, and eternal thought
> Is here extended in a thousand graves.

The conversion of one thing into another is no longer exclusively an imaginative account of origins designed to provide courtly entertainment as in Ovid, or even a poetic representation of daily conscious and subconscious experience, as in the folklore collected by nineteenth-century scholars. It is an attempt to go back to that principle of change, natural to the child and common in dreams, in order to live more adequately our mortal measure of years. It is one of Randall Jarrell's ways of voicing that unfathomable disillusion which informs his poetry without ever quite conquering it, because of the child's hope at its heart.

John Crowe Ransom

The Rugged Way of Genius

NOBODY COULD IGNORE Randall, in those years when I was seeing him daily. He was an insistent and almost overbearing talker. I knew him when he was a child, almost, a sophomore and *enfant terrible* in my writing class at Vanderbilt. But even then, when you came to read what he had written, you knew that he had to become one of the important people in the literature of our time. Later it was hard to reconcile the man with the image I kept of the boy. Not that his ambition failed or even faltered, but that he learned to use his power properly, like a good magistrate; becoming always gentler and less aggressive. He did not have to beat his own drums, or beat the others' brows. Settled at last in Greensboro, it is my understanding that he was loved or admired by everybody in the place; he was both, by his students. I shouldn't be talking in this way perhaps, except that the naked pride of his incisive mind registered early in my affections as a symbol of his courage. More than once I had seen him rising in the academic forum when the official speaker had finished, and bearding the impostor in his lair; ruining him with three or four perfect satirical sentences uttered in that high and piercing voice. His victim rarely found words to reply, and usually would try to laugh his tormentor off, making a horrible smile which meant to be amusing and condescending; but what it showed was not pleasure.

Randall was professional both as a poet and as a teacher of poetry. As fast as his poems were sent out, they were being published and circulated by good houses; at the same time he was teaching poetry, and of course with a salary attached. Critics out in the world, even poet-critics, often tell us that when the poet takes employment in the Academy he compromises his own poetic integrity. Must we buy that idea? Have not the greatest composers and painters suffered gladly the disciples who trooped behind, and even stopped to help them individually? And wasn't this in effect to establish those "schools" of music and painting? The poet in the Academy differs only in having contractual obligations toward those who come to him. His two occupations are very closely related. He studies the same text-poems that they do, though he has more knowledge to start with; and much harder than they do, because as a poet he needs to know poetry. Then he will explain to them why these best poems have established themselves as imperishable. But in Randall's time there were wonderful contemporary poems which looked more than mortal; the courses which he taught were usually in modern poetry. And toward the end of our half century the boys and girls in a sort of mass movement began to try to free their poems almost entirely from the old meters which used to confine the poets, and to write in their own vernacular idiom. The new poetry looks easier to write, but it is hard to write it if the poets care about that distinction which is peculiar and proper to poetry—when it is the property of music. A poem without music is a piece of prose. Now Randall himself was a "modern" poet, if we mean one that comes soon after Pound and Eliot, and even when he was most informal he attended to his music. I think he must have tried in the later years to fix in his pupils' minds the idea of keeping a minimal prosody. That is an old Greek word, but if it still means anything it refers to the sound of the intermittent rhythms made by the phrases; and to the "tone-colors" made by the words in the phrases, where the vowels and the consonants form intermittently into their respective family "clusters," and sound as if coming from the same orchestral instruments.

We will come back to the poetry. But first I will remark upon his prose. It was at least as good as his poetry, and I will offer a sampling of the genius that flowered there. About the year 1952 as I reckon it, when his public manners were perfected but still there were bad critics to reprobate, I was in the audience he confronted when it came his time on a Wednesday evening to read a public lecture at the School of Letters in Bloomington. It was entitled "The Age of Criticism," and I quote one of its paragraphs:

> Critics may still be rather negligible figures in comparison to the composers and painters they write about; but when they

write about writers, what a difference! A novelist, a friend of mine, one year went to a Writers' Conference; all the other teachers were critics, and each teacher had to give a formal public lecture. My friend went to the critics' lectures, but the critics didn't go to his: he wasn't surprised; as he said, "You could tell they knew I wasn't really literary like them." Recently I went to a meeting at which a number of critics discussed what Wordsworth had said about writing poetry. It was interesting to me to see how consciously or unconsciously patronizing they were to—poor Wordsworth, I almost wrote. They could see what he had meant, confused as he was, layman that he was; and because he had been, they supposed they must admit, a great poet, it did give what he had to say a wonderful documentary interest, like Nelson's remarks at Trafalgar. But the critics could not help being conscious of the difference between themselves, and Wordsworth, and my friend: *they* knew how poems and novels are put together, and Wordsworth and my friend didn't, but had just put them together. In the same way, if a pig wandered up to you during a bacon-judging contest, you would say impatiently, "Go away, pig! What do you know about bacon?"

With what a grace is this passage composed; yet it consists with a severe economy of words, which counts every word and does not waste one. The first sentence is introductory; when critics of no repute stop writing about composers and painters and write about writers: "what a difference!" The sentences which follow are strictly consecutive, and the big ones always finish on peaks of comic revelation which rise progressively. The novelist friend at the Writers' Conference: "You could tell they knew I wasn't really literary like them." Randall himself, after hearing the critics discuss what Wordsworth wrote about writing poetry: "How consciously or unconsciously patronizing they were to—poor Wordsworth, I almost wrote." But since Wordsworth's reputation exceeded even theirs, they decided: "It did give what he had to say a wonderful documentary interest, like Nelson's remarks at Trafalgar." Then the single group which Randall makes of the Writers' Conference people and the Wordsworth people: "*they* knew how poems and novels are put together, and Wordsworth and my friend didn't, but had just put them together." The final peak of absurdity, than which there is no higher peak, is the tiny Jarrellian parable about the pig at the bacon-judging contest. Nothing must be said of it. A great joke may be repeated a hundred times, but never explained. It may have to be repeated by any of us a score of times before we quite get the deadly point of it, but finally that is contributed by the laboring understanding which works for us in the underground of consciousness.

"The Age of Criticism" became one of the essays in Randall's book *Poetry and the Age,* published in 1953. The style from which I have quoted is supple as ever, but the pieces are very serious and less funny. In criticism begin responsibilities. The book has great substance, and I believe it is recognized as almost epoch-making in establishing for the first time securely the position which Robert Frost and Walt Whitman occupy in American poetry. Randall uses a very sane and simple method in rating them; though it must be remembered that it is not available to critics who do not know the whole of their authors, nor read the poems without the help of a microscopic judgment which misses nothing. There are two essays on Frost. In "The Other Frost" he writes about the fourteen best poems which are "likely to seem to anybody too new to be true." These are the desperate poems about the facts of life as the New England folk endured them. They confer upon us the Sense of Tragedy, which is one of the most precious wisdoms we can acquire; to poets and their readers it brings some of the gravest and bravest sentiments that our humanity is heir to. I am afraid that is only what I am saying; without saying it, Randall had a great flair for the poetry of desperation. But Randall does not stop there. He writes a much longer second essay on behalf of Frost, addressed "To the Laodiceans," where he names thirty-five poems of all Frost's better kinds, including those named in the first essay; and comments on many of them, but not the easy and familiar ones.

For Whitman, Randall fixes our attention upon "Some Lines from Whitman," rather than whole poems, which might be long and wearisome. He was only amused by the lines and poems of the grosser Whitman, who coined words that philologists would not accept, and misspelled foreign words intentionally by refusing to check them up. He was not too much dismayed by that egregious "I" of Whitman's, by which he identified himself so often as the self-appointed universal American. The quoted lines are many, but:

> To show Whitman for what he is one does not need to praise or explain or argue, one needs simply to quote. He him-

self said, "I and mine do not convince by arguments, similes, rhymes, / We convince by our presence."

At least one comparative judgment is made in Whitman's favor, when his long poems are matched against those of his contemporary Tennyson:

> . . . we are at once aware of how limiting Tennyson's forms have been, of how much Tennyson has had to leave out, even in those discursive poems where he is trying to put everything in.

Randall stands Whitman high on a world pedestal, where he belongs.

I was disturbed at first by his "Reflections on Wallace Stevens." Randall had been ravished by *Harmonium,* Stevens's first book, where he had found "six or eight of the most beautiful poems an American has written"; and poems in later books, till he came to *The Auroras of Autumn.* There he said that Stevens in some places was substituting abstract and logical phrases for the sparkling metaphors we expected. The old bravura was gone; the poet had aged. He had turned to "philosophizing," which a poet must never do. And Randall was right, by that exhibition; I had to confess it. Randall regularly required his own verse to be colloquial, and to deal only with particulars. He read the poem at you, if you were present and questioned it, and explained it if he must in homely terms. (I cannot find any place where he used the term "metaphor.") But Stevens in the book mentioned was engaged upon a philosophical problem, asking whether his high-metaphorical style was telling the truth about reality. In

Transport to Summer Stevens wrote one poem specifically about "The Motive for Metaphor," from which I quote. The motive is to escape from intolerable reality, into

> The ruddy temper, the hammer
> Of red and blue, the hard sound—
> Steel against intimation—the sharp flash,
> The vital, arrogant, fatal, dominant X.

The Greek term "metaphor" is perfectly translated in the Latin term "transformation"; and X is Kant's term for the transformation of the chaotic (and the commonplace) stuff of reality into the fiction of the imagination; because the noble Ideas of the Pure Reason have ineffable longings for expression. That is a simple concept, and Randall would have known it, but would say it, if he said it, in his own words. Metaphor is a "metaphysical" transformation. And the Prince of metaphor and miracle in our language was old John Donne, the metaphysical poet. But Stevens is his successor. We could think of the two as twinned brethren, but for a certain recession of the high style during those centuries which sundered them; for the moral worm had gnawed into Stevens's brain and made him suspicious of his own metaphors.

But I wish Randall had remarked that even *Harmonium* had agitated Stevens in this respect in many poems; and in its most magnificent poem, technically, "Sea Surface Full of Clouds." There the sailor from Tehuantepec observes the reflections of the clouds upon the sea; and the shadows of the clouds upon the deck, which is ordinarily brown, but in the early morning is colored into various chocolates, and transformed in places by the little blobs of clouds into kinds of umbrellas. Few of Stevens's poems have been more admired, but it took me a while to understand it structurally; it was not my luck to come upon a good "explication" in the critical books. The poem is of symphonic form, having five movements of six stanzas each; and the movements repeat the same melody almost precisely, and change the substance only slightly. But there is a progress, unless we call it a regress, because the final movement almost wrecks the sailor's voyage. In each movement there is a middle part, consisting of the third and fourth stanzas, of crucial importance. They are asking, Who could have assembled this miraculous thing? And always in the last line of the fourth stanza the poet admits that he is the one who has done it; but he is too modest or too wary to say it in plain English, he will dress it in a lovely French costume; in both senses that will shelter him. I will show these lines in their order, each preceded by the number of the movement:

I. *C'était mon enfant, mon bijou, mon âme.*
II. *C'était mon frère du ciel, ma vie, mon or.*
III. *Oh! C'était mon extase et mon amour.*
IV. *C'était ma foi, la nonchalance divine.*

But in the final stanza the spirit of the poet is broken, the physical spectacle itself has become too ridiculous, and what he must say in the abysm of his honesty is:

V. *C'était mon esprit bâtard, l'ignominie.*

But "The sovereign clouds came clustering" all the same; "The conch of loyal conjuration trumped," to conjure as usual the winds, which would blow the clouds away till came the "Fresh transfigurings of freshest blue." The poet's loyalty to his art, having gone so far in the other movements, is equal to this one too. But there has been a scare.

There is a happy sequel to Randall's partial alienation from the Stevens of 1953, when he has read the poet's last book, *The Rock,* published in 1954 as part of *The Collected Poems of Wallace Stevens.* In 1955 Randall's long essay was published in *The Yale Review* (I know it only in the Brown and Haller anthology called *The Achievement of Wallace Stevens*). Randall did not take back his former objections, but he gloried in Stevens's grand finale, restoring him to his old stature and making him even larger. He commented on a good number of the new poems, including as a matter of course "The World as Meditation"; the one about Penelope, who thinks in her bed that "A form of fire approaches the cretonnes," and is Ulysses himself, home from his wanderings. But she wakes, and it is only the warmth of the sun upon her pillow. "It was Ulysses and it was not"; either way it would do. "The barbarous strength within her would never fail." If dream or metaphor is the best we can have, let us have it; we can manage with it when reality is not sufficient. That was Stevens's ultimate decision.

But I will remark that Randall must have done his homework there better than most of his fellow essayists. He made two lists of Stevens's poems in descending order. Statistically, they come to twenty-four "best" poems, and twenty-five "bet-

Randall Jarrell, two and a half years old

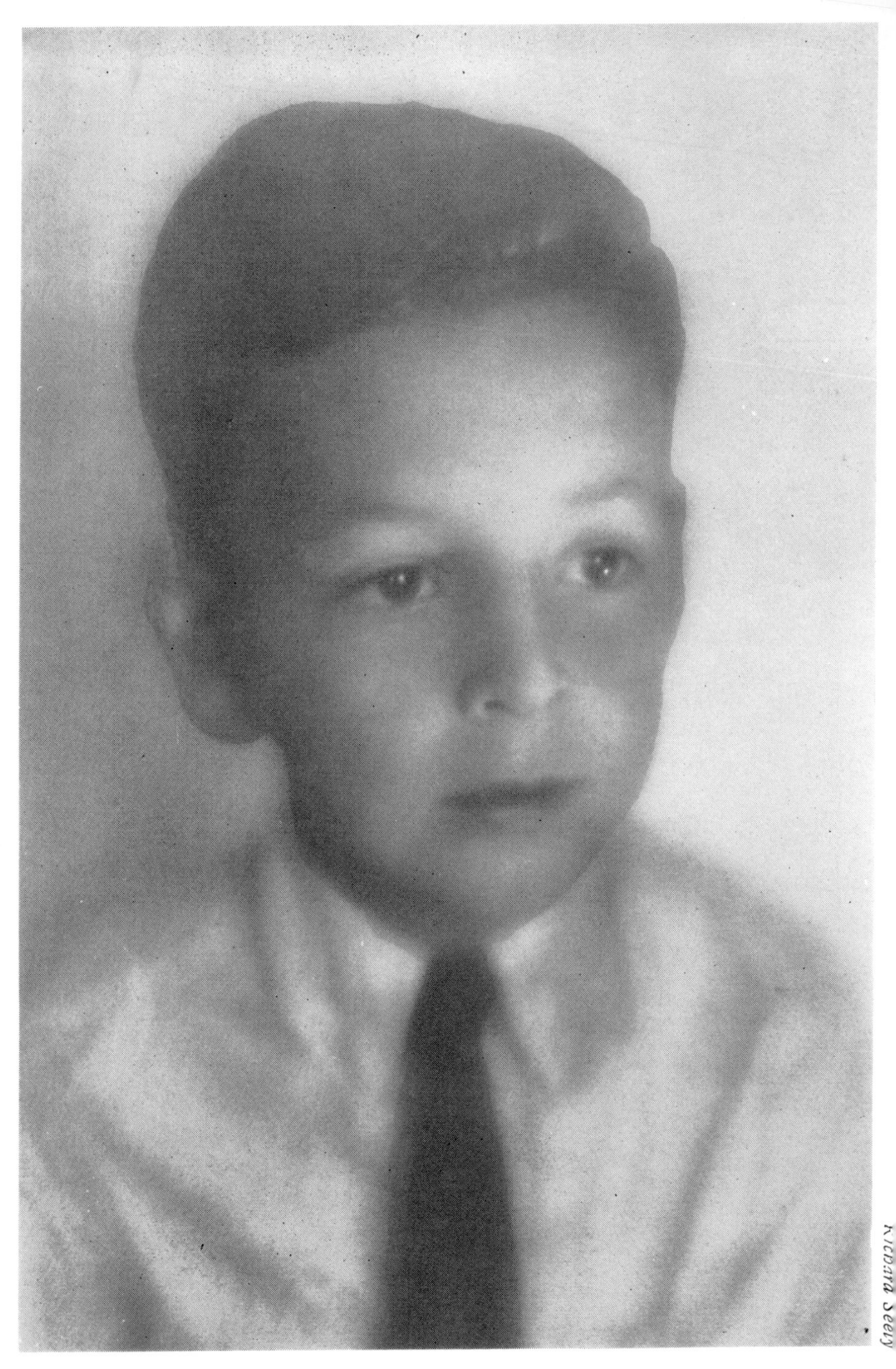

Richard Seely

Randall Jarrell, eight years old. In Long Beach, California

With Mama, Jarrell's paternal grandmother. July 1927, Hollywood

With Dandeen, his great-grandmother. Hollywood, c. 1924

In 1926, with a photograph of Nashville's replica of the Parthenon. (Below) *A section of that photograph, showing the figure of Ganymede for which Jarrell modeled.*

As The Chocolate Soldier *at Hume-Fogg High School in Nashville*

Summer of 1943. The Air Force. Chanute Field, Illinois

Salzburg, summer 1948

Rollie McKenna

At Princeton, c. 1952

Elliott Erwitt

Spring 1954, Manhattan

Bob Willoughby

With Mrs. Jarrell, Alleyne (center), *and Beatrice* (right).
Summer 1954. Laguna Beach, California

June 1957, Washington, D.C.

Ted Russell

Delmore Schwartz and Randall Jarrell at the Library of Congress, 1958

At home in Washington, D.C. June 1957

With Dürer's engraving "The Knight, Death and the Devil." June 1957

Ted Russell

Teaching.
The University of North Carolina at Greensboro, 1963

Randall Jarrell, June 1958

ter" poems. But humanly, I was comforted to find him saying that it had been hard to tell where the dividing line ought to be drawn.

My fellow contributors in this volume will all be honoring Randall, for one thing and another. But it is my impression that he is known most widely as a poet. Is it not possible that our younger readers will not be made to attend sufficiently to his prose? I must insert some notice of what just might be his great masterpiece: *Pictures from an Institution.* And I have elected to recall enough of it to prove that it is really a novel, having a plot and an outcome; not merely a script for filming a lot of odds and ends. It is one of the merriest and wittiest things of our age, and Randall's metaphors are bold and almost innumerable. He equates his characters and their behaviors with stunning figures and figurations from literature. There must be many scholars who know as much literature as Randall did, or more. But scholars are not artists. Outside of Pound and Eliot and Joyce, of course, I think there must be precious few of literary artists in our time and tongue who have had so wide a range of reference.

The great exhibits at Benton are, first of all, President Dwight Robbins, and his English-Colonial wife, his little son, his Afghan, and his swimming pool; and then the most important and high-salaried faculty member, Dr. Whittaker, of Sociology, with a wife who wears outlandish costumes and is dedicated to good deeds, and their two strange children. But there are many other characters, faculty people with or without children, visiting lecturers; and of course the president's secretary, Constance, a very nice young woman who unfortunately has not yet established her identity. Many of them we like very much.

Suddenly, in the fall term, there is the entry of the heroine and star of the show. She is Gertrude Johnson—attended of course by her loyal and undistinguished husband—who comes as Novelist in Residence with a one-year tenure like the reporter's, and conversationally is his most frequent vis-à-vis. All her novels have had one single brutal purpose: to expose the pretensions of the great, by reducing them to the pure original selfishness which really motivates them; to the lowest common denominator of behavior in man as in the beasts. And it does not take her long to plan her next novel with terrifying conviction, as dealing with these very Robbinses and Whittakers; under other names, of course. She tells as much in confidence to the reporter, and he cannot dissuade her. Her first duty at Benton had been to make her formal call upon the president in his office, and it had not come off badly; they thought they might like each other. But very soon there was a party somewhere, and after a few drinks they looked at each other

> and their eyes widened at what they saw. George looked at the dragon and thought, *Why, that woman's a dragon;* and the dragon looked at George and thought, *That's no man, that's an institution.*

Both were right. Gertrude was a dragon, being an Absolute Cynic who was afraid of nothing; and St. George was a professional dragon-killer, and the Institution itself so far as he could manage it.

The year wore on, with Gertrude busily jotting down the ugly facts of life about her victims-to-be, and in the long spring term the Institution people began to tire a little of one another. But something happens. Sidney Johnson has an illness, but under Gertrude's care he recovers in a week. "But Gertrude took longer to recover from his illness." For the first time in her life she had been afraid. What if Sidney should stop caring for her?

> She had trusted Sidney entirely because Sidney needed her entirely: how could Sidney possibly get along without *her?* But now that she saw she could not possibly get along without Sidney, her trust was shaken. When Sidney found out that she was in his power—if he found out, her heart substituted hastily—what would he do? How could you trust *anyone* with such power?
>
> . . .
>
> In the world there were people who were bad to her and people who were good to her, people she was bad to and people she—and Sidney. Sidney was what Gertrude could be good to. From the black steel of Gertrude's armored side there opened a kind of door, and from it a hand emerged and held out to Sidney a glass of lemonade—cold, and with sugar in it, even if it was bad for him—and the hand, seriously and with interest, watched Sidney drink the lemonade. Then the door closed; but still, it had been open for that long: for that long there had been nothing between the world and Gertrude but a hand holding a glass of lemonade.

> It always surprised Gertrude that people, ordinary people, could take themselves seriously; surely even they must see how ridiculous they were! But as she watched Sidney drink the lemonade she did not see how ridiculous he was, but watched seriously and with interest, taking him on his own terms.

That is our first cue to the change that must come over Gertrude, if Randall is the man we think he is. That is, if he wants his book to be more than Pictures; hopeless as it seems, let it come to its point, and be also a Novel. I find in my *Oxford Companion* that Anthony Trollope wrote a novel entitled *The Small House at Allington, Can You Forgive Her?* The title doesn't say what she did, but if we know Trollope we know that his answer will be in the affirmative. I have not read that one, but I did read *Is He Popenjoy?*, and with great pleasure, for I returned to it more than once. Of course he was Popenjoy, and heir to the estate. Randall might have added a flourish to his own title, as follows: *Pictures from an Institution: Will Gertrude Be Saved?* For there is no soul on earth beyond the possibility of redemption if there is in it a single streak of goodness. But Randall did not covet the explicitude of a Trollope.

There is a second cue. The concluding Chapter VII is called "They All Go." It is two or three days after commencement, the students have gone home, and the president and staff, with whatever families they have, are packed up and saying their goodbyes. But there is a strange goodbye which Gertrude makes to the reporter and his wife. They drive her to her train, and here are the last words which Gertrude says to them:

> "I've often thought of writing a book about a—" here, for the smallest part of a second, she hesitated—"about a *writer*."

And in earlier conversations we have been made to understand quite positively that writers respect each other as they must, being a superior breed of people who look down properly upon the greedy herd.

But there is even a third cue, in an odd place: Randall has put it at the very opening of the book, where it occupies a page and a half. It is a flash promoted to this position though the event it deals with belongs in the last chapter. (My wife and I see this trick frequently on our TV.) It is four o'clock in the afternoon of the last day; and her duties in that office are all done forever, but poor Constance, the secretary, is sitting there as she must until the president leaves his office.

> She sat in uneasy content, in easy discontent—she could not tell, for a moment; then she remembered and laughed at herself. . . . Dr. Rosenbaum's old St. Bernard's voice came to her from the tennis courts, and she felt once more the pleasure she always felt at any reminder that he existed; she saved for him St. Augustine's best sentence: I want you to be. Two voices from the President's office—the President's, Gertrude Johnson's—she heard with different feelings; she could not have said exactly what they were.

I can only tell how I interpret these voices. Constance must know now that the president and Gertrude despise one another, but now she cannot understand their tones. I imagine the president as saying goodbye to Gertrude in a nicer voice than usual, because he thinks she will never again get into his hair, or even for better motives; and Gertrude being a little sullen, and quieter than usual, for either of two reasons. Either she has renounced the novel at which she has worked so hard, but grieves because of her sacrifice; or she will publish it anyway as soon as possible and never do another one like it, in which case she is not yet living up to her conversion. But to most intents and purposes she seems saved, insofar as our bright reporter's testimony permits us to judge. So the novel is concluded, if we read it well, without getting out of the one school year at Benton.

And now for Randall's poems. Of course, we'll say that in all of them a new and original voice is speaking. The earlier ones display a more formal music than the later ones, and have a greater dignity. They do not have so much "true-to-life" and prolix detail, nor resort to sprawling long lines, and broken lines, and words and phrases in capital letters. I suppose these are trifles and I am too dainty about them, but I prefer poems of ordinary length to be so compacted that their meanings overflow their spaces. They will expand enormously in the mind of the reader, who as his taste requires finds himself working precisely to that end, and becoming a sort of individual proprietor having special rights in the poet's legacy. But I don't know if the combination of prose properties and poetic properties in the same piece is as good as either prose or poetry by itself; the prose and the poetry seem to adulterate one another. When we read our very young and up-to-date poets, we often suspect that they have not known how to write a pure prose, or a pure poetry. But of course this can never be said of Randall, nor of all of the younger poets.

Following Randall's method with other poets, I have made my list of his fifteen "best" and most permanent poems. If they had appeared suddenly and anonymously in a small volume, it would have been received with wonder as a poetry in a new key and would have made the author famous as soon as he could be identified. I name them in the order in which I find them in *Selected Poems* and the two single volumes that followed; the first eleven I take from the *Selected* ones. Here they are: "A Girl in a Library"; "The Knight, Death, and the Devil"; "The Face"; "Seele im Raum"; "The Black Swan"; "The Island"; "A Soul"; "A Rhapsody on Irish Themes"; "The Skaters"; "A Story"; "The Death of the Ball Turret Gunner"; "Cinderella"; "The Lost World"; "Woman"; and "Thinking of the Lost World."

In these poems I submit myself to the same feelings which they induce in all of us so hauntingly. Probably Randall is the one poet who wears his particular triple crown, which signifies a pure Pity, an all-embracing Weltschmerz, and a wry ironic Wit that steels us (almost) to approve their public presentation. A good half of the listed poems are in the modern style, and ravage us explicitly, while the tighter and more resonant lyrics lodge themselves word by word in our consciousness more obscurely.

I begin by quoting two poems on my list; let them be of two kinds, the informal and the more formal, and among the shortest in those kinds.

THE FACE

Die alte Frau, die alte Marschallin!

Not good any more, not beautiful—
Not even young.
This isn't mine.
Where is the old one, the old ones?
Those were mine.

It's so: I have pictures,
Not such old ones; people behaved
Differently then . . . When they meet me they say:
You haven't changed.
I want to say: You haven't looked.

This is what happens to everyone.
At first you get bigger, you know more,
Then something goes wrong.
You are, and you say: I am—
And you were . . . I've been too long.

I know, there's no saying no,
But just the same you say it. No.
I'll point to myself and say: I'm not like this.
I'm the same as always inside.
—And even that's not so.

I thought: If nothing happens . . .
And nothing happened.
Here I am.
But it's not *right.*

If just living can do this,
Living is more dangerous than anything.

It is terrible to be alive.

The monotone of these flat repetitive phrases makes for a powerful eloquence. The moment is so actual and prolonged, the theme so absolute and simple; it is the tragedy of Every-woman as she stares and speaks into her mirror. Who will cast the first stone upon this ruined face?

And now the other poem, more formal, and as short as a best poem can be:

THE DEATH OF THE BALL TURRET GUNNER

From my mother's sleep I fell into the State,
And I hunched in its belly till my wet fur froze.
Six miles from earth, loosed from its dream of life,
I woke to black flak and the nightmare fighters.
When I died they washed me out of the turret with a hose.

How fast it sticks in the reader's memory, if he will read it twice. This poem is quite worth any half dozen of the many others which Randall wrote about the Air Force in World War II; Randall had served there, heroically, as an instructor, intent first upon the quality of his teaching, then upon the heroism and luck of his fighters. The poem is nearly perfect. (I wish line 3 had been cast in the same rhythm as lines 1, 2, and 4; but as for the grand end-line, *stet!*)

And here is the brilliant "Cinderella." I must quote it all.

Randall Jarrell, 1914–1965

CINDERELLA

Her imaginary playmate was a grown-up
In sea-coal satin. The flame-blue glances,
The wings gauzy as the membrane that the ashes
Draw over an old ember—as the mother
In a jug of cider—were a comfort to her.
They sat by the fire and told each other stories.

"What men want. . . ." said the godmother softly—
How she went on it is hard for a man to say.
Their eyes, on their Father, were monumental marble.
Then they smiled like two old women, bussed each other,
Said, "Gossip, gossip"; and, lapped in each other's looks,
Mirror for mirror, drank a cup of tea.

Of cambric tea. But there is a reality
Under the good silk of the good sisters'
Good ball gowns. *She* knew. . . . Hard-breasted, naked-eyed,
She pushed her silk feet into glass, and rose within
A gown of imaginary gauze. The shy prince drank
A toast to her in champagne from her slipper

And breathed, "Bewitching!" Breathed, "I am bewitched!"
—She said to her godmother, "Men!"
And, later, looking down to see her flesh
Look back up from under lace, the ashy gauze
And pulsing marble of a bridal veil,
She wished it all a widow's coal-black weeds.

A sullen wife and a reluctant mother,
She sat all day in silence by the fire.

Better, later, to stare past her sons' sons,
Her daughters' daughters, and tell stories to the fire.
But best, dead, damned, to rock forever
Beside Hell's fireside—to see within the flames

The Heaven to whose gold-gauzed door there comes
A little dark old woman, the God's Mother,
And cries, "Come in, come in! My son's out now,
Out now, will be back soon, may be back never,
Who knows, eh? *We* know what they are—men, men!
But come, come in till then! Come in till then!"

The story begins with an "imaginary" playmate who sat before Cinderella's fireside, where they told stories to each other. But the author is fettered only for a moment by this twinge of conscience, for the old woman quickly becomes real, and a very godmother. Then the story takes off in earnest. It is at least as honest as the fairy tale which we all know in the text of the decorous Brothers Grimm, and merrier and more adult. It appears that the girl is not quite decided as to which is her true vocation: to be a woman and marry a man, or to be a gnome. The godmother is a perfect gnome; and I suppose that a female gnome is a wise old woman with a sharp tongue who only sits before the fire and talks about the men. In this poem the thought of the two cronies includes even their Father in Heaven, who unfortunately is male. He is said to have created a man's world, but any woman will be emancipated eventually, whether in this world or the next, and then she will have her fun. It is clearly Cinderella's destiny to find her man, so the godmother dresses her regally and sends her off in state to dance with the prince. But even before the marriage she wishes it were all over. The marriage was not a happy one for her, as the godmother must have foreknown; it was the preliminary to happiness. I believe I am paraphrasing Randall's text, and maybe speculating upon his intention, but the "Heresy of Paraphrase" and the "Intentional Fallacy" are the occupational hazards of a critic's profession if he means to do his best for his readers with a strange poem.

The conclusion is magnificent. The fires of Hell are Heavenly to sit by. And the lucky Cinderella acquires again her old familiar, the gossipy godmother; who is better than ever, and now goes by her proper title as the God's Mother. She may have been the origin of all mankind, and of the God to begin with. But Randall was too discreet to propound a systematic theology.

The two other poems upon which I shall make some comment have to do with Randall's memories of his childhood. These he never relinquished, apparently, and at last they became so important to him that they seemed to give a new direction to his life; though we know that it would not be for long, for the poems were first published, in *Poetry,* just two years before his death. The first one for us here is the concluding passage from the first recital of the child in "The Lost World," which is the title poem of his last volume, eleven pages long and showing three recitals by the same child.

A prelude
By Chopin, hammered note by note, like alphabet

Blocks, comes from next door. It's played with real feeling,
The feeling of being indoors practicing. "And yet
It's not as if—" a gray electric, stealing
To the curb on silent wheels, has come; and I
See on the back seat (sight more appealing
Than any human sight!) my own friend Lucky,
Half wolf, half police-dog. And he can play the piano—
Play that he does, that is—and jump so high
For a ball that he turns a somersault. "Hello,"
I say to the lady, and hug Lucky . . . In my
Talk with the world, in which it tells me what I know
And I tell it, "I know—" how strange that I
Know nothing, and yet it tells me what I know!—
I appreciate the animals, who stand by
Purring. Or else they sit and pant. It's so—
So *agreeable*. If only people purred and panted!
So, now, Lucky and I sit in our row,
Mrs. Mercer in hers. I take for granted
The tiller by which she steers, the yellow roses
In the bud vases, the whole enchanted
Drawing room of our progress. The glass encloses
As glass does, a womanish and childish
And doggish universe. We press our noses
To the glass and wish: the angel- and devilfish
Floating by on Vine, on Sunset, shut their eyes
And press their noses to their glass and wish.

If we have full confidence in Randall's moral rectitude, as is very likely, we must agree that this is the way he would have lived and talked as a child, say at the age of eight or ten—provided this was honest autobiography. A prodigy of a child, but no more of one than was in the young man in his teens who later presented himself at Vanderbilt. The child is prodigious in his careful introspection of his own mind, and his easy access to the doggish mind; his remarkable vocabulary, and his not losing his way even in the very complicated sentences. But his sense of style! Take the following passage, after removing the separations between the lines: ". . . the yellow roses in the bud vase, the whole enchanted drawing room of our progress." How can we not feel that a little of Randall's mature knowledge of Henry James was not parceled out to the remembered boy for this occasion?

My own misgivings went even further. It was my impression, and that of my friends, that Randall had spent all of his childhood at Nashville; yet the recitals of the little boy in the poem assumed that the place was Hollywood. Was it a responsible autobiographer who had transferred the scene to Hollywood, because there was more enticing excitement there? But by great luck I was informed, unimpeachably, that Randall had lived as a child for a year or so with his grandparents and great-grandmother, in Hollywood itself. I was chastened of my ugly suspicions.

It does not follow that even at Hollywood there may not be many childish experiences which are common to all stories of children; they may occur in the playroom, on the lawn, at the table, without geographical identification. But Randall had an uncommon degree of the power of "total recall," and evidently he wished that the Lost World could retain many actual recollections of the far-away time. Let us conclude that there cannot have been many writers of distinguished fiction, whether prose or verse, who could manage without calling upon imagination to supplement their own experiences with improvisations, as brilliant as possible. They have wanted their fictions massive, perhaps, but surely with sufficient singularities. This reflection would place Randall's Remembrance of Things Past in the same category with Proust's monumental novel; Proust had testified to using the same technique. Randall would have been quite conscious of that analogy, having said that Proust was the great writer of our century. And while we are about it, let us say that we take Wordsworth's account of his own childhood as substantially true, but that he stylized a great deal more than Randall; and sometimes ponderously, as Randall never did.

"The Lost World" is a revealing and crucial poem; it seems to introduce a fresh and very compelling interest into Randall's intellectual habit. It is true that the book of that title offers a variety of poetical pastimes. But eventually he recognizes the real importance of this particular poem for him, and deals with it like a master who means to put the household of his mind into order.

I am bound to comment on "Thinking of the Lost World," because it is the last poem in Randall's last book, and a sort of announcement of a new stage beginning in his life. It is prompted, of course, by "The Lost World" itself. But here it is Randall speaking, at the age of fifty, and he is declaring that he is going to take up the child's vocation again. A child plays. To his pets, and his artificial animals, and his toys, he assigns just such souls as his own, in order that they may play with him. And the imagination which transforms reality is undoubtedly, after the long interval in which he studies in the hard Schools and Universities of Reality, the same which makes an artist of the man; it served its apprenticeship in the child. Randall grew into a poet-artist, and naturally his imagination was vivid and sure.

I quote from the conclusion of this ultimate poem:

> "Was that the first World War or the second?"
> Moving between the first world and the second,
> I hear a boy call, now that my beard's gray:
> "Santa Claus! Hi, Santa Claus!" It *is* miraculous
> To have the children call you Santa Claus.
> I wave back.
>
> . . .
>
> I seem to see
> A shape in tennis shoes and khaki riding-pants
> Standing there empty-handed; I reach out to it
> Empty-handed, my hand comes back empty,
> And yet my emptiness is traded for its emptiness,
> I have found that Lost World in the Lost and Found
> Columns whose gray illegible advertisements
> My soul has memorized world after world:
> LOST—NOTHING. STRAYED FROM NOWHERE.
> NO REWARD.
> I hold in my own hands, in happiness,
> Nothing: the nothing for which there's no reward.

I felt at first that this was a tragic ending. But I have studied it till I give up that notion. The NOTHING is the fiction, the transformation; to which both boy and man are given. That World is not Lost because it never existed; but it is as precious now as ever. I have come to think that Randall was announcing the beginning of his "second childhood." There is nothing wrong about that, to the best of my knowledge. Out of my more extensive acquaintance with this period of life I can say that it begins gently and develops blissfully. And the first stage of it is when the sons and daughters bring grandsons and granddaughters to bless and to play with; they make a wonderfully compatible company. I have been told of a further stage in which the child in the soul begins to crowd the man out, but evidently the date is indefinite. It should be made known, if I have not already done so, that Randall in all his adult life was a great lover of children and of pets; without that resource, I suppose he could hardly have endured his reporter's job in the Institution.

We must approve this poem. But the thing which really daunts us is the fact that Randall was not permitted by the Overseers to put his beautiful program into effect.

Adrienne Rich

For Randall Jarrell

MY PERSONAL sense of Randall Jarrell began more than ten years ago when he reviewed, to my astonishment, an early book of mine. Reading that review was like getting a letter from someone, a letter of love and exhortation, drenched, like all Randall's criticism, with concern for unfulfilled possibilities, for the life of those poems and all future poems by the same hand. One felt that this brilliant, caustic, affectionate stranger had suddenly involved himself in one's fate—not for his own reputation, or for the sake of purveying a personal influence, but because he was a kind of conscience of poetry. Behind all Randall's joy in particular poems, his insistence that the best be sifted from the merely good, lay, I think, a moralist's realization that virtue exists only in an accretion of particular acts, one of which makes possible the next; and that if the poems of his own generation were not both exemplary and daring, the future of poetics and language itself was in question. Sensing all this, I was too shy to write and tell him, then, how much his dissatisfaction with my book exhilarated me. When, several years later, we met, I knew that an invaluable friendship had entered my life. I was unconsciously counting on years of those meetings, letters written in that musing, coaxing, buoyant voice, the sense that he was there to write for. ("What a strange thing you and I are, if we are, when we are! To have written one good poem—good used seriously—is an unlikely and marvelous thing that only a couple of hundred writers of English, at the most, have ever done—it's like sitting out in the yard in the evening and having a meteorite fall in one's lap; and yet one can't believe that, and tries so hard, by willing and working and wanting, to have the mailman deliver them—and feels disappointed, even, when he doesn't.")

But I will always go on writing for Randall: that is, for an attention, ear, and spirit on which nothing was wasted, and which nothing escaped. A poem—including those very different from his own—was a natural environment for him; he entered a strange poem as a great naturalist might enter a strange forest, every nerve awake—but as a naturalist who was himself part bird, part liana, part jaguar. His influence on the poetry of his time has yet to be fathomed: it worked through his own poems, his published criticism, his teaching, his involvement with the work of his friends. For many of us, if asked that old question: "To what or whom do you address your poems?" the truthful answer would be: "To the mind of Randall Jarrell."

Delmore Schwartz

On Little Friend, Little Friend

IT IS an open secret, and a pity, that Randall Jarrell is known chiefly as the author of overwhelming wisecracks about other poets. Jarrell is not entirely innocent of responsibility for this reputation, nor is the reader: both are perhaps too eager to forget everything for the sake of a good laugh. But only the reader who forgets the jokes and remembers Jarrell's first two books will be prepared for the extraordinary growth in this new book. In his first two books many of the poems were weakened by a thinness and abstractness of texture and reference; it was as if the poet saw his subjects through opera glasses. One was forced to remember Eliot's observation that "the great poets give us real men, talking; set up before us real events, moving." For all the genuineness

This review of *Little Friend, Little Friend* was first published in The Nation, December 1, 1945.

of the poems, the net result resembled the dim and ghostly negative which has to be held up to the light, and not the developed photograph full of daylight and defined objects. And it was impossible not to think of Jarrell's critical prose and to guess that if only the wit might be part of the verse, what a modernist Pope we might have.

The wit remains absent and the abstractness is not entirely dissolved. But in this new book Jarrell has a much closer, much more intimate grasp of his subject, perhaps because he has actually lived through the war with which his first poems were also concerned, but concerned in terms of intuition and premonition, not of the event and the aftermath. From the start Jarrell's sensibility has been avid, ravenous to know, to take in what really exists, to stay awake and to stare at the dark as well as the light. In *Little Friend, Little Friend* this quality of mind, this passion to be aware and awake and alive, comes up against the immense, international, and yet muffled, scattered, masked terror of war, precisely the kind of phenomenon to make such a mind most articulate, as Shakespearean heroes are most eloquent and full of insight when they are dying. Instead of general affirmation or rejection of the war, Jarrell takes the particular part of the dead. In poem after poem the dead soldier says, "*Why did I die?*" And that is the end of the poem. The bombers can't land in the fog, the child does not know why he is in the refugee ship, the prisoners load trucks like automata, the halfwit can accept his mother's death and the drafting of his sister, he can accept everything but that "they took my cat for the Army Corps." "And I cried, and I cried, and I wanted to die." Indeed, the obsessive symbols of the cat, the child, and the dream emerge through most of the book, forced by the pressure of the emotions of hopelessness, helplessness, animal terror and animal tenderness, senseless death, and shrieking over-all perplexity at the fact that men kill each other.

These emotions show their effect in the development of Jarrell's versification. His personal rhythm is now both clear and various. To the ignorant or inattentive reader, who looks in poetry only for the sensational imagery and obvious chanting, Jarrell's writing may seem slack and loose when it is exactly the contrary. By means of justified repetition, hurried anapests, and a caesura fixed by alliteration, Jarrell gets a wonderfully expressive syncopation of movement, a tone which insists, like a passionate stammer, and reiterates nervously because the whole being is compelled by anxiety and guilt:

> They lived, they died. "I am what I am,"
> Someone heard Swift stammer: he was crazy.
> Beethoven, dying, learned to multiply.
> What does it mean? Why, nothing.
> Nothing? . . . How well we all die!

New defects occur also as a result of the poet's growth. In some poems he writes like a *nouveau riche* in ideas, crudely brandishing and flourishing Marxist ideas and permitting himself such a line as "But soon all the *chimneys* were hidden with *contracts,*" a mixture of the visual and the abstract which tries to and cannot become a genuine—which is to say, *seen*—image. An effort is made to versify Marx baldly, to go from statements about trade and credit to a perception of mines and mills. Consequently the poem collapses. Twice, and strangely for an author like Jarrell, he permits his emotions about the war to become an anger against books and the university. The thesis of Archibald MacLeish is renewed when Jarrell attempts to say that if knowledge and scholarship were not actually the causes of war, they ought somehow to have been able to transform capitalist society and prevent war. This banal and sentimental view arrives at hideous absurdity in the poem in which the climax is the burning of the university. Two opposed quotations bear directly on this kind of hysteria: "The letter killeth but the spirit giveth life"; "The spirit killeth, but the letter giveth life." It ought to be possible to remember both of these maxims, for both were spoken with authority and both may be useful pieces of knowledge.

For the most part, however, the motives of honesty, courage, and inconsolable love of life are here submitted to the conditions of poetry and fulfilled in them. If, as one poem declares, this life is a dream from which no one wakes, the dreamer has refused to deceive himself, to let himself go, and to forget what he believes and loves.

On Poetry and the Age

IT HAS BEEN clear for some time that Randall Jarrell is one of the most gifted poets and critics of his generation. The present volume, his first collection of criticism, should do much to confirm and strengthen his reputation. In it he discusses inimitably such poets as Whitman, Frost, Wallace Stevens, John Crowe Ransom, Williams, Walter de la Mare, Robert Lowell, and a good many others. And the book is made a whole instead of a collection of periodical pieces, by two important essays on the obscurity of modern poetry and on the overcultivation of criticism in contemporary writing. Thus it is perhaps the most comprehensive and certainly the most detailed of all studies of modern poetry.

It is a good deal more than that. In his essays on Whit-

This review of *Poetry and the Age* was first published in The New York Times Book Review, August 16, 1953.

man and Robert Frost, Jarrell moves forward to what may very well be the beginning of a new evaluation of poetry and of what poetry has been, what it is, and what it can be. Jarrell goes beyond the standards and the discriminations of T. S. Eliot, which have dominated the criticism of poetry for the past twenty-five years, and he does so by including and assimilating Eliot's views, rather than by the characteristic rejection and exclusion that almost always marks and cripples new movements and new points of view in criticism.

Eliot himself is an example of this kind of one-sidedness: he found it necessary to condemn Wordsworth and Keats in order to praise Dryden and Marvell. Jarrell has achieved—and with great richness and fullness of perception—a point of view from which it is possible to admire all these poets and to admire Whitman and Frost as well as Donne and Mallarmé. The same kind of justice and the same catholic love characterize his essays on Wallace Stevens and Marianne Moore.

Moreover, Jarrell writes in a prose style that possesses some of the best traits of both prose and poetry. He succeeds in being joyous, angry, contemptuous, and gay as well as lucid, direct, and colloquial with complete genuineness and ease. And when he is amusing, as he often is, he is at the same time and unerringly illuminating. Thus, when he says: "To expect Tate's and Warren's poems to be much influenced by Ransom's is like expecting two nightmares to be influenced by a daydream," his formulation may seem at first glance to be merely a piece of wit; but it is, in fact, an exact description and insight.

Behind the witty, passionate intensity of Jarrell's style

there is always a huge, half-rhetorical, half-shocked question: How can any human being in his right mind disregard the power and the glory of poetry? It is as if someone asked: How can you disregard the Atlantic Ocean, the Grand Canyon, and Niagara Falls? Poetry has the overwhelming reality of these natural phenomena, and it is certainly far more interesting. Hence Jarrell is always speaking to the reader as a dedicated, possessed poet. But at times he is speaking only as a poet and purely as a poet. Poetry is one of the most important things in the world to him, as it should be; but at times it is the *most* important thing in the world, which is surely too close to poetry as the *only* important thing in the world.

The result is a certain narrowness of perspective. In his most eloquent and powerful essay, the one on obscurity of modern poetry, Jarrell describes the prevailing modern attitude toward poetry very well. He remarks that almost none of those who accuse modern poetry of obscurity are devoted and habitual readers of the presumably lucid poetry of the past. Indeed, for the most part, there is no reason to believe that they read any poetry whatever, at least to the extent of finding the works of the great poets a necessary part of their lives.

"Most people," he writes, "know about the modern poet only that he is *obscure—i.e.*, that he is *difficult, i.e.*, that he is *neglected*—they naturally make a causal connection between the two meanings of the word, and decide that he is unread because he is difficult." "And yet it is not just modern poetry, but poetry, that is today obscure. *Paradise Lost* is what it was; but the ordinary reader no longer makes the mistake of trying to read it—instead, he glances at it, weighs it in his hand, shudders, and suddenly, his eyes shining, puts it on his list of the ten dullest books he has ever read, along with *Moby Dick*, *War and Peace*, *Faust*, and Boswell's *Life of Johnson*. But I am doing this ordinary reader an injustice: it was not the Public, nodding over its lunch-pail, but the educated reader, the reader the universities have trained, who a few weeks ago, to the Public's sympathetic delight, put together this list of the world's dullest books."

Later, he notes that "one of our universities recently made a survey of the reading habits of the American public; it decided that forty-eight percent of all Americans read, during a year, no book at all. I picture to myself that reader—non-reader, rather; one man out of every two—and I reflect, with shame: 'Our poems are too hard for him.' But so, too, are *Treasure Island, Peter Rabbit,* pornographic novels—any book whatsoever. . . . A sort of dream-situation often occurs to me in which I call to this imaginary figure, 'Why don't you read books?'—and he always answers, after looking at me steadily for a long time: 'Huh?' "

This is in itself a perfect statement. It expresses the anguish of one who does not feel superior but lonely; and the dismay of one who does not want to be cut off from other human beings by his love of literature. But Jarrell writes as if this situation were an arbitrary fact, as if the reading public were merely self-indulgent and irrational in neglecting most poetry and disregarding most serious literature. He is so close to poetry, so involved with the art as such, that the causes of the situation, which are social, cultural, and spiritual, remain quite distant and entirely unexamined.

The same pure and professional concentration upon poetry as poetry circumscribes several other essays, particularly the one on Whitman. But this is Jarrell's first book of criticism; he has just begun to write; and he has written a book that will bring every reader closer to a knowledge of poetry and of experience.

Maurice Sendak

For Randall Jarrell

CHILDREN SELECTING BOOKS IN A LIBRARY

BY RANDALL JARRELL

With beasts and gods, above, the wall is bright.
The child's head, bent to the book-colored shelves,
Is slow and sidelong and food-gathering,
Moving in blind grace . . . Yet from the mural, Care,
The grey-eyed one, fishing the morning mist,
Seizes the baby hero by the hair

And whispers, in the tongue of gods and children,
Words of a doom as ecumenical as dawn
But blanched, like dawn, with dew. The children's cries
Are to men the cries of crickets, dense with warmth
—But dip a finger into Fafnir, taste it,
And all their words are plain as chance and pain.

Their tales are full of sorcerers and ogres
Because their lives are: the capricious infinite

That, like parents, no one has yet escaped
Except by luck or magic; and since strength
And wit are useless, be kind or stupid, wait
Some power's gratitude, the tide of things.

Read meanwhile . . . hunt among the shelves, as dogs do,
grasses,
And find one cure for Everychild's diseases
Beginning: *Once upon a time there was*
A wolf that fed, a mouse that warned, a bear that rode
A boy. Us men, alas! wolves, mice, bears bore.
And yet wolves, mice, bears, children, gods and men

In slow perambulation up and down the shelves
Of the universe are seeking . . . who knows except them-
selves?
What some escape to, some escape: if we find Swann's
Way better than our own, and trudge on at the back
Of the north wind to—to—somewhere east
Of the sun, west of the moon, it is because we live

By trading another's sorrow for our own; another's
Impossibilities, still unbelieved in, for our own . . .
"I am myself still"? For a little while, forget:
The world's selves cure that short disease, myself,
And we see bending to us, dewy-eyed, the great
CHANGE, dear to all things not to themselves endeared.

Karl Shapiro

The Death of Randall Jarrell

THIS LECTURE is not a eulogy, not a memorial, not one of those exercises in the objective perception of value for which the age of criticism is justly infamous. Randall Jarrell was not my friend; nor was he my enemy. But he was the poet whose poetry I admired and looked up to most after William Carlos Williams. This I said many times in many ways in my criticism. I praised his poetry more, and more wholeheartedly, than any other of his contemporaries. My praise, it may be, did not sit comfortably with him, for he spotted me as an outsider, or one who was constantly battling to get on the outside. Jarrell was very much an insider. There was a terrible conflict in his soul between his instinct for freedom and his desire for cultural asylum. This conflict

This lecture was delivered at the Library of Congress, Washington, D.C., on October 17, 1966.

gave him his style, his literary style, his life style. It is a style deceptively free. His bookplate might be the question mark. The most common and significant expression he uses at crucial points in his poetry and in his prose is *and yet.* . . . I thought of naming this lecture "Randall Jarrell—And Yet" but I decided to be more ambitious. I shall try to situate Randall Jarrell among his fellows rather than do his portrait. I think there is a message in his death, for me and for this generation.

Let me dispose of some personal data first, a few observations which will perhaps illumine my not too extensive relationship with him. When I was editing *Poetry* (Chicago) and after I had published hundreds—could it have been thousands?—of poets, I noted that the manuscripts of Randall Jarrell, whether poems or prose, were the only perfect manuscripts I ever saw. I mean that they were letter-perfect. There was no question of a typo or any other kind of graphical error. He was my only scrupulous poet, for most poets write the way they dress and their manuscripts look like somebody else's laundry, thank God. And this minor perfection of Jarrell's was reflected in the precision of thought, especially in his prose, which all the same sometimes took on a slightly euphuistic contour. I think "euphuistic" is the word; "baroque" describes certain of his stylistic processes, a style of inlay in which quotation is so exquisitely handled that everything Jarrell quotes sounds as if he wrote it. He was a great, you might say a dangerous, listener. And yet his style of reportage is comic, for he fears loftiness and bombast like the plague. One looks forward to the publication of his letters. We can be sure that the voice of the poet and of the cultural gossip is there. Charm is overwhelming in all his writing; "wit" is too platitudinous a word for his work, and the sharply outlined involutions of his thought deserve a better word than "wisdom."

He gave a marvelous summation of contemporary poetry from this platform four years ago. I asked him if I could publish it in the *Prairie Schooner*, which I then edited. His reply was: "I'd be delighted for you to print the lecture in the *Prairie Schooner*. You've always been my favorite editor because you're not like an editor at all." I put the best construction on this remark that I could, especially as I knew it to be true, more than true, a complimentary reprimand of *my* style of life and letters. Except for an early merciless review of one of my books, he was always understanding about me—and acidulous. We were of the same group, so to speak, and had fought all the same wars, and he had a right to cry Whoa! when I came galloping by.

All the poets sat on the edge of their seats while Jarrell, who everybody had to admit had earned the right to do so, put together the jigsaw puzzle of modern poetry in front of our eyes. When I was finally fitted into place, with a splash of color, I felt a relief that I fitted, and a regret that that puzzle had been solved. I will repeat what he said of me because it is germane to my evaluation of Jarrell: "Karl Shapiro's poems are fresh and young and rash and live; their hard clear outlines, their flat bold colors create a world like that of a knowing and skillful neoprimitive painting, without any of the confusion or profundity of atmosphere, of aerial perspective, but with notable visual and satiric force." He then goes on to mention my influences—Auden, Rilke, Whitman—and he does not need to say that these are also his influences, more his than mine, because Jarrell assimilated his Auden and Rilke and Whitman, along with his Corbière and Grimm and even Robert Frost. I assimilated nothing but was only influenced by. I rejected Influence out of hand and waged a one-man children's crusade against the Past, the Greco-Judaic-Christian thingamajig, so that Jarrell could say of me with amused amazement: "Both in verse and in prose Shapiro loves, partly out of indignation and partly out of sheer mischievousness, to tell the naked truths or half-truths or quarter-truths that will make anybody's hair stand on end; he is always crying: 'But he hasn't any clothes on!' about an emperor who is half the time surprisingly well dressed." There is a slight concession here: Jarrell admits that the emperor is dressed like an emperor only half the time, while I contend that he is badly dressed even when he is naked.

I will be done with this "interrelationship" in a moment, but I am leading up to something important, a whole or half- or quarter-truth which I am bound to utter. I will read a poem I wrote about Jarrell; it is a prose poem, as prosodists say when they run out of verbiage, and is in my last book. I don't remember Jarrell's reaction to the poem but I aimed to please him when I wrote it.

Randall, I like your poetry terribly, yet I'm afraid to say so. Not that my praise keeps you awake—though I'm afraid it does. I can't help liking them. I even like the whine, the make-believe whiplash with the actual wire in it. Once when you reviewed me badly (you must) I wrote you: "I felt as if I had been run over but not hurt." That made you laugh. I was happy. It wasn't much of a triumph but it worked. When people ask about you I am inclined to say: He's an assassin (a word I never use). I'm inclined to say: Why are you always yourself? Your love of Rilke—if it's love—your intimacy with German and God knows what all, your tenderness and terrorization, your prose sentences—like Bernini graves, staggeringly expensive, Italianate, warm, sentences once-and-for-all. And the verses you leave half-finished in mid-air—I once knew a woman who never finished a sentence. Your mind is always at its best, your craft the finest craft "money can buy" you would say with a barb. I'm afraid of you. Who wouldn't be. But I rush to read you, whatever you print. That's news.

And this is also news. I am quoting from the "News Notes" section of *Poetry* magazine of May 1966. "There was a public ceremony at Yale on February 28th to honor the memory of Randall Jarrell, who was killed last autumn in an automobile accident. John Berryman, Richard Eberhart, John Hollander, Stanley Kunitz, Robert Lowell, William Meredith, Adrienne Rich, Robert Penn Warren, Richard Wilbur, and Peter Taylor came together at Yale to participate in the tribute, for which the chairman was Norman Holmes Pearson. Mary Jarrell, widow of the poet, read 'the last recently written poem that truly pleased him,' 'The Player Piano,' as yet unpublished. The Yale *Daily News* reports that she 'received an impassioned standing ovation as she walked to the lectern.' Elizabeth Bishop, Cleanth Brooks,

Robert Fitzgerald, Marianne Moore, John Crowe Ransom, and Allen Tate, who could not attend, sent testimonials which Professor Pearson read. . . ."

When I read this little notice in *Poetry* I was dismayed at my conspicuous absence from the list. Had Jarrell left it in his will to keep me off the Yale campus? Impossible. I had a blood-boiling moment of suspicion or paranoia that the Bollingen Committee or Professor Pearson or Robert Lowell had blackballed me from the club. My anti-cultural-committee activities span many years and I have tried to sabotage organized culture whenever possible; not always successfully of course. When the National Institute of Arts and Letters elected me a member, I declined. But when their officers called me and said nobody had had that much cheek since Sinclair Lewis declined, and who the hell did I think I was, I chickened out and let them enroll me. When I went to watch the President sign the arts and humanities bill, some writer said: What are *you* doing here? Spying was all I could say. And now Randall had been organized in death by some cultural subcommittee and all I could think was: Now he knows what it feels like to turn over in his grave.

Between the instinct for freedom and the desire for cultural asylum others can make a choice, and always do. Culture committees love funerals. There is, even in one's fellow poets, a touch of the vulture: when the poet lies on the roof of the Tower of Silence, you can hear the shuddering of ragged wings.

I remember once—I think it happened in the Poetry Office of this library, but maybe it didn't happen at all and is just a memorable fancy—that Robert Lowell and Randall Jarrell were playing a game. The game was Who's First and it was Lowell's game. The idea is to grade the poets until the downgrading wipes most of the competition off the board. Two or three remaining contenders then engage in a death struggle. Jarrell played this game with a will but his winning instinct was no match for Lowell.

In Jarrell's bibliography published in 1958 there is a good introduction by Robert Humphrey which contains this sentence: "Most critics predicted the emerging greatness of a Robert Lowell or a Karl Shapiro, but few guessed that Jarrell would outstrip them, especially in so short a time." This judgment is sound, as far as I am concerned, and certainly as far as Lowell is concerned. I'm not playing Who's First, I hope, because I don't think the game is worth my time or anyone else's. Comparisons of Lowell and Jarrell are irrelevant anyhow. Lowell is primarily a figurehead which he himself personally carved out of solid rock. The effort was immense, Churchillian in blood, sweat, and tears. But one feels that Lowell writes poetry to get even, while Jarrell became a poet because he couldn't help it.

Some years ago I volunteered to write an article for the *Evergreen Review* about Lowell. I said I would call it "Robert Lowell as T. S. Eliot." A while later I said I would change the title to "Robert Lowell as Cassius Clay." I finished up by not writing the article at all. It was not Lowell I was after but the maître d'hôtel psychology of literature which Lowell espouses.

In the lecture which Jarrell gave here and which I published in the *Prairie Schooner*, he says this of Lowell (I am paraphrasing): Robert Lowell is the poet of shock. His style manages to make even quotations and historical facts a personal possession. "Make it grotesque" could be his motto. (In the context, Jarrell is contrasting Lowell with Richard Wilbur, a poet who makes poems out of the things of life rather than out of life itself.) Jarrell thought that Lowell possessed and wrote out of a life, yet he knew that this life was at least as unreal as Wilbur's life-by-virtue-of-the-things-of-life. Here is a direct quote: "Lowell has always had an astonishing ambition, a willingness to learn what past poetry was and to compete with it on its own terms." My comment is what Jarrell politely implies, that competition is the sole inspiration of such a poet. Jarrell says in a parenthesis that Lowell bullied his early work, but his own vulnerable humanity has been forced in on him (a statement of tremendous humanity and pardon) with a shadow of fear above. Of Lowell's poems, he mentions their stubborn toughness, their senseless originality (an expression to conjure with), and their contingency. Some of the poems justify the harshness and violence and what Jarrell calls their barbarous immediacy; he ends by complimenting Lowell, without having convinced us why, for his largeness and grandeur, and throws him a fish in this sentence: "You feel before reading any new poem of his the uneasy expectation of perhaps encountering a masterpiece." In an earlier treatment of Lowell in *Poetry and the Age* Jarrell wrote: "Cocteau said to poets: *Learn what you can do and then don't do it*; and this is so . . . As a poet Mr. Lowell sometimes doesn't have enough trust in God and tries to do everything himself . . . But probably the reader will want to say to me . . . what Lincoln said about the drunkard Grant: 'If I knew his brand I would order my other generals a barrel.' "

Our generation—the generation of Jarrell, Wilbur, myself, Roethke, Lowell, Schwartz, Bishop, Ciardi, Berryman, Kunitz, Nemerov, Whittemore—one is almost inclined to add Merrill Lynch, Pierce, Fenner and Smith—our generation lived through more history than most or maybe any. We lived through more history even than Stendhal, who fell, as he says, with Napoleon. We were reared as intellectuals and fought World War II before it happened and then again when it did happen. We witnessed the god that failed and helped trip him up. We predicted the Alexandrianism of the age, and like everybody else, we throve on it. We drove our foreign cars to class to teach. And we bit the hand that fed us, but not very hard, not hard enough. The hand went on signing papers. Once upon a time we were all revolutionaries of one stripe or another, but when we got married and settled down, with tenure, we talked technique instead of overthrow. Half of us stopped rebelling and not because of middle age. The age made it so easy to be a poet, or to survive on lobster, the age gave in so sweetly to our imprecations, the age so needed us to help it hate itself, this spineless age ended by softening the backbone of poetry. Dylan Thomas was the antisymbol of our group, that Dylan who died after he saw the faces of mice in the Bristol crystal. It was Thomas who taught poetry to stop thinking, and we resented that! Though we were or are not all drunks and suicides, we had our goodly share. But all of us felt the rot of institutionalism in our bones. Jarrell got it down in a novel, the kind of novel the age demanded, the exposé of sensibility. Jarrell's novel, *Pictures from an Institution*, is so brilliant that it defeats itself as a fiction; it becomes a hornbook of avant-gardism, sophisticated to the point of philistinism. Jarrell is misleadingly philistine, say, about Modern Art of all varieties. It is because he is impatient with failure or imperfection or goofing around with the Muse. But this impatience of Jarrell's is also a veritable lust for perfection; and both the impatience and the philistinism are what you might call Texan. Jarrell was a good Texan in the sense that President Johnson is a bad Texan. *And yet*, what Jarrell does to Gertrude, his antiheroine in the novel, is almost beyond belief. Can anyone be that worthy of hatred? One wonders what Gertrude thought when she read her portrait. Gertrude is one of those savage Southern female novelists who leaves the world in terror of the art of fiction. The setting of the novel is Benton, a very expensive higher-education academy only six versts from Sarah Lawrence and/or Bennington. Benton's President Robbins doesn't fare any better than the loathed Gertrude, and the only lovable character in the book is a German-Jewish composer-in-residence named Rosenbaum. Jarrell attacks avant-garde institutionalism and everything it implies by immolating President Robbins and all his kinfolk in the way Gertrude might. He attacks dehumanized letters in his lip-smacking crucifixion of Gertrude. True humanity, true culture, true wisdom are preserved in the broken-English Rosenbaums.

Jarrell's love of the good German led him deep into the Black Forest, deep into German childhood. I shared with him his love for *Der Rosenkavalier,* for Elisabeth Schwarzkopf (who is not a very kosher German) and even for Mahler. Germany is the preconscious of Europe, almost all—no, all—her geniuses are maniacs, Germany itself is a maniac, the bright dangerous offspring of the Western soul. "Must you learn from your makers how to die?" Jarrell asks the war spirits in one of so many of his Germany-inspired poems. In a note to the poem "A Game at Salzburg" he says that there is a game that Austrians and Germans play with very young children. The child says to the grownup, *Here I am,* and the grownup answers, *There you are. Hier bin i'*: *Da bist du.* Then Jarrell says: "It seemed to me that if there could be a conversation between the world and God, this would be it." There is an almost unbearable sorrow in this colloquy, a German-Jewish sorrow, so to speak. Jarrell lets Dr. Rosenbaum say: "The people in Hell . . . say nothing but *What?*" To which Jarrell adds: "Americans in Hell tell each other how to make martinis." I am not reviewing the novel but I give it a central place in Jarrell's work as a kind of negative plate of the poetry. The empty intellectualism of America is pinpointed at Benton. The author says: "Nowadays Benton picked and chose: girls who had read Wittgenstein as high school baby-sitters were rejected because the school's quota of abnormally intelligent students had already been filled that year." Jarrell, not quite a Des Esseintes, suffers from a disillusionment of America which all our best artists share, suffers from the disappointment at the failure of the healing powers of poetry in this nation. Benton—American higher education—is only a rarer kind of custom-built Cadillac. One can almost begin to see the coat of arms emerging on the enameled door. One is already afraid of who is inside. He says, lapsing into what he thinks: "Is an institution always a man's shadow shortened in the sun, the lowest common denominator of everybody in it?" It is bitter to answer yes, but so it is in the modern Institution. In his anthology of short Russian novels Jarrell quotes Turgenev on Tolstoy. Tolstoy "never believed in people's sincerity. Every spiritual movement seemed to him false, and with his extraordinarily penetrating eyes he used to pierce those on whom his suspicion fell." The early Jarrell published the beginning of a massive attack on Auden, the most conspicuous idealist of the age. Later he forgave Auden, ideals and all.

Jarrell's generation, my generation, inherited the question of Culture—Mass Culture versus True Culture. It is our *pons asinorum*, and we all had to cross it. Jarrell worried the problem more than most of us because he could not take for granted the purely elite aesthetic of Eliot, the motto of which is High Culture Only: No Foreigners Allowed. Those of us who grew up with *Partisan Review* on our kitchen tables and who wrote for it with great pride had a slightly altered version of High Culture. With us it was High Culture plus social revolution. We won World War II but lost the social revolution. We lost it to what Jarrell called the Medium, the Medium being a kind of symbol for Mass Culture. In the backwash of power and prosperity that engulfed America after our victory, the writers fled to those island citadels called Institutions. Whether it was Benton or Harvard or Berkeley, each of these Mont-Saint-Michels harbored its refugees from the world, from Mass Culture, from the Medium. Jarrell said the acceptably righteous things about Mass Culture, that mass culture either corrupts or isolates the writer, that "true works of art are more and more produced away from or in opposition to society." And yet, he knew the writer's need for contact with the mass and qualified his rejections of the Medium. Part of the artist, he said (I am quoting from "A Sad Heart at the Supermarket"), "wants to be like his kind, is like his kind; longs to be loved and admired and successful." Part of Jarrell longed to be accepted by the Medium but the thought of that depressed him. He asked, "Is the influence of what I have called the Medium likely to lead us to any good life? to make us love and try to attain any real excellence, beauty, magnanimity?" The answer has to be no. The middle-aged woman in the supermarket who buys All and Cheer and Joy for her gleaming washing machine sees only the image of death staring at her in her rear-view mirror. Let me read this poem, which in my mind is already a famous poem.

NEXT DAY

Moving from Cheer to Joy, from Joy to All,
I take a box
And add it to my wild rice, my Cornish game hens.
The slacked or shorted, basketed, identical
Food-gathering flocks
Are selves I overlook. Wisdom, said William James,

Is learning what to overlook. And I am wise
If that is wisdom.
Yet somehow, as I buy All from these shelves
And the boy takes it to my station wagon,
What I've become
Troubles me even if I shut my eyes.

When I was young and miserable and pretty
And poor, I'd wish
What all girls wish: to have a husband,
A house and children. Now that I'm old, my wish
Is womanish:
That the boy putting groceries in my car

See me. It bewilders me he doesn't see me.
For so many years
I was good enough to eat: the world looked at me
And its mouth watered. How often they have undressed me,
The eyes of strangers!
And, holding their flesh within my flesh, their vile

Imagining within my imagining,
I too have taken
The chance of life. Now the boy pats my dog
And we start home. Now I am good.
The last mistaken,
Ecstatic, accidental bliss, the blind

Happiness that, bursting, leaves upon the palm
Some soap and water—
It was so long ago, back in some Gay

Twenties, Nineties, I don't know . . . Today I miss
My lovely daughter
Away at school, my sons away at school,

My husband away at work—I wish for them.
The dog, the maid,
And I go through the sure unvarying days
At home in them. As I look at my life,
I am afraid
Only that it will change, as I am changing:

I am afraid, this morning, of my face.
It looks at me
From the rear-view mirror, with the eyes I hate,
The smile I hate. Its plain, lined look
Of gray discovery
Repeats to me: "You're old." That's all, I'm old.

And yet I'm afraid, as I was at the funeral
I went to yesterday.
My friend's cold made-up face, granite among its flowers,
Her undressed, operated-on, dressed body
Were my face and body.
As I think of her I hear her telling me

How young I seem; I *am* exceptional;
I think of all I have.
But really no one is exceptional,
No one has anything, I'm anybody,
I stand beside my grave
Confused with my life, that is commonplace and solitary.

So in that life which is our Way, there is no excellence. But one wonders, to use Jarrell's pun on the great word *All*, if that is really all. When the prophets of High Culture (I called it Hi-Cult in one of my own essays) all died out, leaving only Dwight Macdonald to rave against the Medium and *Kitsch* and Camp and all those once fashionable diseases of the age; when Eliot fell in love and died, and Pound discovered silence—in short, when the twenties and thirties ended, it was already the sixties, and it had become hard to say where the Medium ended and the isolate poet began. How could a specialized study of the intellectual, say, *Herzog*, be a best-seller? What mass audience was it that picked that up? Even the woman in the supermarket quotes William James. The question with us, with Jarrell, was the probability of accepting the supermarket and its brightly packaged values. Or must one be an Allen Ginsberg and situate Walt Whitman in the supermarket, only to say: "See, I told you so! America has to start over from scratch."

In *Poetry and the Age*, one of the best handbooks of anti-criticism criticism we have, there is an essay on the obscurity of the poet. My edition of the book is dated 1955, a fatal year for pronunciamentos about the Audience, the year when some giant beast slouching toward the City Lights Bookshop gave birth to *Howl*. "Tomorrow morning," Jarrell was saying, "some poet may, like Byron, wake up to find himself famous—for having written a novel, for having killed his wife; it will not be for having written a poem." Jarrell was wrong; the whole generation was wrong about the Audience and the Poet; *Howl* gave us the lie. For myself, I was delighted and immediately sent in my resignation to my generation. They accepted it gingerly but with inquisitorial silence. In the same essay Jarrell had said that "the general public . . . has set up a criterion of its own, one by which every form of contemporary art is condemned." This statement, too, which had for so long been so widely accepted, was already obsolete. A decade after *Howl*—and I see that poem as a symptom rather than as a cause—the general public itself has become the contemporary art audience. There are very few places in our geography any more which resemble a Nebraska of the spirit; and in any case, philistinism today is no longer spontaneous but organized, political. Condemnation of the artist today is no longer mere provincialism; it is, to use a not very old-fashioned term, a form of Fascism. And the general public, whatever that is, is choosing up sides. The Medium still dominates the sensory experience of the masses of people, but the Medium itself has become an initiate of Hi-Cult. The Medium has also had courses in modern poetry and electronic music.

The Berkeley or California Rebellion, like the Whisky Rebellion, was a protest against a central culture. The California Rebellion struck out at every form of institutionalism it could clap eyes on. This too was a generational revolt and continues to be worldwide; it is, as most writers about it have noticed, more a sociological upheaval than a new motion in the arts. There is no innovation in Beat arts: the poetry stems from traditional rebel poets, Rimbaud, Pound, Whitman, Artaud. And the counterrevolt against Beatism stems from what was left over from the old-guard elite and also from members of Jarrell's generation. Jarrell would not, I believe, commit himself to the new barbarians, as some writers call them; he could not; he was too urbane, too civilized, too much a lover of the perfect. I cannot imagine him favoring for any reason the later phase of Beat art, the jazz poetry of Bob Dylan and all those electric guitarists who carry their echo chambers with them wherever they go, portable Æolian winds, and whose motto seems to be Death by Motorcycle. Perhaps finally Jarrell recognized how much of an institution our generation had become, how much an institution he had become. I was in more of a position to face the music, the music of the electric guitar, because of my resignation. It was no surprise to me, when I published a collection of essays called *In Defense of Ignorance*, to receive a letter from a prominent member of our generation that complimented me highly on the book and said how much it was needed, a letter which ended, "but I would appreciate it if you didn't tell anybody." It was of course not Jarrell who penned this. Lowell questioned my adherence to William Carlos Williams. Williams is the godfather of *Howl.*

Jarrell's beautiful fable called *The Bat-Poet* is, like all true fables, open to various readings. A child can read it as well as a philosopher as well as a poet, each with the same comprehension. A little light brown bat leaves the pack to stay out in the world of daylight to "hang there and think." The real bats don't understand the poet bat, who uses such things as colors in his poems, for the bat-poet is a poet. Busy work-a-night bats don't care for color and have no truck with poems.

After trying out his poems on such creatures as the mocking-bird, who criticizes the bat-poet's prosody and complains how hard it is to be a mockingbird; after failing to write a poem about the cardinal, who is perhaps too beautiful even for a poem; after bargaining with the chipmunk, who is the bat-poet's most sympathetic critic (although naturally a poem about the owl gives the chipmunk the primordial Angst), the bat-poet writes his best poem about, of all things, a mother bat zigzagging through the night with her baby clinging to her body. The chipmunk decides that everything the bat does is upside down. At last the bat-poet decides to go and read his bat poem to the bats themselves, but when he gets to the barn where the bats collect, he has curiously forgotten his most important poem and just hangs upside down and goes to sleep like all the other bats.

Whether to be a bat or a poet: that is the question. Maybe the poets of Jarrell's and my generation were all hybrid bat-poets, going back to the institutional barn and then lighting off in broad sunlight to write poems about the righteous and dyspeptic mockingbird, the rich-bitch cardinal, the kindly and existential chipmunk, the owl who gets us all indiscriminately in his claws. When I got my first copy of *The Bat-Poet* I couldn't read it. The title and the drawings bothered me. It was the only thing of Jarrell's I didn't leap to read, and I gave my copy to a student. When I went to find a copy, I found that my library at the University of Nebraska had never heard of it, that no bookstore in my part of the world had ever heard of it, that nobody I knew within hailing distance had ever heard of it, except that there was a mint copy in the State Capitol Building, which I obtained.

The basic assumption, the basic critical theorem, of our generation was that poetry didn't really *go* in this age, that the age demanded everything of the artist except his art, and that the poet was still declassed. Insofar as there was any truth in the assumption, it was a minor truth. When Jarrell defended Robert Frost in calling attention to "the other Frost" he was reminding his intellectual contemporaries that even a popular poet could make the grade. But Jarrell was really saying about Frost that he was a poet whose popularity was perhaps accidental. Conversely, Dylan Thomas, whom Jarrell thought correctly one of the most obscure poets of the age, was popular by default. It might be truer to say that Frost and Thomas were not only creative but also performing artists, not only performing artists but artists in action. Frost and Thomas lived their poetry, on stage and off; they were one with it, while our generation tended to hide or to collect in small conspiratorial groups. We barely learned to *read* poetry, because, as we said a little wearily, we *wrote* it. And because we wrote poetry that we were not necessarily committed to read, because we held to the cold North American delivery, we could seldom muster more than a token audience. Even Robert Frost, finally one of our great readers, insisted on the verb *say* for his recitations. Jarrell's bat-poet picks up the idiom: he says he is going to *say* a poem to the mockingbird. The opposite of *to say* is *to sing*, and even tone-deaf Yeats chanted his works. Pound revived a chant for the

Cantos; it was one of the qualities that attracted him to the Beats. But the classroom voice and the High Church voice were dominant in the generation of Jarrell. And yet, what else were we to do in America, we argued, in a language which is inflected only in moments of violence? We shift between the nasal monotone and the double spondee. Jarrell is the one poet of my generation who made an art of American speech as it is, who advanced beyond Frost in using not only a contemporary idiom (although in Frost it is necessarily fictitious) but the actual rhythms of our speech. Here Jarrell is unique and technically radical. No other poet of our time has embalmed the common dialogue of Americans with such mastery. And because he caught our bourgeois speech he caught our meaning. Here is the beginning of the marvelous essay-poem about, of all uncapturable things, Woman.

WOMAN

"All things become thee, being thine," I think sometimes
As I think of you. I think: "How many faults
In thee have seemed a virtue!" While your taste is on my
    tongue
The years return, blessings innumerable
As the breaths that you have quickened, gild my flesh.
Lie there in majesty!
                        When, like Disraeli, I murmur
That you are more like a mistress than a wife,
More like an angel than a mistress; when, like Satan,

I hiss in your ear some vile suggestion,
Some delectable abomination,
You smile at me indulgently: "Men, men!"

You smile at mankind, recognizing in it
The absurd occasion of your fall.
For men—as your soap operas, as your *Home Journals,*
As your hearts whisper—men are only children.
And you believe them. Truly, you are children.

Should I love you so dearly if you weren't?
If I weren't?

O morning star,
Each morning my dull heart goes out to you
And rises with the sun, but with the sun
Sets not, but all the long night nests within your eyes.

Men's share of grace, of all that can make bearable,
Lovable almost, the apparition, Man,
Has fallen to you. Erect, extraordinary
As a polar bear on roller skates, he passes
On into the Eternal . . .

From your pedestal, you watch
Admiringly, when you remember to.

Let us form, as Freud has said, "a group of two."
You are the best thing that this world can offer—
He said so. Or I remember that he said so;
If I am mistaken it's a Freudian error,
An error nothing but a man would make.
Women can't bear women. Cunningly engraved

On many an old wife's dead heart is "Women,
Beware women!" And yet it was a man
Sick of too much sweetness—of a life
Rich with a mother, wife, three daughters, a wife's sister,
An abyss of analysands—who wrote: "I cannot
Escape the notion (though I hesitate
To give it expression) that for women
The level of what is ethically normal
Is different from what it is in men.
Their superego"—he goes on without hesitation—
"Is never so inexorable, so impersonal,
So independent of its emotional
Origins as we require it in a man."

It is a long deep poem of a couple of hundred lines such as

You call to me, "Come"; and when I come say, "Go,"
Smiling your soft contrary smile . . .

—two lines packed with as much meaning as "The Death of the Ball Turret Gunner."

An age's poetry does not purify the dialect, or any of that nonsense which aesthetic moralists believe, but an age's poetry fixes the age for those who care to gaze upon it in another age. Most of the poets of Jarrell's generation, when they were not simply describing, setting up the landscape of the city dump or suburbia or attacking the gleaming machinery of our brilliant kitchens, most of our poets dealt in minor points of ideology, lives of the saints or of boxers, or the symbolism of automobiles. Our technique was irony and nothing but irony, more kinds of irony than the Arabs have words for camel. But Jarrell, for all his indirection, spoke directly to the theme and in the direct idiom of our semiliterate educated classes. He listened like a novelist—I have already alluded to his ear—he heard the worst of us as well as the best. Things like iambic pentameter hypnotized him not. He used it as one sits in a Victorian chair in a friend's house, but how well he knew a Victorian chair when he saw one.

No one has ever caught a French writer or a German writer or an English or Irish or Scotch writer asking what a French, German, English, Irish, or Scotch writer is. But American writers ask practically nothing but what is an American writer, meaning what is an American? It is the great theme of American literature and in a sense the only one. Jarrell says, for instance, about Walt Whitman: "If some day a tourist notices, among the ruins of New York City, a copy of *Leaves of Grass*, and stops and picks it up and reads some lines in it, she will be able to say to herself: 'How very American! If he and his country had not existed, it would have been impossible to imagine them.' "

Jarrell is almost as pro-American as Whitman himself. He applauds Marianne Moore's saying about America that it is not Niagara Falls, the calico horses, and the war canoe that matter, or the resources or the know-how; "it is not the plunder, / but 'accessibility to experience.' " He praises her Americanness and makes more famous the famed line about our language: "grassless / linksless, languageless country in which letters are written / not in Spanish, not in Greek, not in Latin, not in shorthand, / but in plain American which cats and dogs can read!"

For *Paterson* (*Book I*) Jarrell reserved greater praise, predicting, because it was the most American poem ever, that it might become the "best very long poem that any American has written." *Paterson* didn't pan out that way, for Jarrell or for anyone else, but Williams did. Williams revealed America, New York on its horizon, "a pillar of smoke by day," says Jarrell, "a pillar of fire by night." Williams and Jarrell play with the remark of Henry James that America "has no ruins." "America is full of ruins," says Jarrell, "the ruins of hopes."

M. B. Tolson, the great and practically unsung Negro poet —he too is dead—says somewhere in *Harlem Gallery* that the dilemma of the Negro between the white and the black bourgeoisie is: To be or not to be—a Negro. The Negro has a choice, is what Tolson argues, and he (and I) would rather the Negro become a Negro. But this dilemma does not exist for the paleface American: there is no choice of to be or not to be an American. Once an American, once an American poet, one can only ask: I am an American (or an American writer). Is there anything I can do about it? American poets even as late as Jarrell's generation tried to do something about it by remaining only as American as their passports demanded. A few of us, following Williams, wore the stars and stripes in secret, like The Man Without a Country. Jarrell and I are two of these. The generation of our fathers wore the flag with the cross of St. George or the flag of the stars and bars, and some of them sported the ribbon of the Legion of Honor and one or two the Red, White, and Black. None of my generation sported the Iron Cross, which one sees nowadays in dime stores in America for little boys to play Nazi. But almost all of the generation of Jarrell at one time or another played Red or Pink.

The value and the quality of poetry, unfortunately or fortunately, have nothing to do with moral or political contents. *The Divine Comedy* is banned in Pakistan, or used to be, for religious reasons; modern art and poetry are or used to be banned in Red Russia, also for religious reasons. Sad to say, many poets are political or moral idiots, even among the great. In our own time we have to fight the tendencies which threaten what is dear to our own lives and ideologies. But in Jarrell's generation we were almost to a man humane humanists, and unlike our predecessors, were democratic in politics, agnostic in religion, and baroque in literature. Among us only Robert Lowell and myself could be described as extremists, and our extremism had different derivations and opposite goals. Jarrell suffered deeply through the Stalinist-Francoist-Mussolini-Hitler years, hoping against hope for a betterment in the human condition. His first book was called *Blood for a Stranger* and was printed in 1942, a war book. He retained only a few of these poems when thirteen years later he published his *Selected Poems*, but the themes of war and Fascism—war as Fascism—were always in his mind. Jarrell has written more good poems about the wars and about Jews and Germany, the good Germany perhaps, than anyone else. He has written also the most famous and the best war poem of anyone in the twentieth century, in five lines.

The volume called *Little Friend, Little Friend*, though it has some of his best-made single poems, is a thematic book, a war book in which the poet is personally absent. The title page carries the penetrating explanation of the poems, the pathos of modern war in the code language of flyers: ". . . Then I heard the bomber call me in: 'Little Friend, Little Friend, I got two engines on fire. Can you see me, Little Friend?' I said 'I'm crossing right over you. Let's go home.' "

The anguish of the soldier is shown less in his anonymity, his exile from the human race, than in his emotional sentimental desperation. The chief symbols—though Jarrell did not write to manipulate symbols *qua* symbols—are the mother and the cat. It is no Baudelairean cat (woman the destroyer), no T. S. Eliot cat (a kindly figure from the bestiary); Jarrell's cat is the object of love, if not a love-object, a cat who listens. The mother is pure mother who "thinks heavily: My son is grown." That's all; he's grown, therefore he is a soldier. The pilot falling from his plane sees the smoking carrier and its guns as children's toys. For it is true that in the elemental iconography of war everything is stripped down to a child's arithmetic: mother, soldier, cat, gun. There is a salient difference between our war poetry such as Jarrell's and that first great war poetry written in our fathers' war by Wilfred Owen and Sassoon and Rosenberg and Blunden and so on. The British war poets who showed everyone how to write antiwar poetry were themselves all outstanding warriors and heroes. They cried out against war but were as conversant with blood as Lawrence of Arabia. None of my generation was a war hero, that I remember, or even an outstanding soldier. It says in a note in one of Jarrell's books that he "washed out" as a combat pilot and became a celestial navigator, a much more suitable classification for a poet. In a sense, we waited out the war in uniform. Jarrell's ball-turret gunner is also washed out—of the turret with a hose. Unlike the war poets of World War I, who never recovered from the experience, our generation did. We inherited a historical perspective which was denied our fathers. We foresaw and witnessed the whole world turning into the state. The war was of secondary importance to us even while we were part of it. When we came home there was grass growing on all the highways of the forty-eight states, but not for long. Our army went from demobilization to college or to television school; our poets became the university poets. But the tragedy of our generation—and I believe it is the tragedy—was that our army never melted away. It remained, it grew bigger, it was more and more all over the world. It became the way of life, the state—if not the garrison state itself, then something resembling it mightily. The war never came to a stop; only the protocols of armistice were suspended. Our poetry, from the forties on, records the helplessness we felt in the face of the impersonal character of the age—the Impersonal itself, which is always death to poetry.

There is a literary commonplace that American literature is essentially a child literature. That *Moby Dick* is a boy's book—I was given a copy when I was seven—that every

American hero is Huckleberry Finn in disguise, that poets are really little girls in mufti, that the artist has to prove his masculinity, and so on. A culture without mythos is forced into ideology. Whitman is an ideologue; his negation of mythology is one hundred percent American. Our poets when they deal in the myths do as Jarrell did, following Rilke and other modern artists, analyze and psychologize Orestes or Orpheus. We understand without belief. This is the opposite of using comparative mythology in order to revive and enforce belief, as Eliot did. Our poetry studies behavior and leads us back to the child. With Jarrell, too, the child becomes the critic and the center of value. Our mythology is the First Impression, the earliest consciousness; all the big people are giants out of Grimm and most of them are bad. When a little girl is moving to a new house she thinks:

> The broody hen
> Squawks upside down—her eggs are boiled;
> The cat is dragged from the limb.

She thinks:

> We are going to live in a new pumpkin
> Under a gold star.

Theodore Roethke was a modern kind of nature poet, a biology poet with the eyes of a microscope. Jarrell was the poet of the *Kinder* and the earliest games of the mind and heart. All those wounded soldiers and shot-down men turn back into children, for a wounded man is again a child. In the poem called "The State" the child says:

When they killed my mother it made me nervous;
I thought to myself, It was *right:*
Of course she was crazy, and how she ate!
And she died, after all, in her way, for the State.
But I minded: how queer it was to stare
At one of them not sitting there.

In his earliest collected work, one of those five-sided anthologies which New Directions invented to launch young poets, Jarrell worried the bone of Romanticism, trying to find a rationale for his departure from what he called Modernism. The crux of the problem of our generation was the Modernism which Eliot and Pound and Joyce represented and which Jarrell said did not apply to him or to us. He pretended that Modernism was dead but knew how well it would flourish in the academies. He catalogues the faults of Modernist poetry as well as has been done: the emphasis on connotation, texture, extreme intensity, forced emotion, violence, obscurity, emphasis on sensation, perceptual nuances, emphasis on the part rather than on the whole, and much more. He even enumerates the Modernist poet's attitudes: antiscientific (Jarrell was one of the few poets of our age who was not antiscientific and who understood that science was not necessarily the intruder in the house), anticommonsense, and antipublic. He ends this essay, which is very early and very fine, with a touch of the style to come. He has his hypothetical reader ask him a question: ". . . the reader may have thought curiously, 'Does he really suppose he writes the sort of poetry that replaces modernism?' " And he replies with an ambiguous, a diplomatic yes.

It was, say, Eliot, who is yet the most convenient target of attack for new poets, because Eliot erected targets wherever his mind led him; it was Eliot who invented Modernism and had it patented. And it was Auden who first shot at the target, and missed. Jarrell took care of Modernism in practice better than in theory, as later he took care of Auden. It became necessary for everyone my age to attack Auden, as sculptors must attack Mount Rushmore. Nevertheless, Auden and Mount Rushmore still stand and probably always will. Jarrell, I think, failed to help establish our generation as a separate force and simply, not so simply, went his way to write some of the most quietly agonizing poetry of our time. His overestimation of Lowell represented a kind of fear that, generationally speaking, we did not exist. He half feared being ingested by the Lowells. But I am a child, said Jarrell, I am the bat-poet; let me go and I will send you many much juicier poets. I will send you my mother and father and a fat girl in the library and even my cat. When John Ciardi put together an anthology of our generation with self-introductions, Lowell was too busy to write his (as I was too), and Jarrell reprinted his encomium about Lowell for Lowell's introduction. The roster of the generation in that version of it reads: Richard Wilbur, Peter Viereck, Muriel Rukeyser, Theodore Roethke, Karl Shapiro, Winfield Townley Scott, John Frederick Nims, E. L. Mayo, Robert Lowell, Randall Jarrell, John Holmes, Richard Eberhart, John Ciardi, Elizabeth

Bishop, and Delmore Schwartz. It is an impressive list, in my view, a loose confederation of states which had no president.

I must say something about Schwartz. Dwight Macdonald wrote a memorial about him in the September 8, 1966, issue of *The New York Review of Books*. In it he said all the things an editor of *Partisan Review* should say, all the Hi-Cult clichés which *Partisan Review* takes as gospel. It is strange, to say the least, that this great publication, one of the great intellectual quarterlies of our century, should always have been so obtuse about poetry, as if (which I believe was the trouble) they didn't understand it. They took a Stalinist view of poetry, which is that poetry should go back where it came from, and then modified that view with Trotsky's rather nineteenth-century bohemian view of poetry, which reminds one, touchingly, of perhaps Verlaine. They could swallow the *Four Quartets* hook, line, and sinker and turn on the Beat poets like the OGPU. Macdonald, politically brilliant, a jaded libertarian with the old Marxist leadership principle in his heart, Macdonald says that Schwartz was killed by America, a statement that wouldn't stand up five minutes in a provincial psychiatrist's office, any more than that same college cheer that went: America killed Dylan. Macdonald says: "Poetry is a dangerous occupation in this country, as the biographers of too many of our best twentieth-century poets show, from Ezra Pound on, including the recent deaths of Randall Jarrell and Theodore Roethke. This is not a new thing. . . ." And then Macdonald quotes Baudelaire on Poe. ("For Poe the United States was nothing more than a vast prison . . ." and so forth.) This dismal, sociologically oriented view of poetry (now being taught in junior high but no further) was shared neither by Schwartz or Jarrell or myself nor by any of the other poets I know of. Whether poetry is a more dangerous occupation in America than tree surgery or insurance salesmanship is hard to say. Macdonald points to Delmore Schwartz's tremendous urge toward self-destruction but contents himself with the easy out that America got Delmore. It is one of those facile aesthetic lies which lead to the formation of poetry committees.

There is this about Schwartz as about Jarrell. Both refused that lie; and both were tormented by the strategy of escaping from the elite committees which survive by virtue of the lie. Macdonald, discussing his friendship for Schwartz, cites the Jewish-Gentile difference between them, as if this were an area of misunderstanding for an editor of *Partisan Review* or even *McCall's*. Jarrell, unlike Schwartz, did not become a part of *PR*, although he edited poetry and did the poetry reviews for *The Nation*, a magazine which is intellectually unidentifiable. *The Nation* in our time was more congenial to poetry than the great quarterlies, which always subordinated the poem to the ideology of the magazine. Jarrell wrote some of his best critiques for *The Nation*, in that kindly intellectual morass where one was allowed to Become rather than Be. In the quarterlies one must have already arrived.

So, after all, Jarrell was hung up, as we all were, by the sense of common sense, Thomas Paine's or Henry Ford's or the scientist's. And, after all, Macdonald has a truth in his craw, that poetry (he meant I think *being* a poet) is dangerous. *In danger* would be a better phrase, as children are in danger. It comes to the sadness about us that poets are not loved or are loved in the wrong way for the right reasons or—whatever that saying is. It comes to the fact that America the Mother wants to love her children but is much more successful at killing them off, or just making them successful. Jarrell had a brilliant, sure, and subtle mind, and would have been the greatest poet since whoever the last great poet was, had he not lacked the sense of power. He lacked it, to his disaster. It is what you might call a psychological factor, *the* psychological factor. He came of a generation that could not hate Mother America but which was afraid of her and for her. There is no one of our generation who betrayed her or who tried to topple the Victorian Statue of Liberty into the drink. Jarrell was the least anti-American of all of us, and the most. He recoiled from the boredom and the horror and the glory of the day-to-day life. But what he did in his poetry, which had never really been done before, was to face the modern scene and to—what more is there to say—to face it. He faced the music of the American Way of Life. But the subject wasn't anything that Dwight Macdonald would know about, because the elites never stoop to the observation of the actual. It wasn't anything that the power-mad poets would ever see, because they are so busy climbing Mount Everest that they don't know what millennium they are in. Jarrell tried to do the impossible: to observe and make poetry of a chaos, without being either inside or outside of it. He did it better than anyone else, better than it can be done. He did it passionately and with superb control. He did it with lies and subterfuge and great prose. He did it by hiding and spying, reporting and keening. I would imagine that he wept himself to death, out of frustration for the Kafka-like manias of our time, including those of the intelligentsia; out of the ambition which he denied himself because he was more intelligent than any of us; out of the love of the natural which denies the political. He died, you might say, because his heart was in the right place and his heart was even stronger than his intellect. Jarrell was split between his heart and mind. He was modern, which means hating being modern. He was born after Humpty Dumpty fell off the wall, and he knew that T. S. Eliot Scotch tape couldn't put anything back together again.

That is all I have to say. Thank you.

Allen Tate

Young Randall

IT WAS in 1931, I believe, when Randall was a freshman at Vanderbilt, that I first met him. Red Warren was then teaching there; at his house one Sunday afternoon I saw a tall, languid boy of eighteen rise to acknowledge the introduction to my wife and me, and then sit down, ignoring my extended hand. It was shyness, or the kind of awkwardness that comes of one's not knowing who one is. He must even, at that early time, have been conscious of his superior gifts and chafing under the restraints imposed by youth. I remember Red leading me into another room and showing me some of the boy's poems. There was one beginning "The cow wandering in the bare field" which struck me as prodigious; I still think it one of his best poems. I gathered from people who knew him better than I did, or ever came to know him, that he was a proud and difficult young man who studied all the time and had few or perhaps none of the purposeless diversions of the undergraduate. Although he seemed as an undergraduate to have read all English poetry —John Ransom once said to me that Randall knew more than he did—he was I believe a psychology major almost to the time of his graduation; this interest continued in a less formal way and is discernible in his later as well as in his youthful poems. It struck all his older friends at that time that his technical knowledge of verse must have come to him without labor: an early poem, "A Description of Some Confederate Soldiers," had a formal mastery that I, nearly fifteen years older, could not have equaled.

In those days I lived about forty miles from Nashville, and I saw him only at intervals when I came to the city for parties at the houses of the old Fugitives, to which he would be invited. But he would have none of the Fugitive tradition: from the beginning he was his own man. Nor would he allow himself to be a Southerner. He was of Tennessee parentage, brought up, I believe, in California. If he ever looked at the writings of the Agrarians, he would have thought it all nonsense, or at any rate an irrelevant excursion into history without value to a poet. The other prominent literary undergraduate of Randall's time was the late George Marion O'Donnell. We, the elder retired statesmen, marveled that these young men did not form a post-Fugitive group or a collaboration modeled on Wordsworth and Coleridge. Our rather highfalutin talk about the Southern tradition left Randall cold. When he came to see us in Tennessee, and later in Princeton, he would leave the company to play with my small daughter and her friends, whom he enjoyed more than he did us. For an inscrutable reason—I never understood Randall—he liked me very much for some years around 1940, but not much later on. He dedicated to me his first book, *Blood for a Stranger*; he had previously asked me to go over the manuscript and arrange the order of the poems; this I did; but he then gave them his own order, writing me a letter in which I appeared to be a little obtuse.

This is not the time to appraise Randall Jarrell's entire work. It is enough to say that he was one of the best poets of his generation, along with Lowell, Schwartz, Berryman, Wilbur, and Roethke, and that his work will last. As a critic, he had, like most of us, his poet-heroes in whom no fault could be found. His prose was powerful and impeccable. If this were an ad interim report, I should sum it up by saying that he was a fine poet and a great prose-stylist.

Eleanor Ross Taylor

Greensboro Days

MY FIRST memory of Randall's face is animated, laughing, talking—a face dominated by intense dark eyes —in the car that drove up to Allen Tate's house in Sewanee one spring afternoon in 1946. I had heard of Randall Jarrell —had admired him—while an undergraduate at Woman's College; I had read with excitement his poems in *Partisan Review,* his brilliant reviews of poetry; had dug up his master's thesis on Housman at the Vanderbilt library, and delighted in Fanny Cheney's story of how he had come running at her across the Vanderbilt campus on his hands and knees, saying, "I'm a saber-toothed tiger!" I had heard stories of his Kenyon days from Peter. I felt well prepared for what he would be like. I now added to it tallness, an impression of strength and coordination, juxtaposed with a certain remoteness and quiet intensity.

I had my first opportunity that afternoon to offend him

with one of his obsessions—I gave them instant coffee. Mackie had said in the kitchen, "Just don't tell Randall," but after I had extracted his approval I did tell him, and he laughed, "I have to stand on my judgment!" As he was seldom "polite," it may be instant coffee was better in those early days, but years later when I used to discuss with Mary chocolate recipes to which I added "just a spoon of instant Sanka," he would intone between sadness and contempt, "Instant—Sanka!"

Once he admired some particularly pretty yellow pears in our apartment; when I admitted I had added the blush with lipstick, he was obviously repelled, yet impressed that he had been taken in. Nobody was more concerned with distinguishing between artifice and art.

We—Jarrells and Taylors—bought a duplex at 1924 Spring Garden Street in 1947. Randall was customarily ensconced on the couch in their living room with an afghan over his legs, looking out the window behind the couch (where Kitten was often perched), a coal fire going in the grate, with his writing in his lap—the athlete in invalid's trappings—or, perhaps, the wolf in grandmother's nightgown. His voice could express more affection and welcome than anybody's. Peter and I were there often and long. If we made as if to go, saying, "You're working on your writing"—for he did write down things in the course of our visit—he would always insist he could write and talk at the same time—*liked* to. He was usually listening to Mahler or Hindemith or Bartok—mostly Mahler, that era—while we talked and he also wrote. I said little in sessions with the Jarrells (I would have been an idiot to chatter when it was possible to listen to Randall)—applied to him occasionally for an interpretation of something, once, I remember, Katherine Anne Porter's *The Leaning Tower.* No matter how elementary my questions, he answered them patiently and brilliantly. I often felt the secret of my success with Randall was that he preferred honest ignorance to superficial knowledge!

He had no use for work in the sense of *toil* or *duty.* And while he had boundless energy for tennis and didn't know what it was not to find time to write, he must have had some hard moments that spring as we got the duplex into shape. Once we found them painting a room, and Randall said almost tearfully, "I don't *like* it. I just happen to be good at it!" We persuaded the Jarrells to join us in planting rye grass over the whole yard, telling him—I'm not sure whether in good faith or by deliberate deceit—it didn't have to be cut. It grew especially rank on "their side" of the yard, and he held us to our statement that it didn't have to be cut.

Shortly after the Jarrells arrived in Greensboro in 1947, we all spent an afternoon with Clara May and Marc Friedlaender (one of many wonderful gatherings with them) on their pier beside the lake. We were talking about survival and overrefinement. Marc said he didn't like to feel that, if his survival depended on being able to kill and dress an animal, for instance, he couldn't do it. The rest of us agreed we felt ashamed of our squeamishness, but Randall disagreed. "I consider myself the ornament of civilization!" he declared. "When it perishes, let me perish!"

Another time we were talking about the Orson Welles invasion-from-Mars program that made such a stir in 1938. Randall refused to see anything upsetting in such an idea: "I'd like nothing better than for some creature from outer space to come and make me its pet!"

He found small talk deadly. Once when Mackie and I were discussing the price of stockings, or brands of coffee, he burst out histrionically, "Oh, what a petty, ignoble conversation!" He talked about serious things simply and about simple things with a wit that elevated them. "These cinders taste almost like toast."

He did not gossip (though he could characterize each of us in the most murderously comic aphorisms) and half listened in boredom when we did. He found our pattern laughable. At one point, he said, somebody always asked, "Is he the one who—" or "Is that the one with—" in pursuit of even peripheral subjects for gossip.

I was sometimes sassy to Randall, but I remember only one occasion when I was sarcastic to him and I don't, fortunately, remember what I said—some poor "But isn't it a strange thing that if thus-and-so—then thus-and-so"—sort of remark. He was on that couch in the Spring Garden living room and looked at me quickly, taken aback, then looked out the window and said with a lofty smile, "This isn't the Eleanor I know." I think I felt the way the television interviewer must have who reportedly made a reference to "highbrow" matters and turned to Randall with a sardonic smile, "You don't mind being called 'highbrow,' do you, Mr. Jarrell?" and who was answered instantly, cooly, simply, without a flicker of apology or qualification, "No, not at all."

I sometimes suspected he had a nearly superstitious belief that your insight and vision would be taken away from you in proportion to the extent you lied, that as you sought the truth, you would find it. He was most awfully honest. His highest regard (next talent) was for the "disinterested" person who had swept away prejudice and self-deceit, and he seemed to me to have succeeded in being that person. His busy, expert separation of the sheep from the goats made you pretty uncomfortable when you were among the goats, and nobody was ever assigned an unquestioned chair on the side of grace. This obligation to be honest was coupled with his belief in one's obligation to talent. When I used to reply to him, no, I had no new poems, he would taunt, "You'll be sorry—in heaven!"

His honesty was related to his generosity to students, to me, and, I think, to people like Christina Stead and Corbière. We were likely to do nothing for him in return, as people not on committees, not writing recommendations, not mentioning things to powerful people, not promoting, arranging, appearing. He battled for the survival of such people. After Peter led me across the hall that day and made me show Randall those first poems, I never made another request of him. It was always a gratuitous act on his part that asked to see my poems, consoled my rejections, asked to send them out, asked to write a preface, read them to groups.

He never modified his opinion of a book for a politic or

expedient reason, though he sometimes changed his mind, when he saw the pear's blush was lipstick. He called names in his reviews, the names of the obtuse and the vicious. He had bitter enemies in the casualties of his honesty, but he never seemed to feel this price too much for self-honor, though I think he suffered sometimes, in rare moments, at certain worldy honors appropriate to him he never got. Such considerations were really beneath his notice. The important thing was that your work was good and that you did it. We all believe this, but who else lives by it?

He liked to give presents, too. Once he took down from their wall and gave to Peter a picture Peter had admired once too often. In Levanto, where Mary and Randall and Beatrice were in the summer of 1958 (and we Taylors were in nearby Bonassola), he could never ignore a beggar and seemed to feel real pain that he had more than they did. When I suggested that some who begged were probably better off than others who worked, he replied that if they could bring themselves to ask us for money their poverty was too great to refuse.

The natural shore at Levanto was pebbles. Sand had been brought in for the beach, but to get into the water you had to cross an excruciating length of marble-sized fragments, usually set at frying temperature and bound to incapacitate your arches by halfway out. Randall found a way around this. He sat down and slid out. The rest of us pretended not to know the bearded American who went through this ceremony, but Randall was not abashed. He smiled a lofty smile when other people nursed their bruised insteps.

Randall and I sat under one of the beach umbrellas at Levanto to go over my poems. I think he was wearing a tennis cap with a green eyeshade. The trains skittered by just behind us, and beside us an Italian family who came to their umbrella every day with a wicker trunk full of lunch, china, silver, and serving dishes, ran out and held their plates into the breakers to be rinsed. Nothing could interfere with Randall's concentration, but I will never forget my agitation, in spite of the privacy speaking English gave us, at the distractions, the shame of exposing my poems to Randall (I knew him so well that his gentleness could not conceal his real outrage at a bad line or a bad poem), of having to explain myself here and there, and at his praise. When he said my poems were almost more like natural beauties than works of art, that the poems taken as a body seemed better than any single poem, when he commented on my obsessions and compulsions, I felt these attributes more enviable than their opposites! When Randall set out to praise you, you felt permanently Praised.

Altogether, we had three sessions going over my poems. The last in Levanto in 1958, when the book was ready to be sent to the publisher; the first in their apartment in 1949, when I had about half a dozen poems; the other in his office, about 1951, when I was going over to Greensboro on the bus once a week, from Hillsborough, to sit in on his class for a semester. The astonishing thing about his criticism (other friends who profited by it say the same thing) was that he so keenly respected your own individuality, could see what you were trying to do, and so could help you to help yourself. No rewriting, just a long finger unhappily indicating certain lines, "I think you might make this better," "I believe I'd just throw this one away—it's sort of cooked-up" and—just when you were rock-bottom—a dazzling smile, "Gee, this is magical!" We talked about punctuation and the breaking of lines. He disliked lines broken unnaturally—against syntax—and would press for a reason if an unrhymed line were broken in the middle of a clause or phrase.

All the wonderful things he said, so indelibly I thought, seem to evaporate now. They were spontaneous and meant for the moment, but Peter and I can't help wishing we had remembered better, even had written things down. He wrote us few letters. We once talked about that, with Randall saying letter-writing was part of self-discovery when you were young, and after that it was just agony, the sort of work he found sinful. The two I have are addressed not to "Mrs. Peter Taylor," but to "Mrs. Eleanor Taylor," as those of Mrs. Malcolm Hooke, in whose house and confidence Randall so much was during the twenty years he was in Greensboro, are addressed to "Mrs. Lucy Hooke." Randall characteristically insisted on giving woman her individuality apart from her husband, no matter how fond he was of the husband.

It is useless to dwell on the twenty years he might have had, the poems he might have explicated for our daughters and sons, and the other poems he might have written, the other wonderful things he might have turned to. How lucky we are to have known him!

Peter Taylor

Randall Jarrell

THE FIRST I ever heard of Randall was that he was a boy who knew a lot and that he had posed for the figure of Ganymede in the pediment of the Parthenon—our Parthenon, that is, in Centennial Park, Nashville, a full-sized model of the original, with the exact Athenian dimensions. The sculptors who were making a reconstruction of the pediments—Belle Kinney and L. F. Scholz, I believe they were—asked Randall to pose as Cup Bearer to the gods. That was in 1922. The child Randall is there in Centennial Park today, perhaps as good a justification as you could ask for the existence of our Parthenon.

Anyway, the first I ever heard of Randall Jarrell was that he was a boy who knew a lot. I heard it from one of my childhood friends in Nashville, Avery Handley. But I really didn't know Randall until I was living in Memphis and came back to Vanderbilt as a freshman in 1936. The gods of the literary undergraduates at Vanderbilt in those days were, of course, the Fugitives, the Agrarians. Not all of the group were teaching there then, but Nashville was still the gathering place. The atmosphere was made to order for aspiring young Southern writers who as restless young men longed to leave home, but who as restless young writers had the feeling that they ought to remain in their own country.

Among the literary students at Vanderbilt there were two parties. Each had taken for its master a brilliant graduate student. One of these was George Marion O'Donnell. The other was Randall. The two graduate students were not congenial. They lived very different kinds of lives. They addressed each other as Mr. O'Donnell and Mr. Jarrell. O'Donnell and his followers met by night in a beer joint called Melfi's. Randall held sway, held court, held class—that's the word for it—on a grassy plot outside the student union building either at midmorning or in the early afternoon. His would-be disciples—for he only tolerated us—met there not to drink beer but to play touch football with the master. By temperament some present were much better suited to the life at Melfi's, but we gave up all that and tried instead to play "touch." It was Randall's talk we wanted of course, and his talk on the sidelines and even while the game was in progress was electrifying. It was there that I first heard anyone analyze a Chekhov story. I have never since heard anything to equal it. On the sidelines of one of those games I once suggested to him that probably we couldn't know just how good Chekhov's stories were unless we could read them in Russian. He laughed at me—somewhat cruelly, I'm afraid. Or it may have been gleefully that he laughed, and his laughter may have been at his own thoughts. I was never able to hold it against him, at any rate—not for longer than overnight—whenever he laughed at something I said or at his thoughts about something I said. Because Randall's laughter, cruel *and/or* gleeful, really *was* irrepressible. And often when he laughed he was about to make one of his best cracks. On that occasion he said, "Even in Constance Garnett's translation, Chekhov's stories are the best in the English language." I have never since those days outside the student union heard anything to equal his analyses of Chekhov stories. Even then Randall could talk about a story you had read, and make you feel, make you realize, that you had never really read it before.

Although O'Donnell's thinking was much closer to the Agrarians' than Randall's was (O'Donnell had already published an essay in *Who Owns America*), Randall's admiration for the literary productions and for the men themselves was surely no less than O'Donnell's. He constituted a sort of loyal opposition on campus. His loyalty was such, in fact, that when Mr. Ransom was hired away by Kenyon, it was Randall who headed the student group petitioning the administration to keep him at Vanderbilt. The morning we went to present our petition to Chancellor Kirkland, Randall was spokesman. The old chancellor sat at his desk and read through the letter, which had been largely composed by Randall. Finally he looked up and said, "Boys, I'll have to have a signature on this letter." Randall, bursting into gleeful and perhaps cruel laughter and bouncing around the desk to stand beside the old chancellor, replied, "Oh, sir, we have signatures," and he began turning over the pages and pages of student signatures that were underneath the letter.

During the next two years, of course, Randall himself was teaching at Kenyon. Mr. Ransom had brought him along as his loyal friend, if also as the kind of loyal opposition Mr. Ransom enjoys. Both men admired Robert Frost's poetry. Eventually both were to become Frost's good friends. It was something to have those three poets, as we sometimes did at Kenyon, in the same room talking poetry. It is not what they said I can remember—I frequently didn't understand what they were saying—but I recognized and remember the intense feeling. One night in a rather large gathering, Randall made some reference to sprung rhythm. Frost stood shaking his jowl angrily. Finally there came from Frost's corner a deep growl: "Loose iambic, Jarrell, that's just loose iambic."

In addition to persuading Mrs. Ransom to remodel an old fur coat of his mother's for him, Randall set a good number of other ladies and young girls on the campus and on Gambier Hill to sewing for him. I remember seeing him one night in Mt. Vernon, with one of the high school teachers he dated over there. The two of them were looking in a shop window, and Randall was pointing out a sweater he admired. Already you could practically see the knitting needles flying in the girl's hands. And in the Kokosing Restaurant in Gambier, a grimy little store building like something out of a Western movie and next door to the house where we all lived, the sisters who waited tables there and their old mother too, who tossed hamburgers, were somehow persuaded to darn Randall's socks. They may even have done his laundry. I can see him stopping by there in the morning to deliver a handful of socks and to ask what kind of pies were there for lunch. They were crazy about him—called him Randall, whereas they called the rest of us by our last names. When I went back to Kenyon to teach a dozen years later, it was Randall, of all my contemporaries, that the villagers wanted news of.

Among his friends at Kenyon there were the tennis players. There was Don McNeil, and there was Maury Lewis, with whom he most often played tennis. Maury was a boy from Arkansas with a high, Southern voice who, when they had a tennis engagement, would come to the foot of the stairs in Douglass House and call out, "Randy, are you ready?" I never knew anyone else who presumed to call him Randy. But by the end of the second year you would see members of Kenyon's champion tennis team sitting about the soda shop reading Auden and Chekhov and Proust. Apparently he was able to teach literature on the tennis courts as well as on the touch field.

I enrolled in an eight o'clock class in American literature which he taught at Kenyon. It was held on the third floor of Ascension Hall. Since it was an eight o'clock, Randall was frequently late meeting it. We would look out the third-floor windows and see him sprinting down the Middle Path, often eating his breakfast as he ran. The rule at Kenyon was that the class had to wait on a professor only until the second bell. The boys would cup their hands and shout to Randall how many minutes or seconds he had, and he kept coming. Sometimes the bell would ring when he was already on the stairs, but regardless of that, when the bell rang, the class, most of it, would stampede down the stairs. I don't know how many times this happened—more than once or twice. Anyhow, I see him standing on the stairs when the stampeding students were gone, smiling and shrugging his shoulders. The good part, though, was that there were a half-dozen students who would remain, and those sessions with the devoted half dozen were, of course, the best sessions. It was more like a literary club than a class. To Randall's friends there was always the feeling that he was their teacher. To Randall's students, there was always the feeling that he was their friend. And with good reason in both cases.

After the war I saw Randall again in Nashville, and then he and I migrated with our wives to New York. We lived there for only a short time, but it was then that we became really close friends. I doubt I could have ever got started again after the war if I had not had Randall to talk to or to listen to. He was wonderful, of course, about reading what you had written and wonderful about telling you the truth about it—often the terrible truth. His talk was about literature, painting, music, about your own work, seldom about his. I remember once at Kenyon there was a student who had done a painting, a landscape, and had it proudly displayed in his room. When Randall came in and saw it there, he exclaimed, "Gosh, that's good!" He pointed out all the fine qualities. The painter sat soaking up the praise. They talked of other things for a while, and when Randall got up to leave he said, putting his fist on his hip and frowning, "You know, I've changed my mind about that picture. There's something wrong, awfully wrong, about the light in it. You ought to work on it some more, or maybe you really ought to just throw this one away and do another." As usual, of course, he was right about it.

He was that way about stories and poems too—never hesitated to tell you what he thought about something you had written, never hesitated to change his mind about what he thought. If you published something he didn't like, he behaved as though you had been disloyal to him in some way—or not that so much—more as if you had been disloyal to some other friend of his—your other self, that is, your artist self. And that he would not tolerate. He might avoid seeing you for days afterward. But oh, if you published something he liked! One winter when I was staying in London, I had two ten-page letters from him about two stories of mine he had seen in print. And if one were on the same side of the Atlantic with him, there would be long-distance telephone calls that went on and on. Or if there were no call or letter when you published something, the silence was awful and seemed bound to reach out to you wherever you were. Once you were a student of Randall's, once you were a friend of Randall's, it was for life.

After New York, we were together in many places. Intermittently, over a period of nearly twenty years, we taught together at the University of North Carolina, at Greensboro. We once bought a duplex apartment there, financed largely by our GI loans and by our working wives. When, in 1947, I reported to a mutual friend that Randall was coming down to Greensboro to be interviewed for a teaching appointment, at what was then the Woman's College of the university, the friend refused to believe me. In effect, he said that in that "Southern female seminary" Randall would be like a caged beast. But Randall knew what he was doing. He had already lived in New York, which he found very distasteful, and he had taught for a while in a very advanced, very experimental institution there, where the teaching was done in conferences and where no grades were given. He knew that he wanted to live in what he called "real America" and he knew that he could do with a little more of the seminary atmosphere in the college where he was to settle down to serious teaching and writing. . . . At lunch, on the day of Randall's interview with the six senior members of the English Department at Greensboro, he behaved very well, except that he insisted upon talking about books instead of letting us ramble on about whether we preferred the fish cakes or the roast pork. But I must add that I think the senior members of the English Department behaved rather well too. Randall's view of the two spinsters and the four middle-aged men in the group was that they were types he had known all his life. And, as a matter of fact, their attitude toward him was not too different from his own toward them. Why, they had, so to speak, known Randall all their lives. Other gifted, young, Southern literary men had passed through their lives. And so they were able to recognize one when they saw him. The others had not been so brilliant in conversation or such gifted writers, but, still, their having known the others helped. They knew who he was. Later on, several of those present at that luncheon became friends of Randall's. One of the ladies present boasts today that she is the original of Miss Batterson in *Pictures from an Institution*. Not only can she recognize herself, but, after all, Randall once *told* her that she was the original. It is a very affectionate portrait that he painted of the sensitive, cultivated Southern gentlewoman who has given her life to teaching.

We spent summers together in the Tennessee mountains, and one summer we took our families to the Italian Riviera and rented places near each other. By that time my wife and I had two small children and weren't able to make many excursions away from home base. But when the Jarrells would go off to Florence for a few days, they would return with presents for us. It would be a Uccello reproduction for my wife or toys for the children or a hat for me like the one Randall had bought himself on their last trip and which I had admired. On the occasion of the hat, we were down at the little station to meet them when they came in on the afternoon train, and there was Randall—he had his beard then—leaning out the train window, grinning and waving the little green hat at me. I'd earned the hat by having recently done a story he approved of. What he always let one know was that he cared about how one's writing was going; and there is no better friend than that.

Once when I was living in the country in North Carolina, about fifty miles from Greensboro, Randall came out to spend the day. When he got out of his car, he was carrying a briefcase. He didn't often carry a briefcase in those days. My wife and I eyed it without comment until at last he said, "Guess what! I've written a novel!"

"You're kidding," I said.

He burst out at me, "Are you crazy? You know I don't kid about things like that!" And of course he was right. He didn't kid about things like that. It was *Pictures from an Institution.*

I suppose that nothing is more interesting than to hear what someone else—especially Randall Jarrell—has said about you. A friend reported to me once something that Randall had said of me and my literary efforts: "He is like a great white horse doing tatting." I loved so hearing him say the witty things he said about people that I used to wish I could have been hiding under the sofa the night he brought forth that about the white horse. He found gossip tedious and boring, yet it was worth making him endure it occasionally just to hear the final word he would come up with, once and for all settling the hash of the subject. And of course the whole method of *Pictures from an Institution* is that of letting us hear what the characters in the book have to say about each other. It is mainly a book of Randall's witty talk, and in it we see to what serious places his witty talk could take one. And since I have never done what I always said I intended to do—that is, to write down the things he said—I should like to conclude with two passages from *Pictures* that will make us hear his voice as nothing else can. I have chosen one of the subjects that he was best on: important people and their fondness for important people.

Ordinary people think that very important people get along badly with one another—and this is true; but they often get along worse with you and me. They find it difficult not simply to get along with, but to care about getting along with, ordinary people, who do not seem to them fully human. They make exceptions, real or seeming, for school friends, people who flatter them enough, relatives, mistresses, children, and dogs: they try not to bite the hand that lets them stroke it . . . but all power irritates—it is hard for them to contain themselves within themselves, and not to roast the peasants on their slopes. But they eye one another with half-contemptuous, half-respectful dislike: after all, each of them *is* important, and importance, God knows, covers a multitude of sins.

This earth carries aboard it many ordinary passengers; and it carries, also, a few very important ones. It is hard to know which people are, or were, or will be which. Great men may come to the door in carpet-slippers, their faces like those of kindly or fretful old dogs, and not even know that they are better than you; a friend meets you after fifteen years and the Nobel Prize, and he is sadder and fatter and all the flesh in his face has slumped an inch nearer the grave, but otherwise he is as of old. They are not very important people. On the other hand, the president of your bank, the Vice-Chancellor of the—no, not of the Reich, but of the School of Agriculture of the University of Wyoming: these, and many Princes and Powers and Dominions, are very important people; the quality of their voices has changed, and they speak more distinctly from the mounds upon which they stand, making sure that their voices come down to you.

The very important are different from us. Yes, they have

more everything. They are spirits whom that medium, the world, has summoned up just as she has the rest of us, but there is in them more soul-stuff, more ego—the spirit of Gog or Magog has been summoned. There is *too much* ectoplasm: it covers the table, moves on toward the laps of the rest of us, already here, sitting around the table on straight chairs, holding one another's hands in uneasy trust. We push back our chairs, our kinship breaks up like a dream: it is as if there were no longer Mankind, but only men.

P. L. Travers

A Kind of Visitation

OCCASIONALLY, very rarely—like the spirit of delight—comes a book that is not so much a book as a kind of visitation. I had not known that I was waiting for *The Animal Family* but when it came it was as though I had long been expecting it. This is what happens when one encounters poetry. "Never seek to tell thy love," or "Fear no more the heat o' the sun," or "Out of the cradle endlessly rocking" the voices cry, and between the reader and the poem there is an immediate recognition—as though one's own thoughts, till now mute, unknown, unquickened, leapt to life at the announcement.

Nothing could be simpler than this story of Randall Jarrell's, if indeed one can call it a story. A lonely hunter finds a

This review of *The Animal Family* was first published in The New York Times Book Review, November 21, 1965.

mermaid, takes her to live in his hut, and with her adopts successively a bear cub, a lynx kitten, and a boy from a drifting lifeboat. That is all—and yet, reading it, one is convinced that this all is everything, each happening inevitable, essential, right. The secret lies, of course, less in the plot than in the telling. The author lingers over the facts with the absorption, the inner delight of the true storyteller, letting them play and range as they will; he listens to what they say, he notes down every informing detail, above all he takes his time.

Taking time takes one into timelessness. And thus the story, like the traditional fairy tale, seems to be without beginning and without end in the sense that one is aware of it existing long before the flyleaf and long after the back page. Was, is now, and ever shall be is the meaning both of Once Upon a Time and Happy Ever After; and this is the world the book inhabits.

All good stories have this feeling of continuity, of going on and never ending. Moreover, the good story never explains. The courtship of the hunter and the mermaid is taken as a matter of course, much as it is in the old Scottish ballads, where, after all, mermaids who wive with humans are two-a-penny. There is nothing here of Hans Andersen's mawkish portentousness and nostalgia, no longing for an immortal soul, no craving for a pair of legs. *Our* mermaid accepts herself as she is, a sea-creature in love with the land, eager to understand its language, willing to submit to its limitations. She toils happily, if awkwardly, over the meadows, propelling herself by her own tail, lives on a diet of raw fish and when she takes up her abode in the hut proves to be an indifferent housewife.

But there is more to homekeeping than sweeping floors or stirring the stew; it is relationship that matters. And here every domestic detail of their mutual life throws light upon the characters of the hunter and the mermaid and the affinity between them. They "were so different from each other that it seemed to them, finally, that they were exactly alike; and they lived together and were happy."

The book, indeed, is a paean to family life and its long unending thread. The reciting of its small, factual, intimate daily round constitutes, as it were, an epic in reverse. The reader is made party to all its lights and shadows, its souvenirs, heirlooms, problems; one grieves with the hunter when he dreams of his dead parents, is concerned for him in his moments of masculine uncertainty in front of the mermaid's feminine sureness, rejoices with them both when with the advent of the first child—the bear cub—two and one make three.

The animal children are beautifully drawn and juxtaposed; the clumsy, slow-witted bumbling bear and the quick lithe lynx each becomes more truly himself when placed beside the other. After two such fully realized characters the author could artistically go no further in the world of beasts. The third child *had* to be a boy and with him the family is complete—at peace, with the charm wound up.

The story is a medley of lyrical factuality. Never once does its sentiment decline into sentimentality—"The bear's table manners were bad. But so were the mermaid's"—nor our belief into skepticism. There is the truth of fact and the truth of truth, as D. H. Lawrence said, and any child reading this book would know to which category *The Animal Family* belonged.

Is it a book for children? I would say yes because for me *all* books are books for children. There is no such thing as a children's book. There are simply books of many kinds and some of them children read. I would deny, however, that it was written *for* children. But is any book that these creatures love really invented for them? "I write to please myself," said Beatrix Potter, all her natural modesty and arrogance gathered into the noble phrase. Indeed, whom else, one could rightly ask. And this book bears the same hallmark. Someone, in love with an idea, has lovingly elaborated it simply to please himself—no ax to grind, making no requirements, just putting a pinch of salt on its tail—as one would with a poem—and setting it down in words. How, therefore, could a child—and children come in all ages, remember—fail to read and enjoy it?

Robert Watson

Randall Jarrell: The Last Years

WRITING ABOUT Randall Jarrell, I can only think how much better he would have written this essay than I. I imagine him looking over my shoulder and sighing, You call *that* prose. If God were a writer and wrote a book that Randall did not think was good, Randall would not have hesitated to give it a bad review. And if God complained, I think Randall would then set about showing God what was wrong with his sentences. Actually Randall could have written this essay if I had been on my toes. What was interesting about him beyond his writing was what he said. In an hour's visit he could shower us with a hundred epigrams; we all thought these wonderful sentences would appear in his essays: they didn't, he made up new ones. Had we known they would die on our living-room rug, I think my wife, Betty, and I would have sat, notebooks in hand, during his visits. With Betty, who is a painter, he talked art; with me he talked poetry. Randall had no small talk. Four days before he died, we talked at great length about Gerard Manley Hopkins and also several living poets. During the conversation he repeated this remark of Heine's about someone: "He was immortal until the day he died." Randall Jarrell was the only person I have ever known well who was unquestionably a genius and destined for immortality.

He was reading *The Wind in the Willows* when I first talked to him on a hot September morning in 1953 in the gymnasium of what was then called the Woman's College of the University of North Carolina, where I was a new instructor and he an associate professor just back from a two-year leave of absence. During that year Randall usually wore a Glen plaid suit and had a mustache—the beard, the large colorful wardrobe, and expensive sports cars came later. I had read his war poems and I was in the middle of reading *Poetry and the Age*, published only a few months previous to our first meeting, but I had not read his poems in any thoroughgoing fashion. We were both early at registration; the students were beginning to line up at the door, which would open at 9:00 A.M. Randall would read a little of *The Wind in the Willows,* then laugh and say what a marvelous book it was. I asked him what the students were like. "Read my poem 'A Girl in a Library,'" he answered. "Gee, I'm glad to get back here. This college is like Sleeping Beauty." And his eyes returned to the pages of *The Wind in the Willows.*

Frequently his face expressed boredom or a wordless misery, but most often a flashing vitality and enthusiasm. His passion for books made him exciting to know because he was always praising a book we had somehow missed, such as *The Man Who Loved Children*, or encouraging us to reread Grimm or Wordsworth. Unlike academics, he paid no attention to literary fashion, had no systematic theory about literature, and did not talk over anyone's head. Few could explain the very difficult more simply. He had more compelling interests in life than most of us, and whatever subject interested him he knew with the depth, but not the dryness of the specialist. I don't know many who had, for instance, more interest in professional football than he—a sport he was fond of comparing to poetry. A colleague of ours once said half jokingly, "The only thing I have in common with Randall Jarrell is a love of clothes, and damn it, he knows more about clothes than I do." We always felt he wanted to know more than anyone in the world about what interested him. One of his boyhood fears that he often expressed was of not having any new books at home to read. During the years I knew him, he seemed to be reading around the world. In 1953 he was winding up German literature and beginning his march through Russian literature. If he had lived, I imagine him crossing the border into China, then on down to India.

When he liked a person, a book, or a painting, he was wild with joy. His introductions of visiting speakers were famous—some of us attended lectures and readings more to hear Randall's introduction than to hear the visitors. A few winters ago Jean Stafford arrived on the campus to give a lecture on fiction. During the night ten inches of snow fell, and the Jarrells found themselves snowbound at home several miles from the university. Randall called me on the telephone and asked me to give the introduction. If I would get a pencil and paper, he would tell me what to say: what to say turned into a fifty-minute lecture on the works of Jean Stafford. In the middle of the lecture he said he had to leave the phone and would I hang on for a moment. The moment turned into five minutes before he returned to the phone. "I saw a wolf go by the window," he said, "and I wanted to watch it." Pause. "No, it wasn't really a wolf. It was only a dog that looked like a wolf."

On campus one year he asked me to bring our small children around on Halloween, but I assumed the invitation was simply polite talk and we did not drive the children out to the Jarrells for "trick or treat." In hurt tones the next day he said that he and Mary were all dressed up for Halloween. Where were we? He loved to dress up. He had a hat he called his Sigmund Freud hat. And he had a coonskin hat he said he bought with Tootsie Roll wrappers when he was a boy. He also loved to pose for pictures. He and Mary offered to pose for my wife Betty, who did one painting of Mary and two of Randall. Less than a month before he died, he saw a painting Betty had done of our son Winthrop asleep, with Uccello's *The Battle of San Romano* as the background. He asked if Betty would paint him reading or daydreaming with one of his favorite paintings as background or dream-work. We never knew what painting, if any, he selected.

He loved the perfect and he loved being right. Since he believed that the enemy of the best was the good, on occasion some of us whose manuscripts he read felt consigned to a circle of hell reserved for those who write imperfectly. His criticism was strenuous, detailed, and accurate. I recall very clearly his comment on the words "heavy coffin" I had used in a poem. "Heavy coffin," he said scornfully. "Everyone knows coffins are *heavy*. Now *light* coffin, that would be much more interesting." Whenever he told anyone a poem was not good, he always said it in a tone that implied he was as distressed as the poet himself must be.

What endeared him to his writing students was the seriousness with which he took their writing; he spoke to them as if they were all potential Homers. Once we called all the writing students together because too many had enrolled in the courses for us to handle. He told them that if their ambitions were to write works that would be published in the *Saturday Evening Post*, they should drop the course and go read the *Saturday Evening Post*. The *Post* would be their best teacher. But if they aspired to be Homers they could remain in the writing classes. Student after student told me that Mr. Jarrell seemed to know ten times better than they what their poems and stories were about. He never tried to impose any rules or any system. The best teachers of writing, he always claimed, were the best works of the best writers. He knew that imaginative writing could not be taught; he knew too that only rarely would he have students who could really write. From his writing classes he expected mostly to turn out skilled and dedicated readers who would know that imaginative writing was a normal though difficult occupation.

Most writers who teach are reluctant to serve on university committees because they wish to protect their writing time. Randall, though, was very conscientious about both committee meetings and faculty meetings. He served twice in Greensboro as chairman of a committee to revise the freshman and sophomore English courses. He turned his committee meetings into lectures on books he thought all students should know—or diatribes against works he detested: he hated *Tom Jones*, for instance, a novel which annoyingly crept back onto the syllabus whenever he was not on the committee.

By some standards he was a prude—he didn't drink, smoke, or use profanity, and did not like conversations or jokes about sex. Yet when he himself lectured about a story or a poem he never dodged any sexual implications. He was very fond of his step-daughter Beatrice, who was enrolled in my sophomore English class. After a very free-wheeling class discussion of "The Wife of Bath's Prologue," I wondered whether he would hear about it and be disconcerted. Sure enough, the next day in the corridor he hailed me. Much to my surprise, he complimented me on what he had heard was a tactful and reticent handling of sex in the class. Either the class was much less bawdy than I had thought, or Beatrice, a young lady of great taste and delicacy, had been very discreet in her account.

His love of being right all the time was troublesome. He always won an argument—even when he was wrong, which was not often—because he knew his subject in more detail, had a marvelous memory, and had a mind that worked with a matchless velocity. Years ago I recall him telling me how much better a novel *The Idiot* was than *Crime and Punish-*

ment. Later I found him in his office reading *Crime and Punishment.* What a great book it was, he told me, really much better than *The Idiot.* I said that I was very happy he had come around to my opinion. He looked very pained because he was not the kind of man who liked to come around to the opinions of others, especially younger colleagues. No, he said. He hadn't really come around at all: he had based his earlier preference on a reading of *Crime and Punishment* in high school when he was not old enough to appreciate it.

Randall was awkward at parties attended by more than a few people even though he could address a thousand from the platform with ease. At parties many interpreted his silence and apparent indifference as disdain of the company. Actually he was shy and uncomfortable. What he liked to do most at parties was to sit on a sofa with Mary and one other person he knew with whom he could discuss books, or paintings, or perhaps sports. New people who talked with him were apt to find him unnerving, not through any fault of his, but because his reputation for genius tended to keep his listeners quiet: they did not want to make fools of themselves. I recall a shy young lady telling Randall at a dinner party how much she liked the poems of Yeats. "What particular poems of Yeats do you like best?" he asked. In fear that she would like the wrong ones, she lost her nerve and could not bring herself to name a single poem.

My mind goes back to our first conversation when I found him reading *The Wind in the Willows.* He was engaged in a favorite occupation, reading, and with my arrival turned to another favorite occupation, telling what he enjoyed about a book. In the years that followed, he began to translate fairy tales and then to write children's books of his own. (During this period he was also writing the essays that appeared in *A Sad Heart at the Supermarket,* the poems included in *The Woman at the Washington Zoo* and *The Lost World*, and many translations, Goethe's *Faust* being the most ambitious.) He identified with children and the cozy world of the child. When we asked callers what they would have to drink, he was the only guest who would call for "milk and cookies." And, like many children, he sometimes seemed to have little grasp of the practical world. One day when the Jarrells were going on a trip he left his canary with us. We asked him what we should feed the canary. Obviously he did not know, so he simply said, "Three meals a day, three meals a day." His identification with children helped, I think, to give him a clarity of expression—he wanted to be understood by everyone, not just intellectuals.

He had, as most of us have, a dark side. How well he translates these dark feelings into poetry. "90 North" is a poem about a little boy who has dreams of going to the North Pole and then as an adult takes a journey to the "actual pole."

In the child's bed
After the night's voyage, in that warm world
Where people work and suffer for the end
That crowns the pain—in that Cloud-Cuckoo-Land

I reached my North and it had meaning.
Here at the actual pole of my existence,

Where all that I have done is meaningless,
Where I die or live by accident alone—

Where, living or dying, I am still alone;
Here where North, the night, the berg of death
Crowd me out of the ignorant darkness,
I see at last that all knowledge

I wrung from the darkness—that the darkness flung me—
Is worthless as ignorance: nothing comes from nothing,
The darkness from the darkness. Pain comes from the darkness
And we call it wisdom. It is pain.

The pain of life, though, could be eased by reading. "Change me," so many of his characters cry. In "Children Selecting Books in a Library" he gives an explanation of the meaning of books in our lives, of how they can bring about transformations. Books, to both the child and the adult, can become a protection against the horror of life, "the capricious infinite / That, like parents, no one has yet escaped / Except by luck or magic." Our adult lives may be full of fears, but so are the lives of children. "Their tales are full of sorcerers and ogres / Because their lives are."

Read meanwhile . . . hunt among the shelves, as dogs do, grasses,
And find one cure for Everychild's diseases
Beginning: *Once upon a time there was*
A wolf that fed, a mouse that warned, a bear that rode
A boy. Us men, alas! wolves, mice, bears bore.
And yet wolves, mice, bears, children, gods and men

In slow perambulation up and down the shelves
Of the universe are seeking . . . who knows except themselves?
What some escape to, some escape: if we find Swann's
Way better than our own, and trudge on at the back
Of the north wind to—to—somewhere east
Of the sun, west of the moon, it is because we live

By trading another's sorrow for our own; another's
Impossibilities, still unbelieved in, for our own . . .
"I am myself still"? For a little while, forget:
The world's selves cure that short disease, myself,
And we see bending to us, dewy-eyed, the great
CHANGE, dear to all things not to themselves endeared.

One day a few years ago I found Randall in a very dejected mood in his office. He had been reading Eleanor Taylor's poems over and over in preparation for writing his essay on her. "No one will believe me," he said, "if I say directly how great a poet she is. Her poems are so good," he continued, "that they make my own poems seem weak in comparison." But after talking about Eleanor Taylor's poems for a few minutes, he forgot his sadness over his own work and became cheery and exuberant. What his friends most admired in Randall Jarrell was that he gave praise and enthusiasm where it mattered in our lives.

By some quirk of the "capricious infinite," *The Lost World,* his last book of poems, received less attention and less favorable attention than any book he wrote during the last dozen years of his life. *The Lost World* is a powerful and richly varied book of poems. For the first time he wrote extensively about his own life, a subject that had seldom entered his poems directly. In this book he altered his style somewhat to give most of the poems a surface simplicity. He also reduced the frequency of his "learned" allusions and changed in general the pitch of his poems from the rhetorical relentlessness of much of his previous work—especially the war poems—to quieter speech, more subtle rhythms, which to the unobservant ear may sometimes seem like prose. Since many of these poems seem so deceptively easy in comparison with the earlier poems, his last poems have occasionally been dismissed with nods and sad faces which say, "How could such an intellectual giant go against the grain of his mental powers to write such simple, prosy, sentimental poems. Poor Jarrell. Such a falling off." In his essay "The Obscurity of the Poet," he says, "When critics first read Wordsworth's poetry they felt that it was silly, but many of them *said,* with Byron, that 'he who understands it would be able / To add a story to the Tower of Babel.' " And later on in the same essay he repeats a frequently asked question and gives the answer: "when the old say to us, 'What shall I do to understand Auden (or Dylan Thomas, or whoever the latest poet is)?' we can only reply: 'You must be born again.' " We have a tendency to like more of what we have liked, of what seems familiar. And when we hear the phrase "How he's changed," the phrase usually means "How he's changed for the worst"; how seldom "changed for the better."

In the long title poem of *The Lost World* and its epilogue, he re-creates scenes from his childhood in Hollywood, yet as in all genuine works of art the private and particular childhood of Randall Jarrell is tranformed into a childhood we all share. In its own distinct and different way the beauty of this poem is comparable to the beauty of the passages in Wordsworth's "Prelude" in which he describes his childhood. At one point Wordsworth says, "Fair seed-time had my soul, and I grew up / Fostered alike by beauty and by fear: / Much favoured in my birthplace, and no less / In that belovèd Vale to which erelong / We were transplanted." The child in "The Lost World" together with his family is transplanted from the farm to Hollywood, where he is nourished by a kind of beauty and fear undreamt of by Wordsworth.

The child grows up among the props of make-believe: a papier-mâché dinosaur on the set of the motion picture *The Lost World*, an artificial igloo, the set of his school play, *The Admirable Crichton*; or the make-believe of his storybooks. The child half-nurtured on make-believe tries to understand the habitual, work-a-day world of adults (what we are fond of calling the "real" world) by seeing it in terms of fiction: when the child watches a laborer in the factory where "Pop" works, he sees "a dwarf hammering out the Ring / In the world under the world." Often after his schoolwork the child, as children do, puts on homemade armor to play a game of war as if unconsciously the small child already knew that in fact all men must prepare themselves for a world of brutal contention.

So many nostalgic memories of childhood are re-created:

a boy's love of animals, his listening in bed through earphones to the crystal set, the taste of chocolate tapioca, a game of dominoes with his great-grandmother. My particular favorite describes the child seated beside a police dog in the back seat of a car:

> So, now, Lucky and I sit in our row,
> Mrs. Mercer in hers. I take for granted
> The tiller by which she steers, the yellow roses
> In the bud vases, the whole enchanted
> Drawing room of our progress. The glass encloses
> As glass does, a womanish and childish
> And doggish universe. We press our noses
> To the glass and wish: the angel- and devilfish
> Floating by on Vine, on Sunset, shut their eyes
> And press their noses to their glass and wish.

The poem is a brilliant reconstruction of the freshness, the wonder of life to the child, held in contrast to the routine, the habit life of his elders.

The boy's life, though, is certainly not all pleasure; he is also nourished on fear. In a startling and agonizing passage Jarrell describes the boy watching "Mama" wring the neck of a chicken. Horrified, the boy worries that perhaps she will someday kill one of his pet rabbits for supper. And the boy also has been worried about a story he has been reading concerning a scientist who is preparing to destroy the world. "He couldn't really, could he, Pop?" "No, that's just play, / Just make-believe," answers Pop. But at the edge of the boy's mind he knows that Mama *might* kill one of his rabbits, just as one side of his mind tells him that, as we all know, the atomic scientists *might* very well destroy our planet. And, as all constant readers know, make-believe is true, often cruelly true, a fact which Jarrell demonstrates throughout this book and many other of his earlier poems.

The title of the poem is richly suggestive, referring not only to the lost world of prehistoric life, but also to the lost world of our childhood, so lost that not even the houses or trees remain, and perhaps to the final loss of life on our planet itself, through atomic destruction. In the adult, speaking in the epilogue "Thinking of the Lost World," is still the frightening boyhood memory:

> The chicken's body is still going round
> And round in widening circles, a satellite
> From which, as the sun sets, the scientist bends
> A look of evil on the unsuspecting earth.

Certainly "The Lost World" is a poem that speaks directly to us in mid-twentieth-century America, to our lives, just as Wordsworth spoke to his contemporaries in the early nineteenth century.

At times throughout the book Jarrell expresses a bleakness about life, a kind of cosmic despair reminiscent of Thomas Hardy or even A. E. Housman when the latter says, "high heaven and earth ail from the prime foundation." But this bleakness, so justified in view of the history of the twentieth century, is balanced with joy. As the child has his joys, so does the adult. Randall Jarrell insists, for instance, that man and his life can be made exalted through works of art, which are one of the redeeming miracles of life. On this subject I would especially recommend the poem called "In Galleries," in which, alas, the miracle of art is so powerful it renders the guards invisible.

With an eye for detail as sharp as Pope's, he captures the surface, the specific content of a society in which we buy Cheer and Joy, ironically, in packages at supermarkets, eat Cornish game hens, get X-rayed by roentgenologists, fly in jet planes, wear gold lamé gowns, use electric toothbrushes, paint abstract paintings, drive Bentley automobiles, live in fashionable suburbs like Montecito, eat breakfast in the Plaza Hotel in New York, and take vacations on islands in the Caribbean. But beneath the surface glitter of affluent life (so affluent in "Three Bills" that it is crippling), he shows us that the dark, primitive powers, like the wild life in the forest, move ominously in the deepest regions of our minds. Many of these poems, such as "Field and Forest" and "The House in the Wood," are forceful reminders of these nightmarish forces.

Other poems present the plight of the aging and dying inhabitants of our world. In "Next Day" a woman who is shopping in a supermarket laments what age has done to her. Once pretty with the kind of attractiveness men stare at with desire, she discovers, now that she is no longer an object of men's stares:

> I'm anybody,
> I stand beside my grave
> Confused with my life, that is commonplace and solitary.

"The Lost Children," one of the most piercingly sad poems I have read and my favorite short poem in the book, gives us a mother's reflections on her two daughters, one who dies in childhood and the second who is now a mother too. The woman feels that through time and change she has lost her living daughter as truly as she has lost her dead daughter. Few poets can capture man's feelings of loneliness and loss as poignantly as Jarrell. For a poem with quite a different feeling, one of flat domestic horror, I recommend "A Well-to-Do Invalid."

He can move us with the sentiments of a Wordsworth by his memories of childhood life, by his concerns with the process of aging, but he has another voice that can be instructive in the manner of Pope or Swift. The long poem "Woman" is a wildly amusing poem, tender and witty and instructive. The poem is an essay on the nature of women, on all their fascinations and, to men at least, follies. Karl Shapiro once joked that Randall Jarrell knew too much about women. After we read the poem "Woman," we are all wiser about Woman, a subject that is an obsession of all men, and most women too.

In trying to convey what *The Lost World* is like as a book, I have not been able to say much about the many fine single poems—"Washing," "Well Water," and "The Bird of Night." Nor have I been able to describe the fluency and naturalness with which he handles difficult verse forms and the ease with which he shifts moods from poem to poem. With lightning intelligence and deep feeling, Randall Jarrell looked open-eyed at the delights and horrors of our time, nothing too small and tender to escape his attention and nothing too large, too frightening, such as the awesome ending of "The Old and the New Masters" where he describes an imaginary modern painting.

in abstract
Understanding, without adoration, the last master puts
Colors on canvas, a picture of the universe
In which a bright spot somewhere in the corner
Is the small radioactive planet men called Earth.

Mrs. Randall Jarrell

The Group of Two

I CAME INTO Randall's life after Salzburg and Rilke, about the middle of Mahler; and I got to stay through Goethe on up to Wagner. It was in the early fifties, in what Karl Shapiro called Randall's "both sides of the Rhine" period. It was the time of his Prussian officer's leather coat, when everything German mattered (I was Mary Eloise von Schrader, though German in name only) as well as—as always—when *everything* mattered. How could so much matter to one man!

Randall's Enthusiasms, negative and positive, could put a spell on him—and you, too. I've watched many a sensible person who met him during one of his Enthusiasms get enthralled and leave for home sure in the knowledge that Randall's main side interest was Groddeck. The next sensible person was sure it was gear ratios; and the next, graphology. Small, commonplace matters Randall made himself pay at-

tention to the way his Gertrude Johnson would, As A Novelist, and then he'd pass on. With a *real* subject—anthropology, Renaissance painting, psychoanalysis, Romantic composers—he dwelt in it and it dwelt in him.

He was an active spectator, too. In fact, if he was merely watching a performance I could be sure he was about to say, "Let's wash this out." Anything worth staying for made him twist and untwist his legs, clasp and unclasp my hand, jerk, hum, and sweat with empathy until he almost rang like that line of Rilke's he translates: *Whenever I saw something that could ring, I rang.* On the way home he'd say, "I *ought* to write Ingmar Bergman a letter." Or Tanaquil Le Clercq. Or Pancho Gonzales. Or Johnny Unitas. In the case of Sviatoslav Richter he went so far as to have a Gucci handbag delivered to Mrs. Richter, but while he could discourse at length to me about the great pianist he couldn't express himself directly with more than a conventional note of greeting before the concert.

When we met, Randall quickly saw what a hodgepodge I was and supplied me with all of Rilke, Eliot, Lowell, Chekhov, Auden, Peter Taylor, and Jarrell to read. Proust followed these in the mail; then *The Charterhouse of Parma*; then, in with all the recorded Mahler of that time, some Learn German records "to play when you don't have anything to do."

He was always dazzling me with a feat such as turning on the car radio in the midst of some music and crying out at the *first* notes Liszt! Strauss! Berlioz! In the campus bookstores he liked to flip through the art postcards, identifying them: "Piero—Uccello—van der Goes—wicked old Tiepolo—Goya—Daumier—Caravaggio, that wretch!—Vuillard—Rousseau—dopey old Braque—Kokoschka." "Doesn't he look like *Peter*?" he'd say of the Kokoschka self-portraits. And at home, by ourselves, he liked to ask me what sentence I was reading in Proust and then tell me the ones that came before and after it.

His Enthusiasm at this time was sports cars and for as long after as I can remember we were always going out for the "new" *Road and Track*. Summers at Monteagle or Montecito, that magazine pulled us into one drugstore and out another, and off to faraway small towns "that might not be sold out." Winters in Greensboro—after breakfast, after class, after dark—the idea could strike Randall to "go out into the Great World," and we did: two Chicken Littles in their TD or their XKE, off to a "lovely magazine stand where—who knows, eh? Who knows?"

I didn't read *Road and Track*, Randall read it to me after he'd read it himself: then he'd read it to himself again. When the new one came, the old one went under the bed with old Schwann and L. L. Bean catalogues and *High Fidelity*.

In *Road and Track* Randall got a world peopled and costumed and behaving as imaginatively as he could have made himself; and best of all, he hadn't made it himself. It came nearer than anything else to satisfying that leitmotiv of yearning, in certain poems, for "people from another planet." On our deck in Laguna, looking past the Seal Rocks at the Pacific, he'd dream over those drawings of dreams—The All-Possible Car. He *believed* in *Road and Track*'s theocracy of old, holy motors whose Dalai Lama was the adorable Bugatti. And he'd marvel at the exotic vernacular critics used to review drivers and drivers used to review cars. "Baby doll! What prose," he'd say. "Listen to this."

There in that magazine, among dates of rallies and *concours d'élégance* and races, man found the dates of consequence to man. "Just think, pet cat," the groom said when he'd found ours. "We're probably the only people in the world getting married on the eighth so we can be at Madera on the tenth."

It was a fine, bright, smog-free eighth in Pasadena, as dry and glittering as California used to be in the twenties. *That,* and being able to see Mt. Wilson Observatory, seemed the main topic of the guests and Randall muttered to me, "One touch of weather makes the whole world kin." But it was *Gemütlichkeit* there, with my friends of thirty years perpetuating us in Kodachrome in front of portraits and brasses in my mother's home. Randall's dark eyes lingered on mine above our champagne as we toasted *ewig Freundschaft* to each other, *ewig, ewig*. Ländlers on Helen's accordion ebbed and flowed in the rooms, and it was dark when our last goodbyes drifted off into that eucalyptus-Vicks-scented air. *Im augenblick* Madera, and two Jarrells perched on a rail fence oblivious of all save ourselves and Phil Hill racing the first C-Jag in this country.

To be married to Randall was to be encapsulated with him. He wanted, and we had, a round-the-clock inseparability. We took three meals a day together, every day. I went along to his classes and he went along on my errands. I watched him play tennis, he picked out my clothes. Sometimes we were brother and sister "like Wordsworth and Dorothy" and other times we were twins, Randall pretended. "The Bobbsey Twins at the Plaza," he'd say up in our room at the Plaza. And laugh and be gay: "The silliest one in the family. That's Masha." He got us trading scarves and gloves the way he and Peter traded hats and jackets and he and Bob Watson traded ties.

Like that boy in Rilke's "Requiem," Randall "printed" on himself the names of Chekhov and Proust and Freud *so far off now, already so long ago*, and Gogol, too. When he discovered Freud's birthday was the same as his, we stopped calling it his and celebrated Freud's. When some guests mistook our small framed picture of Chekhov for Randall's father, Randall sighed after they had gone (he was never prepared for the world's uncultivatedness), "People, *people*! Is there no limit to what people don't know?" But before we went to bed that night, he took a long look at Chekhov's picture and a long look at himself in the mirror. "You know what?" he said. "What?" I said. "If you blur your eyes . . ." And I said, "It's so, Randall. It's so." And with that he made up his mind to have a beard.

Years after, when people said he looked like Renoir's gentleman with the opera glasses in *La Loge* or like Donatello's head of Goliath, he'd ask with boyish delight, "Really? Do you really think so?" And gradually, with no overt plan, our bearded paintings outnumbered the others and every room has its Solomon, or Odysseus, or Constantine, or John the Baptist, or *der heilige Hieronymus.*

Randall (so it seemed to me) had an affinity for what he thought of as his Other: that One he saw in ponds and photographs and mirrors. He had his favorite mirrors and his "un-favorites," but I believe he looked into every one we ever saw. After a day in bed with a cold, when he'd read and written and slept too much, he'd ask me, like the Mariner's "three years' child," for the hand mirror. Unconcerned by my watching, he'd study himself for minutes, thinking—I know not what. Then he'd turn playful and perform for me and *the old friend who lives in my mirror* a pantomime of Tsar Nicholas turning into Rasputin and Mephistopheles turning into Faust. Waiting for traffic lights in the Jaguar or the Mercedes 190SL, Randall might seem to be looking off in space, but if I followed his eyes there we'd be, *windowed ones within their windowy world*, in the plate glass of a store front. I would wave to the delectable car, the man in the ascot, the woman over his shoulder, waving. I'd say, "There they are." And Randall, staring back at them, would say, "America's dream."

Two little girls, one fair, one dark—one Alleyne, one Beatrice, my daughters—came into the marriage with me. To them Randall was more of a friend, or pet, or affectionate encyclopedia than a father. Kitten—who was not a kitten but a big, black Persian cat—came with Randall. They had taken walks and naps and trips together for years; they trusted and admired and "went-out" to each other. To Randall *every part of him had a clear, quick, decided look about it.* That sentence is quoted from a description of the mockingbird in *The Bat-Poet,* but Randall said it first about Kitten. They were Kitten's qualities and Randall wanted them from tennis partners and automobile mechanics and critics. At certain intellectual moments Randall had that look himself and he and I often caught a glimpse of it when Ted Williams was at bat or when President Kennedy was fielding questions at a press conference. Simultaneously we would say, "Look. Look. He's looking like Kitten."

Randall said, "Kitten has a general's eye for terrain." And in any new district Kitten soon had in his head which houses he could get under and which trees and roofs would serve best for ambush and reconnaissance; then he went off on his own. After some three-day bivouac (worrisome for us), he'd emerge from a hedge and Randall would drop anything to run out and pick him up and hug him and say in a breaking voice, "Oh, Kitten. *Kitten.* Clever one to take such good care of yourself."

They played a game based on mutual anticipation and fast reflexes, something like tennis, that consisted of Randall's flicking the end of a necktie in imaginative ways just out of Kitten's reach—if he could. They would range over the floors and furniture, high and low, and play several "sets" with the easy skill of two "clear, quick, decided" intelligences that had never failed, or been clumsy, at anything they'd ever done.

When Kitten thought Randall had been writing too long, he sometimes stepped into the middle of the room and made a long, drawn-out, vexed cry of impatience that brought Randall to his feet. Other times he took a stance directly in front of his chair and with his ankles together and his tail floating he'd gaze up at Randall, giving off rays of invitation. Soon I'd hear the familiar melody, "Little ambassador, are you bored? All right. We'll play. Come now. We'll laugh and play. Oh, yes. Oh, yes."

When Randall relaxed in the bathtub after tennis, and read, Kitten often sat nearby and purred. He could purr until he almost sang. When his heart was especially happy he'd stand with his front paws on the edge of the tub and stretch until Randall met him halfway with his bowed head and they'd bump and rub heads. If Randall were lying on the sofa reading, Kitten would lie along the arm of it with his head near Randall's, black on black, and stroke his hair with the same patient, purposeful, impressive strokes he used to take care of his own.

Once at a cocktail party on a campus we were visiting, a professor began drawing Randall out on Kitten. Delighted to escape from General Conversation, he was animated and voluble and a circle soon formed. At this point, to be funny perhaps, the professor interjected a story he'd heard about Randall giving his meat ration coupons to the cat during the war. "Why of course!" Randall flashed sparks. "What would you *expect*? He's only a poor cat, and has to eat what he can. People can eat anything. What an absurd remark."

At home anyone holding Kitten on his lap had, as the

girls said, King's X. If the music on the FM "went bad" while Randall was holding him, I'd hear him in the other room saying, "Away, away, base Menotti." (Or Sibelius, or Hindemith.) And in another instant, "Help! Help! Someone come change the music. I'd do it myself but I'm holding Kitten—as *that* phrase goes."

On many clear nights, back from the library, we'd put the car in the garage and be looking up to find Orion's belt and sword when a downy, faintly warm, almost invisible presence wound itself in and out between us, leaning lightly on us. "Isn't that po*lite*?" Randall said. "To want to come and meet us!" One night he didn't come. Kitten was hit at the side of the road by a car. Like Randall, one blow on his skull killed him instantly. Again like Randall, the beautiful eyes and face, and the graceful body were not hurt in any way. Alone together we buried him in the dark under a deodar tree. When I laid some fern leaves down in his grave first, Randall *thanked* me. Then we curled him in a circle "like a little fox" and covered him over. At class the next day, Randall could scarcely teach and we decided to drive to Charleston for a few days. When we came back to Greensboro, people spoke so kindly to Randall. Alleyne and Beatrice were so loving; and I did all I could to comfort him, but in the end he had to suffer by himself all the zigzag work of mourning, with the guilt and the longed-for dreams and the dreaded fading and the reluctant giving up.

Something we never got to the end of talking about was California in the Old Days. We so nearly must have met back then that we thought we *must* have met. Randall and I had lived in Long Beach at the same time. We knew each other's houses. Mr. Jarrell worked for a photographer named Richard Seely. My parents knew Mr. Seely. Randall's father called on prospects for the Seely Studio and once someone, *someone*! called at my father's office and arrangements were made for a series of photographs to be taken of me. They are gently lighted, altogether winning studies, as are the ones he made of Randall at that time and of Mr. Jarrell, too: and all signed by him in India ink.

The ones of Randall's father are of a fair, gray-eyed, aquiline young man not even thirty. He is jaunty in his double-breasted vest and his well-tailored cap. In another, wearing a wide-brimmed fedora, he looks like Wallace Reid. (I heard with a pang how hard he'd been scolded for buying the pretty, striped shirt he has on, when they were short of money.)

We talked a lot about the reception room my father shared with another doctor, Dr. von W., who was treating Mrs. Jarrell for that *recurrent / Scene from my childhood, / A scene called Mother Has Fainted*. I went there after school sometimes, to wait for my father to see his last patients and then give me a ride home. Randall went there to wait for his mother. I clearly remember chatting with the receptionist and feeling important because she knew me. And I dimly recall that some schoolboys in sneakers were often sitting by the window, absorbed in magazines.

We could recall to each other the cinnamon bearclaws we'd bought from the *blue windmill* bakeries in Southern

California. And as small, weary passengers out for a Sunday spin in the back seat of our family's sedans, we'd both seen the cheering signs of the Albers Milling Company, *The old prospector with his flapjack in the air.* Randall knew as well as I did those golden-oak, dwarf-sized tables and chairs we were too big for in the Children's Reading Room in Lincoln Park. We shared one more memory in the *pink sphinx* mentioned in "The Lost World." It had once starred in a Pharaoh movie and then wound up as a failed real estate office across from Randall's school in Hollywood. By chance, or design, this was just next door to my Uncle Fritz's house and when my parents went to see my uncle I went and played in the pink sphinx. That world, where the M-G-M lion was young and where every child knew a lady with an "electric," existed for us both *so uncannily / That* [. . .] */ I believe in it* [. . .] */ I keep saying inside:* [. . .] */ I* know *those children. I know all about them. / Where are they?*

After his parents were divorced, Mrs. Jarrell and the little brother left Long Beach and went back to Nashville. Randall stayed on in Hollywood with his grandparents and great-grandmother on his father's side, who are the Mama and Pop and Dandeen of "The Lost World." He was with these old-fashioned old people for about a year and the poem says they delighted in *this last child* of theirs *in pride or bewilderment.* The household in "A Street off Sunset" did reassure and guarantee so much in the interim before Randall's mother sent for him; and he says *real remorse / Hurts me, here, now: the little girl is crying / Because I didn't write. Because— / of course, / I* was *a child, I missed them so.* Randall told me he hated to leave. "How I cried!" he said. And he'd begged them so hard to keep him that when they wouldn't—or couldn't—he blamed them for being cruel and resolved never to think about them again or write them a word. Later on he wrote them a poem instead (though they may not have lived to read it), "A Story."

In Nashville, Randall said, he was "covered with relatives." The Campbells (pronounced Cam'll) were an intimate, dominating family of strong wills, the whole of which was not as formidable as its parts. None of them was a listener or a relaxed person, but each on his own level was effective and, as Randall's mother said, "left tracks." She was the poor and pretty one who "had to work" and Uncle Howell (Brother) was the president of Bell-Camp Candy and her mainstay. In Campbell minds, Randall was expected to Be a Little Man and to aim toward supporting his mother, which, unhappily for Randall, Uncle Howell had done at a very early age.

"They had real gifts for finding me the most *awful* jobs," Randall said. "I wouldn't have minded delivering papers so much—though it was hell-ish—if I could have hired somebody to do the collecting. The people were so *bad*. They wouldn't pay, and they told lies. And I had to keep going back." They made him sell Christmas seals and ribbons from house to house, and Randall said, "*Imagine*, pestering people like that in their houses. Wasn't that a wicked thing to make a child do?"

When the sculptors for the Nashville Parthenon invited him to model for Ganymede, they were enchanted with this child who told them myths of the gods while he posed. He soon had the run of their studio, spent whole days with them. After they finished the pediments, though, they had to go back to whatever planet they'd come from and Randall was left desolate. Long afterwards his mother said the sculptors had asked to adopt him, but knowing how attached to them he was she hadn't dared tell him. "She was right," Randall said bitterly. "I'd have gone with them like *that.*"

He went on "growing up" in the library and at the backboard of the tennis courts and writing in his room with the door locked. In high school he played on the tennis team, edited the literary magazine, starred in some plays, and headed the Honor Roll. It was the Depression and at graduation Uncle Howell offered him a job in the candy company, provided he learned bookkeeping and shorthand at the secretarial school. Randall sat through the classes but said he couldn't make himself pay attention and would sketch or write poetry or put his head down on his desk. Eventually, Uncle Howell sent him to Vanderbilt—the first one in his family to go to college—and Randall was grateful.

He was still poor. He told me about playing tennis with one nickel in his pocket and how it distracted him from his serve—in the Tennessee heat—trying to decide whether to keep the nickel for carfare home or spend it on a bottle of Tru-Ade to pour over his head. When we were married he was temporarily hard up again. Strewn through the handwritten pages of *Pictures from an Institution* are little sums like $23.80 plus $41.50 with $14.95 taken away. He would sigh, "When I get through this, all I want is enough money not to have to think about it." Even then, Randall was above thinking about change, and pennies poured out of his pockets into the sofa and car and onto the bear-fur rug by our bed. Alleyne and Beatrice called these "Randall's oil wells" and he let them have them. "A penny is more trouble than it's worth is my motto," he said. Bills got crammed into any pocket in midsentence at a store and weeks later he'd come into a room all smiles and say to us, "Guess how much money I found in assorted jackets this morning?" Randall never had a savings account, only a spending account, where his royalties and honorariums and salaries were transubstantiated into Baltic amber, boxes at the Cuvilliéstheater, the house in Montecito . . . His idiosyncrasy for Sears, Roebuck handkerchiefs might be a contradiction, but was it? After a childhood in which a good handkerchief had been a miserable present, he used them, as a grown man, for tearing into strips when he wanted to tie something, or wiping the grease off the wire wheels of the Jaguar.

The last time we were in Europe we saw a spotted fur hat with a Garbo-dipped brim that Randall said was "right up my alley." I thought so, too, but I was ashamed to spend so much for a mere hat. And I didn't want him paying for it because he'd already bought me something and it was my turn to find him a present. I hated to take off the hat and kept looking at myself in the glass, not knowing what to do. "How much have you spent on hats in the last ten years?" Randall asked me. "Nothing!" I said. I couldn't remember when I owned a hat last. "O.K.," he went on. "Pro-rata it. If you allow yourself ten dollars a year for the past ten years, does it seem so bad?" I laughed and took out my checkbook and said, "Fur hat, will you marry me?"

We forgot all about this until Randall was ill, when in Rilke's words "rain starred the stream" and we saw "the naked tree Trouble . . ." Then we talked over how much real trouble we'd had in our years together. It seemed so little to both of us that we said if we'd pro-rata our bad time just now against the rest we'd still come out way ahead.

After our two years in Washington we bought a rustic, improbable house in a small forest of pines and hardwood the bulldozers forgot. The Bobbsey Twins in Their Hunting Lodge, Randall called us. (I think this was the time that, just to be mischievous, I said to him about the twin-ing, "How can that be, Ramble? I'm four days older than you." "Only chronologically," he sang to me over his shoulder.) We fed and read-about birds and bought and read-about trees, and Randall learned how to put up hammock hooks. He put up a dozen. It was his idea to surround the house with rooted ivy plants in hopes they would "take the place" as the neighbors warned. "The first year it sleeps. The second year it creeps. The third year it leaps," they told him. By the fourth year the house was thickly covered and ivy strayed across the window screens and, to Randall's delight, sent tendrils indoors. The neighbors, horrified and triumphant, asked him what he was going to do *now*? And Randall said, serenely, "Let 'em. They won't harm me if I don't harm them is this house's motto."

Cal Lowell's letters at this time were full of the grim realities of the bomb and mass death, and they stuck in Randall's mind and made him sad. "But Cal is right," he said and wouldn't be comforted. "What an age to be part of!" He was gloomy that spring until he found a sentence of Luther's that seemed to ward it off: *And even if the world should end tomorrow I still would plant my little apple-tree.* He quoted this to Cal, and to classes, and put it in the front of his book *A Sad Heart at the Supermarket.* Then he bought us a six-tree apple orchard, hollies, firs, golden willows, ginkgos, a magnolia for me, and a birch for "good, sweet Chekhov."

Alleyne and Beatrice married and Randall and I were having "meals at all hours" and playing *Tristan and Isolde* in the moonlight. In the dark, far across from us, the tuner's green lights made it Daisy's dock that Gatsby watched, we said; and the amplifier's many-heighted tubes glowed for us "like a little city." Randall—editing his collections of Kipling, then—liked to quote what Kipling said about some time he spent with his parents: "Not only were we happy, we knew we were happy." On Sundays we had pasties with Löwenbrau and watched the National Football League on television. Beside quarterbacking plays, Randall was continually appreciating scenes of the crowd, half in light and half in shadow, or of half stadium and half turf with the athletes in combat on the bright limed lines of the grid. "Wouldn't that make a painting!" he'd say. "Oh, if only I could *paint.*"

Randall didn't join things, unless you count Phi Beta Kappa, the National Institute of Arts and Letters, and the Army. If he "had a hard time knowing what to do at parties," it was even worse at meetings. He went when he had to, protesting innocently, "The trouble is, there's nothing to *do.*" And when he got home I'd ask what happened and he'd say blankly, *"Happened?"* and add, "Well, I cleaned out my billfold." Once, at an *American Scholar* meeting, he sketched all evening and brought back a "speaking likeness" of Margaret Mead. At graduations he passed notes to the other professors and made funny signals to me out in the audience. I never joined things either, not even church, and when people asked if I belonged to this League or that Club I'd have to say truthfully, "I just belong to Randall." When Chancellor Otis Singletary—whom Randall was "nuts" about—tried to get a mailing list of our friends for the university file, Randall's brow got wrinkly. Finally he said, "Otis, we know more chipmunks than we know people."

In a hammock at one of his stations "out in Nature" and with the FM on loud, Randall wrote his *Bat-Poet.* His creatures were the half-tamed ones we fed. Some of them, or ones just like them, live on in these woods; and the *real* cardinal, the one who knew Randall, is the red bird in the green pine who still calls birdie-birdie-birdie-birdie for his sunflower seeds. In Life, Frost and Cal were Mockingbirds; Michael di Capua and I were Chipmunks, of sorts; and Bob Watson and Randall were Bats.

In 1963 Randall got a sabbatical. We bought our Jaguar in Coventry and drove across Europe on what a gentleman in Bamberg called our "secondt vedding moon." We hadn't planned much time for England because Randall had once gotten along badly with some English academics and he was "against England." In the lamplighted evenings at the Taylors' house, talking over our itinerary, Peter ventured some of his "That won't do's." And he and Eleanor (such a James-ite, castle-combing, monarchistic, Anglophile pair) forced Somerset, Goathland, Doncaster, etc., on Randall with the same sweet unreasonableness he'd used to force Freud, *War and Peace*, and Bosch on them.

Randall couldn't get over his astonishment at the way London looked compared to New York. "Why it's like a time machine," he said. Everything cozy and well made and stable that had fallen out of America in this century seemed —seemed to Randall—*there* in England. He still liked Germany but it was hard on him to be cut off from magazines and newspapers, even menus. "Oh, I'm so ill-educated," he complained. "Imagine knowing *one* language!" The language we got fondest of in England we heard on a television program called *Steptoe and Son* and Covent Garden had to carry on without us on their night. This and a curiosity about cricket made us feel somewhat residential. More and more, England seemed the fulfillment of Randall's wish for a foreign country where they spoke English. And more than once, over his game pie at Fortnum and Mason's, he said, "We *ought* to get a flat here some summer."

While the Wimbledon matches were televised, we started our days early to do a gallery or some shopping in the morning. Then, comfortably propped in bed with our tea trays and sultana cake, we watched in bliss the mounting Australian sweep before those hushed outdoor stands, with only the bup-bup cotton-bubble sound that tennis makes.

In the long twilights we liked to watch the black and white parents in our district strolling in the park with their golden children. "English trees *are* like Constable trees," Randall noted interestedly when he looked out the window of our hotel on the Bayswater Road, across from Kensington Garden. Our sightseeing was a joke: no Westminster Abbey, no St. Paul's, or Towers, or tours—but we extended our stay. And the next thing I knew, Randall had appointments on Savile Row with "this dovey tailor!" He even took me there and we browsed through the wools together, thinking of more things for him to order. One pale, almost rainbow-hued check kept drawing Randall back. Of course it was too *jeune fille* for a jacket, he said, and too overwhelming for a suit, and yet . . . and yet . . . When I suggested a topcoat, Randall burst out, "A coat! A summer overcoat! I'll be just like someone in a Russian novel." He carried a stick for one day, but after he snapped off the tip in a grate he forgot all about it in a cab. And when he remembered it later, he said, "Alas, poor stick," and laughed and added, "Well, it was hardly my style." (A Burberry from Burberry's was, and a trilby from Lock's.)

Cal was passing through London then and we spent a few hours together, talking on a bench in Kensington Garden. Cal was for Plath that day, and Gunn—and Larkin. Randall was for Larkin, Larkin, and Larkin: that was normal. Cal's and Randall's temperaments, it seemed to me, were about as opposite as some of the poets they compared. But the two friends' intelligences were complementary. At each visit they roused each other up once or twice, whether they meant to or not; and then, like physicists on different hemispheres who advance their own knowledge on each other's papers, Cal and Randall (when their initial resistance passed) often pushed with their paws and found something palatable in each other's latest Enthusiasms. "Cal's right," Randall might say. "I was dumb about X——. He's better than I thought." Or he might say, "The people Cal likes!" For a day or two after being with Cal, Randall was more Randall than ever.

Randall's former phobia about England came down hard on France. Since he'd learned and *liked* to "maintain the orderly sequence of the queue," he was appalled at the brother-against-brother ways in Paris. At *Tannhäuser* one night and at other public places where it seemed apropos, Randall said loudly, "Good *night*! What a way to behave." One weekend "did" for France.

A few days among the hill farms of the Moselle and a few days of alp-viewing and miniature golf on the Boden See got us in the right mood for Munich. Mornings there started with a frantic routine: the Jarrells half through their breakfasts and urging on the half-asleep Michael di Capua with his, so we could be first at the box office for the turned-back opera tickets of the day. By ten-thirty the crisis would be passed—either we were going that night, some of us were going, or none of us were going—and we could calm ourselves over *Weisbiers* on the sidewalk at Luitpold's. There Randall and I stared with tender fascination at a waitress who would never know she looked "like the perfect Gretchen for *Faust*." And there the now-awake Michael became—with his repository of opera knowledge—that rare kind of good company Randall so often longed for: "Someone who knows more than I do about a subject I'm interested in."

By ourselves in Vienna we had a month of choosing between the Theater an der Wien, the Staatsoper, and the Redoutensaal every day; sometimes this could mean choosing between Bergonzi and Seefried and Rysanek. For over-all quantity and quality the Kunsthistorische became our latest "unfashionable enthusiasm." To have the nude Saskia and Titian's *Susanna and the Elders*; Vermeer's magical *Artist in His Studio*, and that Adam and Eve with the reptile that Randall called "the one inspired Cranach," *and* his beloved *St. Sebastian Mourning St. Irene*, was to us, rich fare. The Velázquez Room with, among others, nine Infantas made Randall cry out, "Mama-Mama! The paintings Franz Josef stole." And all this before you got to the fourteen Brueghels. When we went into that room, Randall whispered fiercely, "That Louvre! Isn't it over*rated*?" We sat among the Brueghels often, and in silence got free of ourselves and into those scenes in water, or snow, or fields, where the least crow flapping home was intended and where man's small, coarse, mystical, pitiful, vigorous, doomed efforts in his world took place. Before we left Vienna for a Donatello tour of Tuscany, Auden's "Musée des Beaux Arts" was rankling in Randall's mind to make him write a little later his own feelings in "The Old and the New Masters."

Home in Greensboro again, Randall finished the last work on his translation of *The Three Sisters* for the Actors Studio Theatre in New York. He was back to playing tennis with his old singles partner on fine winter days. On other days he'd dress warmly in the ochre twill "Danish nobleman's jacket" and the briarproof trousers and Bean boots he is wearing in Betty Watson's portrait. And he'd roam the Quaker farms near our house, finding winged elm branches and boughs of wild persimmon to bring back with the news of the ponies he saw, a little boy named David, and a red dog that all got written into an unpublished story called *Fly by Night.*

Randall liked us to have "cottage-y" meals; that is, omelette-and-salad meals with the teapot and the toaster on the table. He invented omelettes with quartered radishes and avocado cubes in them and was deliciously enterprising with his salad dressings. Herbs and spices would be strewn about in lavish disarray, but I was never sure which ones he'd used. Randall wasn't sure, either. He was always flattered, though, to be questioned and would try helpfully to remember and finally say, laughingly, "All that comes to me is what Frost said— 'A little of anything goes a long way in a work of art.' "

When the lettuce was especially nice, Randall sorted it over himself. Sometimes he'd call to me, "Come see your Randall. He has something to show you. You'll be glad you came." And when I got there he'd show me a perfect little lettuce leaf about as big as a canary feather. "Isn't it *dear*? I knew you'd want to see it." And he'd pop it in his mouth, saying, "It was much too good for this world."

Sections of his autobiographical poem "The Lost World" were being written then, to so much Liszt and to so many Richter recordings that I still hear the music when I read it. Just before he wrote "The Player Piano" and forgave his parents everything, we were listening to the Richter record of *Pictures at an Exhibition.* Randall was sitting with his eyes closed and his face turned upward and was playing chords on his knees. When the music finished, he said with sudden vehemence, "You'd have thought *somebody* would have given me piano lessons!"

At this same time there were three or four songs from Part One of *Faust* that he kept retranslating and wishing Goethe hadn't written. They "weighed on his spirit" and finally he told me he'd made up his mind to put them into literal prose in an appendix at the back of his translation, "Where they can't stick out and ruin everything."

Then something unexpected happened. After a false start or two, a book took hold of him and got written almost consecutively to its end. Daily, like a small glacier, it gathered up objects such as deerskin rugs from Salzburg, the new window seat we'd added, the Gucci hunting horn over our brick hearth and our female satyr figurine from Amsterdam. Into this setting Randall put a bearded hunter and a mermaid, the lynx from the Washington Zoo, the seals from Laguna days, and finally he gave these a boy who wanted to be adopted by *The Animal Family.*

Randall's nervous breakdown was showing signs that all but we could see. Before the worst of it happened, he was granted a few magic weeks of Lisztian virtuosity when nothing in his lectures or readings was veiled to him any longer. Everything his heart desired seemed possible to him. (He even met and *talked* to Unitas one day—and wrote a poem about it the next.) Poems flew at him, short ones, quatrains, haiku, aphorisms, parts of poems, ideas for poems until just words beat at his head like many wings. Before it was through with us, this ordeal called forth a desperate valor we'd never have known we had; and Donne's lines " . . . for affliction is a treasure, and scarce any man hath enough of it . . . that is not . . . ripened by it and made fit for God . . ." came to have more meaning for us than I'd have wished. When the doctors let him come home again, Randall was not as good as new, but he was recovering.

It was summertime and we got a Hoyle from the library and taught ourselves a beginner's pinochle, then an advanced pinochle. Then Randall scrambled those two together with some added attractions of his own that made a superior pinochle we kept a daily score on. Many afternoons we took our Bicycle playing cards out to the university's lake and played pinochle in the grass inbetween swims. We were both rereading *The Inspector General* before Randall was to teach Gogol in his Russian literature class that fall. It was Randall who transposed our old Bobbsey Twin formula into Bobchinsky and Dobchinsky at Piney Lake. He had me reading Ludwig's *Bismarck* to keep him company in his new interest in nineteenth-century Germans. His classes were big and enthusiastic and he was glad to be teaching again. At home he was sorting over poems on hand and making decisions about a book to be called *Let's See*. "The Player Piano" was to be in it; and "The Augsburg Adoration"; and this one.

Randall Jarrell

A Man Meets a Woman in the Street

Under the separated leaves of shade
Of the gingko, that old tree
That has existed essentially unchanged
Longer than any other living tree,
I walk behind a woman. Her hair's coarse gold
Is spun from the sunlight that it rides upon.
Women were paid to knit from sweet champagne
Her second skin: it winds and unwinds, winds
Up her long legs, delectable haunches,
As she sways, in sunlight, up the gazing aisle.
The shade of the tree that is called maidenhair,
That is not positively known
To exist in a wild state, spots her fair or almost fair
Hair twisted in a French twist; tall or almost tall,
She walks through the air the rain has washed, a clear thing
Moving easily on its high heels, seeming to men

Miraculous . . . Since I can call her, as Swann couldn't,
A woman who is my type, I follow with the warmth
Of familiarity, of novelty, this new
Example of the type,
Reminded of how Lorenz's just-hatched goslings
Shook off the last remnants of the egg
And, looking at Lorenz, realized that Lorenz
Was their mother. Quacking, his little family
Followed him everywhere; and when they met a goose,
Their mother, they ran to him afraid.

Imprinted upon me
Is the shape I run to, the sweet strange
Breath-taking contours that breathe to me: "I am yours,
Be mine!"
Following this new
Body, somehow familiar, this young shape, somehow old,
For a moment I'm younger, the century is younger.
The living Strauss, his moustache just getting gray,
Is shouting to the players: "Louder!
Louder! I can still hear Madame Schumann-Heink—"
Or else, white, bald, the old man's joyfully
Telling conductors they must play *Elektra*
Like *A Midsummer Night's Dream*—like fairy music;
Proust, dying, is swallowing his iced beer
And changing in proof the death of Bergotte
According to his own experience; Garbo,
A commissar in Paris, is listening attentively

To the voice telling how McGillicuddy met McGillivray,
And McGillivray said to McGillicuddy—no, McGillicuddy
Said to McGillivray—that is, McGillivray . . . Garbo
Says seriously: "I vish dey'd never met."

As I walk behind this woman I remember
That before I flew here—waked in the forest
At dawn, by the piece called *Birds Beginning Day*
That, each day, birds play to begin the day—
I wished as men wish: "May this day be different!"
The birds were wishing, as birds wish—over and over,
With a last firmness, intensity, reality—
"May this day be the same!"

Ah, turn to me
And look into my eyes, say: "I am yours,
Be mine!"

My wish will have come true. And yet
When your eyes meet my eyes, they'll bring into
The weightlessness of my pure wish the weight
Of a human being: someone to help or hurt,
Someone to be good to me, to be good to,
Someone to cry when I am angry
That she doesn't like *Elektra,* someone to start out on
Proust with.
A wish, come true, is life. I have my life.
When you turn just slide your eyes across my eyes
And show in a look flickering across your face
As lightly as a leaf's shade, a bird's wing,

That there is no one in the world quite like me,
That if only . . . If only . . .
                                        That will be enough.

But I've pretended long enough: I walk faster
And come close, touch with the tip of my finger
The nape of her neck, just where the gold
Hair stops, and the champagne-colored dress begins.
My finger touches her as the gingko's shadow
Touches her.
                    Because, after all, it *is* my wife
In a new dress from Bergdorf's, walking toward the park.
She cries out, we kiss each other, and walk arm in arm
Through the sunlight that's much too good for New York,
The sunlight of our own house in the forest.
Still, though, the poor things need it . . . We've no need
To start out on Proust, to ask each other about Strauss.
We first helped each other, hurt each other, years ago.
After so many changes made and joys repeated,
Our first bewildered, transcending recognition
Is pure acceptance. We can't tell our life
From our wish. Really I began the day
Not with a man's wish: "May this day be different,"
But with the birds' wish: "May this day
Be the same day, the day of my life."

Notes on the Contributors and the Editors

HANNAH ARENDT, a member of the National Institute of Arts and Letters, is the author of *The Origins of Totalitarianism* (1951), *The Human Condition* (1958), *On Revolution* (1963), and *Eichmann in Jerusalem* (1963).

JOHN BERRYMAN's books include *Homage to Mistress Bradstreet* (1956); *77 Dream Songs* (1964), for which he received the Pulitzer Prize; and *Berryman's Sonnets* (1967). He is a member of the National Institute of Arts and Letters and in 1967 was awarded the Fellowship of the Academy of American Poets.

ELIZABETH BISHOP received the Pulitzer Prize for *Poems* (1955), a volume that combines *North and South* (1946) and *A Cold Spring*. Her other book of poetry is *Questions of Travel* (1965). She is a member of the National Institute of Arts and Letters and received the Fellowship of the Academy of American Poets in 1964.

PHILIP BOOTH's first book of poems, *Letter from a Distant Land*, was the Lamont Poetry Selection for 1957. It was followed by *The Islanders* (1961) and *Weathers and Edges* (1966).

CLEANTH BROOKS is the author of, among other books, *Modern Poetry and the Tradition* (1939), *The Well-Wrought Urn* (1947), *The Hidden God* (1963), and *Understanding Poetry* (with Robert Penn Warren, 1938).

JAMES DICKEY received the National Book Award for *Buckdancer's Choice* (1965). His other collections of poetry are *Into the Stone* (1960), *Drowning with Others* (1962), *Helmets* (1964), and *Poems 1957-1967*. He is now Poetry Consultant to the Library of Congress.

DENIS DONOGHUE is Professor of Modern English and American Literature at University College, Dublin. He is the author of *Connoisseurs of Chaos* (1965), a study of modern American poetry, and *The Third Voice: Modern British and American Verse Drama* (1959).

LESLIE A. FIEDLER's books of criticism include *An End to Innocence* (1955), *Love and Death in the American Novel* (1960), and *No! In Thunder* (1960); his novels, *The Second Stone* (1963) and *Waiting for the End* (1964).

ROBERT FITZGERALD received a Bollingen Prize for his translation of *The Odyssey* (1961). His poetry has been collected in *A Wreath for the Sea* (1943) and *In the Rose of Time* (1956). He is the Nicholas Boylston Professor of English at Harvard.

R. W. FLINT's criticism appears in *Partisan Review, The Kenyon Review, Commentary,* and *The New York Review of Books.* He is presently editing and translating a new edition of works by Cesare Pavese.

ALFRED KAZIN is a member of the National Institute of Arts and Letters. His books include *On Native Grounds* (1942), *A Walker in the City* (1951), *Contemporaries* (1962), and *Starting Out in the Thirties* (1965).

STANLEY KUNITZ was awarded the Pulitzer Prize for his *Selected Poems 1928-1958.* He is a member of the National Institute of Arts and Letters.

ROBERT LOWELL's books include *Lord Weary's Castle* (1946), for which he was awarded the Pulitzer Prize; *Life Studies* (1959), for which he received the National Book Award; *Imitations* (1961), for which he received the Bollingen poetry translation prize; *For the Union Dead* (1964); and *Near the Ocean* (1967). His plays include *The Old Glory* (1965) and *Prometheus Bound* (1967). He is a member of the American Academy of Arts and Letters.

WILLIAM MEREDITH has translated Apollinaire's *Alcools.* His own poetry has been collected in *Love Letter from an Impossible Land* (1944), *Ships and Other Figures* (1948), *The Open Sea and Other Poems* (1958), *The Wreck of the Thresher and Other Poems* (1964).

MARIANNE MOORE received the Pulitzer Prize and the National Book Award for her *Collected Poems* (1951). That same year she was awarded the Bollingen Prize for poetry and in 1953 the National Institute of Arts and Letters awarded her its Gold Medal for Poetry. Her other books of poems include *Like a Bulwark* (1956), *O To Be a Dragon* (1959), and *Tell Me, Tell Me* (1967). She has translated *The Fables of La Fontaine* (1954) and Perrault's *Puss in Boots, The Sleeping Beauty & Cinderella* (1963). She is a member of the American Academy of Arts and Letters.

ROBERT PHELPS edited *Earthly Paradise,* an autobiography of Colette drawn from the writings of her lifetime. He is the author of *Heroes and Orators* (1958), a novel, and his criticism appears frequently.

SISTER M. BERNETTA QUINN, O.S.F., author of *The Metamorphic Tradition in Modern Poetry* (1955), is referred to by Randall Jarrell in "A Conversation with the Devil" ("Indulgent, or candid, or uncommon reader / —I've some: a wife, a nun, a ghost or two—").

JOHN CROWE RANSOM was awarded the Bollingen Prize for poetry in 1951 and the Fellowship of the Academy of American Poets in 1962. His books include *Selected Poems* (1945, revised edition 1963) and *World's Body* (1938), a collection of essays. He is a member of the American Academy of Arts and Letters.

ADRIENNE RICH's books of poems are *A Change of World* (1951), *The Diamond Cutters* (1955), *Snapshots of a Daughter-in-Law* (1963), and *Necessities of Life* (1966).

DELMORE SCHWARTZ's poetry includes *In Dreams Begin Responsibilities* (1939), *Vaudeville for a Princess* (1950), and *Summer Knowledge: New and Selected Poems, 1938-1958;* he was awarded the Bollingen Prize for poetry in 1959. His stories are collected in *The World Is a Wedding* (1947) and *Successful Love and Other Stories* (1961). He died in July 1966.

MAURICE SENDAK's books for children include *The Nutshell Library* (1962); *Where the Wild Things Are* (1963), for which he was awarded the Caldecott Medal; *Hector Protector and As I Went Over the Water* (1965); and *Higglety Pigglety Pop! or There Must Be More to Life* (1967). He made the pictures for Randall Jarrell's *The Bat-Poet* (1964) and *The Animal Family* (1965) and for George MacDonald's *The Golden Key* (1967).

Notes on the Contributors and the Editors

KARL SHAPIRO received the Pulitzer Prize for *V-Letter and Other Poems* (1944), which was followed by *Poems 1942-1953, Poems of a Jew* (1958), and *The Bourgeois Poet* (1964). His prose books include *Beyond Criticism* (1953) and *In Defense of Ignorance* (1960). He is a member of the National Institute of Arts and Letters.

ALLEN TATE was awarded the Bollingen Prize for poetry in 1956 and the Fellowship of the Academy of American Poets in 1963. His most recent books include *Poems* (1960), *Collected Essays* (1960), and *The Man of Letters in the Modern World* (1955). He is a member of the American Academy of Arts and Letters.

ELEANOR ROSS TAYLOR's poems are collected in *A Wilderness of Ladies* (1960). She is the wife of Peter Taylor.

PETER TAYLOR is the author of *A Woman of Means* (1950), a novel; *Tennessee Day in St. Louis* (1957), a play; and four collections of stories, *A Long Fourth and Other Stories* (1948), *The Widows of Thornton* (1954), *Happy Families Are All Alike* (1959), and *Miss Leonora When Last Seen* (1963).

P. L. TRAVERS is the author of the *Mary Poppins* books. Her other books for children include *I Go By Sea, I Go By Land* (1941) and *The Fox at the Manger* (1962).

ROBERT PENN WARREN received the Pulitzer Prize for his novel *All the King's Men* (1946) and both the Pulitzer Prize and the National Book Award for *Promises: Poems 1954-1956*. His most recent books include *Selected Essays* (1958); *The Flood* (1964), a novel; *Who Speaks for the Negro?* (1965); and *Selected Poems* (1966). He is a member of the American Academy of Arts and Letters.

ROBERT WATSON is the author of *Three Sides of the Mirror* (1966), a novel, and two books of poems, *Advantages of Dark* (1966) and *A Paper Horse and Other Poems* (1962).

MRS. RANDALL JARRELL lives in Greensboro, North Carolina. She frequently reads Randall Jarrell's poems at colleges and before literary groups.